COMPUTER
BOOK SERIES
FROM IDG

Access For Windows® For Dummies®

C000140640

Where to Find Help (Chapter 3)

- ✔ this book (you figured that out already— you're looking here!)

- ✔ the online help system (whack the F1 key)

- ✔ use keyword PCAPPLICATIONS on America Online, GO MSACCESS on CompuServe, OR JUMP MICROSOFT on Prodigy

- ✔ the `comp.databases.ms-access` Internet newsgroup

- ✔ `http://www.microsoft.com/ Support/` on the World Wide Web

- ✔ call Access 95 phone support at 206-635-7050 from 6:00 a.m. to 6:00 p.m. Pacific Standard Time

A Few Fields to Get You Started (Chapter 4)

Name	Type	Size	Notes
First Name	Text	15	person's first name
Last Name	Text	20	person's last name
Company	Text	25	company name
Address 1, Address 2	Text	30	include two fields for address; some corporate locations are pretty complicated
City	Text	20	city name
State, Province	Text	4	state or province; apply the name appropriately for the data you're storing
Zip Code, Postal Code	Text	10	zip or postal code; note that this is stored as text characters, not numbers
Country	Text	15	not needed if you only work within a single country
Office Phone	Text	12	voice telephone number; increase the size to 17 for an extension
E-mail address	Text	30	Internet e-mail address
SSN	Text	11	U.S. Social Security number, including dashes

. . . For Dummies: #1 Computer Book Series for Beginners

COMPUTER
BOOK SERIES
FROM IDG

Access For Windows® 95 For Dummies®

Cheat Sheet

Field Types to Know and Love (Chapter 4)

Text	Stores any kind of text (letters, numbers, even letters *and* numbers)
Memo	Use these for really *long* text (descriptions, reports, and such)
Number	Any number you intend to *count* or *do math* with
AutoNumber	Automatically fills in a unique number for every record
Currency	A specialized number field for storing your money
Date/Time	Dates, times, or both (depending on how it's formatted)
Yes/No	Logical field that holds Yes/No, True/False, or On/Off
OLE object	Wildly technical field type that can do anything, including wash your car

Reverse Index to the Good Stuff

IDG
BOOKS
WORLDWIDE

. . . For Dummies: #1 Computer Book Series for Beginners

References for the Rest of Us!®

COMPUTER BOOK SERIES FROM IDG

Are you intimidated and confused by computers? Do you find that traditional manuals are overloaded with technical details you'll never use? Do your friends and family always call you to fix simple problems on their PCs? Then the . . .*For Dummies*® computer book series from IDG Books Worldwide is for you.

. . .*For Dummies* books are written for those frustrated computer users who know they aren't really dumb but find that PC hardware, software, and indeed the unique vocabulary of computing make them feel helpless. . . .*For Dummies* books use a lighthearted approach, a down-to-earth style, and even cartoons and humorous icons to diffuse computer novices' fears and build their confidence. Lighthearted but not lightweight, these books are a perfect survival guide for anyone forced to use a computer.

"I like my copy so much I told friends; now they bought copies."

Irene C., Orwell, Ohio

"Quick, concise, nontechnical, and humorous."

Jay A., Elburn, Illinois

"Thanks, I needed this book. Now I can sleep at night."

Robin F., British Columbia, Canada

Already, hundreds of thousands of satisfied readers agree. They have made . . .*For Dummies* books the #1 introductory level computer book series and have written asking for more. So, if you're looking for the most fun and easy way to learn about computers, look to . . .*For Dummies* books to give you a helping hand.

ACCESS
FOR
WINDOWS® 95
FOR
DUMMIES®

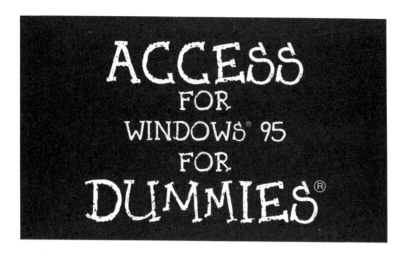

by John Kaufeld

IDG Books Worldwide, Inc.
An International Data Group Company

Foster City, CA ♦ Chicago, IL ♦ Indianapolis, IN ♦ Southlake, TX

Access For Windows® 95 For Dummies®

Published by
IDG Books Worldwide, Inc.
An International Data Group Company
919 E. Hillsdale Blvd.
Suite 400
Foster City, CA 94404

Library of Congress Catalog Card No.: 95-81426

ISBN: 1-56884-929-X

Printed in the United States of America

10 9 8 7 6 5 4

Distributed in the United States by IDG Books Worldwide, Inc.

Distributed by Macmillan Canada for Canada; by Computer and Technical Books for the Caribbean Basin; by Contemporanea de Ediciones for Venezuela; by Distribuidora Cuspide for Argentina; by CITEC for Brazil; by Ediciones ZETA S.C.R. Ltda. for Peru; by Editorial Limusa SA for Mexico; by Transworld Publishers Limited in the United Kingdom and Europe; by Al-Maiman Publishers & Distributors for Saudi Arabia; by Simron Pty. Ltd. for South Africa; by IDG Communications (HK) Ltd. for Hong Kong; by Toppan Company Ltd. for Japan; by Addison Wesley Publishing Company for Korea; by Longman Singapore Publishers Ltd. for Singapore, Malaysia, Thailand, and Indonesia; by Unalis Corporation for Taiwan; by WS Computer Publishing Company, Inc. for the Philippines; by WoodsLane Pty. Ltd. for Australia; by WoodsLane Enterprises Ltd. for New Zealand.

For general information on IDG Books Worldwide's books in the U.S., please call our Consumer Customer Service department at 800-762-2974. For reseller information, including discounts and premium sales, please call our Reseller Customer Service department at 800-434-3422.

For information on where to purchase IDG Books Worldwide's books outside the U.S., contact IDG Books Worldwide at 415-655-3021 or fax 415-655-3295.

For information on translations, contact Marc Jeffrey Mikulich, Director, Foreign & Subsidiary Rights, at IDG Books Worldwide, 415-655-3018 or fax 415-655-3295.

For sales inquiries and special prices for bulk quantities, write to the address above or call IDG Books Worldwide at 415-655-3200.

For information on using IDG Books Worldwide's books in the classroom, or ordering examination copies, contact the Education Office at 800-434-2086 or fax 817-251-8174.

For authorization to photocopy items for corporate, personal, or educational use, please contact Copyright Clearance Center, 222 Rosewood Drive, Danvers, MA 01923, or fax 508-750-4470.

 is a trademark under exclusive license to IDG Books Worldwide, Inc., from International Data Group, Inc.

About the Author

John Kaufeld

John Kaufeld got hooked on computers a long time ago. Somewhere along the way, he discovered that he really enjoyed helping people resolve computer problems (a trait his Computer Science pals generally considered a character flaw, but that everyone else seemed to appreciate). John finally achieved his B.S. degree in Management Information Systems from Ball State University, and he became the first PC Support Technician for what was then Westinghouse, outside Cincinnati, Ohio.

Since that time, he's logged nearly a decade of experience working with normal people who, for one reason or another, were stuck with a "friendly" personal computer that turned on them. He's also trained more than 1,000 people in many different PC and Macintosh applications. The vast majority of them not only survived the experience, but thrived on it. Today, John is president of Access Systems, a computer consulting firm. He still does troubleshooting, conducts technical and interpersonal skills seminars for up-and-coming computer gurus, and writes in his free moments.

John's other IDG titles include *FoxPro 2.6 For Windows For Dummies, Paradox 5 For Windows For Dummies,* and the best-selling *America Online for Dummies* (he regularly uses AOL, where he's knows as Jkaufeld, and he loves to get e-mail, answering every message he gets). John lives with his wife, two children, one overbearing canary, and a lovable American Eskimo puppy in Indianapolis, Indiana.

Welcome to the world of IDG Books Worldwide.

IDG Books Worldwide, Inc., is a subsidiary of International Data Group, the world's largest publisher of computer-related information and the leading global provider of information services on information technology. IDG was founded more than 25 years ago and now employs more than 7,700 people worldwide. IDG publishes more than 250 computer publications in 67 countries (see listing below). More than 70 million people read one or more IDG publications each month.

Launched in 1990, IDG Books Worldwide is today the #1 publisher of best-selling computer books in the United States. We are proud to have received 8 awards from the Computer Press Association in recognition of editorial excellence and three from Computer Currents' First Annual Readers' Choice Awards, and our best-selling ...*For Dummies*® series has more than 19 million copies in print with translations in 28 languages. IDG Books Worldwide, through a joint venture with IDG's Hi-Tech Beijing, became the first U.S. publisher to publish a computer book in the People's Republic of China. In record time, IDG Books Worldwide has become the first choice for millions of readers around the world who want to learn how to better manage their businesses.

Our mission is simple: Every one of our books is designed to bring extra value and skill-building instructions to the reader. Our books are written by experts who understand and care about our readers. The knowledge base of our editorial staff comes from years of experience in publishing, education, and journalism — experience which we use to produce books for the '90s. In short, we care about books, so we attract the best people. We devote special attention to details such as audience, interior design, use of icons, and illustrations. And because we use an efficient process of authoring, editing, and desktop publishing our books electronically, we can spend more time ensuring superior content and spend less time on the technicalities of making books.

You can count on our commitment to deliver high-quality books at competitive prices on topics you want to read about. At IDG Books Worldwide, we continue in the IDG tradition of delivering quality for more than 25 years. You'll find no better book on a subject than one from IDG Books Worldwide.

John J. Kilcullen

John Kilcullen
President and CEO
IDG Books Worldwide, Inc.

IDG Books Worldwide, Inc., is a subsidiary of International Data Group, the world's largest publisher of computer-related information and the leading global provider of information services on information technology. International Data Group publishes over 250 computer publications in 67 countries. Seventy million people read one or more International Data Group publications each month. International Data Group's publications include: **ARGENTINA:** Computerworld Argentina, GamePro, Infoworld, PC World Argentina; **AUSTRALIA:** Australian Macworld, Client/Server Journal, Computer Living, Computerworld, Digital News, Network World, PC World, Publishing Essentials, Reseller; **AUSTRIA:** Computerwelt, PC TEST; **BELARUS:** PC World Belarus; **BELGIUM:** Data News; **BRAZIL:** Annuário de Informática, Computerworld Brazil, Connections, Super Game Power, Macworld, PC World Brazil, Publish Brazil, SUPERGAME; **BULGARIA:** Computerworld Bulgaria, Networkworld/Bulgaria, PC & MacWorld Bulgaria; **CANADA:** CIO Canada, ComputerWorld Canada, InfoCanada, Network World Canada, Reseller World; **CHILE:** Computerworld Chile, GamePro, PC World Chile; **COLUMBIA:** Computerworld Colombia, GamePro, PC World Colombia; **COSTA RICA:** PC World Costa Rica/Nicaragua; **THE CZECH AND SLOVAK REPUBLICS:** Computerworld Czechoslovakia, Elektronika Czechoslovakia, PC World Czechoslovakia; **DENMARK:** Communications World, Computerworld Danmark, Macworld Danmark, PC World Danmark, PC World Danmark Supplements, TECH World; **DOMINICAN REPUBLIC:** PC World Republica Dominicana; **ECUADOR:** PC World Ecuador, GamePro; **EGYPT:** Computerworld Middle East, PC World Middle East; **EL SALVADOR:** PC World Centro America; **FINLAND:** MikroPC, Tietoverkko, Tietoviikko; **FRANCE:** Distributique, Golden, Info PC, Le Guide du Monde Informatique, Le Monde Informatique, Reseaux & Telecoms; **GERMANY:** Computer Business, Computerwoche, Computerwoche Extra, Computerwoche Focus, Electronic Entertainment, GamePro, I/M Information Management, Macwelt, PC Welt; **GREECE:** GamePro, Macworld & Publish; **GUATEMALA:** PC World Centro America; **HONDURAS:** PC World Centro America; **HONG KONG:** Computerworld Hong Kong, PCWorld Hong Kong, Publish in Asia; **HUNGARY:** ABCD CD-ROM, Computerworld Szamitastechnika, PC & Mac World Hungary, PC-X Magazine; **INDIA:** Computerworld India, PC World India, Publish in Asia; **INDONESIA:** InfoKomputer PC World, Komputek Computerworld, Publish in Asia; **IRELAND:** ComputerScope, PC Live!; **ISRAEL:** PC World 32 BIT, People & Computers; **ITALY:** Computerworld Italia, Computerworld Italia Special Editions, Lotus Italia, Macworld Italia, Networking Italia, PC Shopping, PC World Italia, PC World/Walt Disney; **JAPAN:** Macworld Japan, Nikkei Personal Computing, SunWorld Japan, Windows World Japan; **KENYA:** East African Computer News; **KOREA:** Hi-Tech Information/Computerworld, Macworld Korea, PC World Korea; **MACEDONIA:** PC World Macedonia; **MALAYSIA:** Computerworld Malaysia, PC World Malaysia, Publish in Asia; **MEXICO:** Computerworld Mexico, GamePro, Macworld, PC World Mexico; **MYANMAR:** PC World Myanmar; **NETHERLANDS:** Computable, Computer! Totaal, LAN Magazine, Macworld, Net Magazine; **NEW ZEALAND:** Computer Buyer, Computerworld New Zealand, MTB, Network World, PC World New Zealand; **NICARAGUA:** PC World Costa Rica/Nicaragua; **NIGERIA:** PC World Africa; **NORWAY:** Computerworld Norge, Computerworld Privat, CW Rapport Klient/Tjener, CW Rapport Nettverk & Telecom, CW Rapport Offentlig Sektor, IDG's KURSGUIDE, Macworld Norge, Multimedia World, PC World Ekspress, PC World Nettverk, PC World Norge, PC World's Produktguide, Windows Spesial; **PAKISTAN:** Computerworld Pakistan, PC World Pakistan; **PANAMA:** GamePro, PC World Panama; **PARAGUAY:** PC World Paraguay; **P. R. OF CHINA:** China Computerworld, China Infoworld, Computer & Communication, Electronic Product World, Electronics Today, Game Camp, PC World China, Popular Computer Week, Software World, Telecom Product World; **PERU:** Computerworld Peru, GamePro, PC World Profesional Peru, PC World Peru; **POLAND:** Computerworld Poland, Computerworld Special Report, Macworld, Networld, PC World Komputer; **PHILIPPINES:** Computerworld Philippines, PC Digest, Publish in Asia; **PORTUGAL:** Cerebro/PC World, Correio Informático/Computerworld, Mac•In/PC•In Portugal; **PUERTO RICO:** PC World Puerto Rico; **ROMANIA:** Computerworld Romania, PC World Romania, Telecom Romania; **RUSSIA:** Computerworld Rossiya, Network World Russia, PC World Russia; **SINGAPORE:** Computerworld Singapore, PC World Singapore, Publish in Asia; **SLOVENIA:** MONITOR; **SOUTH AFRICA:** Computing S.A., Network World S.A., Software World; **SPAIN:** Computerworld España, COMUNICACIONES WORLD, Dealer World, Macworld España, PC World España; **SWEDEN:** CAP&Design, Computer Sweden, Corporate Computing, MacWorld, Maxi Data, MikroDatorn, Nätverk & Kommunikation, PC/Aktiv, PC World, Windows World; **SWITZERLAND:** Computerworld Schweiz, Macworld Schweiz, PCtip; **TAIWAN:** Computerworld Taiwan, Macworld Taiwan, PC World Taiwan, Publish Taiwan, Windows World; **THAILAND:** Thai Computerworld, Publish in Asia; **TURKEY:** Computerworld Monitör, MACWORLD Turkiye, PC WORLD Turkiye; **UKRAINE:** Computerworld Kiev, Computers & Software Magazine, PC World Ukraine; **UNITED KINGDOM:** Acorn User, Amiga Action, Amiga Computing, Amiga, Appletalk, CD Powerplay, CD-ROM Now, Computing, Connexion, GamePro, Lotus Magazine, Macacction, Macworld, Open Computing, Parents and Computers, PC Home, PC Works, The WEB; **UNITED STATES:** Cable in the Classroom, CD Review, CIO Magazine, Computerworld, Computerworld Client/Server Journal, Digital Video Magazine, DOS World, Electronic, InfoWorld, I-Way, Macworld, Maximize, MULTIMEDIA WORLD, Network World, PC World, PUBLISH, SWATPro Magazine, Video Event, WebMaster; **URUGUAY:** PC World Uruguay; **VENEZUELA:** Computerworld Venezuela, GamePro, PC World Venezuela; and **VIETNAM:** PC World Vietnam   10/17/95

Dedication

To Jenny, because without you I'd be completely nuts.

To J.B. and the Pooz, for reminding Daddy to smile when all he could do was write.

To IDG Books, for the opportunity of a lifetime.

My sincere thanks to you, one and all.

Acknowledgments

Another one's out the door...

As with any good magic trick, there's more to putting out a book than meets the eye. Kudos and candy (lots of chocolate!) to my Project Editor, Kathy Cox, for her diligent efforts in making my ramblings follow commonly accepted semantic guidelines. An equally significant quantity of thanks (and chocolate) are thrown in the direction of my Technical Editors, Jim McCarter and Kevin Spencer, for making sure I'm not making this stuff up.

Thanks also to Stuart J. Stuple and Bjoern Hartsfvang for their deft touch with Parts III and iV; their help was important in completing this book. Without them, I'd still be writing.

Special thanks to Anne in Microsoft Outside Sales for having *information at her fingertips* when I needed to know about the impending release of Access 95. I can't tell you anything more about her because she's a Microsoft Trade Secret and I'm under nondisclosure. It's a legal thing.

Cindy in Microsoft's Access Support Group gets a special tip o' the hat for helping me track down a particularly irksome *feature* with a beta release of Access 95. Without her help, I'd have even less hair than I currently have (and these days, every hair counts).

(The Publisher would like to give special thanks to Patrick J. McGovern, without whom this book would not have been possible.)

Credits

**Senior Vice President
and Publisher**
Milissa L. Koloski

Associate Publisher
Diane Graves Steele

Brand Manager
Judith A. Taylor

Editorial Managers
Kristin A. Cocks
Mary Corder

Product Development Manager
Mary Bednarek

Editorial Executive Assistant
Richard Graves

Editorial Assistants
Constance Carlisle
Chris Collins
Kevin Spencer

Production Director
Beth Jenkins

Production Assistant
Jacalyn L. Pennywell

**Supervisor of
Project Coordination**
Cindy L. Phipps

Supervisor of Page Layout
Kathie S. Schnorr

Supervisor of Graphics and Design
Shelley Lea

Reprint/Blueline Coordination
Tony Augsburger
Patricia R. Reynolds
Todd Klemme
Theresa Sánchez-Baker

Media/Archive Coordination
Leslie Popplewell
Melissa Stauffer
Jason Marcuson

Project Editor
Kathleen M. Cox

Editors
Jeannie Smith
Diana R. Conover

Technical Reviewers
Jim McCarter
Kevin Spencer

Graphic Coordination
Gina Scott
Angela F. Hunckler
Carla Radzikinas

Production Staff
Brett Black
Jill Lyttle
Jane Martin
Laura Puranen

Proofreaders
Kathleen Prata
Christine Meloy Beck
Gwenette Gaddis
Dwight Ramsey
Carl Saff
Robert Springer

Indexer
Sherry Massey

Cover Design
Kavish + Kavish

Contents at a Glance

Cartoons at a Glance

By Rich Tennant

page 252

page 45

page 269

page 299

page 7

page 172

page 290

page 123

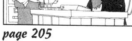

page 205

page 100

Table of Contents

Introduction

*B*eing a normal human being, you probably have work to do. In fact, you may have *lots* of work piled precariously around your office. Someone, possibly your boss (or if you work at home, your Significant Other), suggested that Access 95 might help you get more done in less time, eliminate the piles, and generally make the safety inspector happy.

So you picked up Access 95 and here you are. Whee.

If you're confused instead of organized, befuddled instead of productive, or just completely lost on the whole database thing, *Access For Windows 95 For Dummies* is the book for you.

This is a book with a purpose: to explain Access 95 without turning you into a world-class nerd in the process. What more could you want? (Well, you *could* want a chocolate malt, but Marketing said I couldn't package them with the books.)

You Don't Need to Be a Nerd to Use This Book

Becoming a nerd is totally out of the question. In fact, you only need to know a few things about your computer and Windows 95 to get the most out of *Access For Windows 95 For Dummies*. In the following pages, I presume that you

- ✔ Use Microsoft Windows 95 and Access For Windows 95 on your computer.
- ✔ Know the basics of Windows 95.
- ✔ Work with databases other people have created.
- ✔ Use and create queries, reports, and an occasional form.
- ✔ Want to make your own databases from scratch every now and then.
- ✔ Perhaps have used Access 2 (but that's certainly not a requirement).

The best part is that you *don't* have to know (or even care) about table design, field types, relational databases, or any of that other database stuff. What you need to know to make Access 95 work for you is right here, waiting to be found.

Sneaking a Peek at What's to Come

To give you an idea of what's ahead, here's a breakdown of the six parts in this book. Each part covers a general topic of Access 95. The part's individual chapters dig into the details.

Part I: Which Came First: the Data or the Base?

Right off the bat, the book answers the lyrical question "It's a data-*what?*" By starting with an overview of both database concepts in general and Access 95 in particular, you get the information you need to make sense of the whole database thing. This part also contains suggestions about solving problems with (or even *without*) Access 95. If you're about to design a new Access database to fix some pesky problem, read this section first — it may change your mind.

Part II: Truly Tempting Tables

Arguably, tables (where the data lives) are at the center of this whole database thing. After all, without tables there wouldn't be any data to bully around. This part explores what you need to know about designing, building, using, changing, and generally coexisting in the same room with Access 95 tables.

Part III: Finding the Ultimate Answer to Everything (Well, Not Really)

If tables are at the center of the Access universe, then queries are the first ring of planets. In Access, queries ask the power questions; they unearth the answers you *know* are hiding somewhere in your data. This part also explains how to answer smaller questions using Find, Filter, and Sort, Query's little siblings.

Part IV: Turning Your Table into a Book

Seeing your data on-screen just isn't enough sometimes. To make things *really* shine, it's time to commit them to paper. Part IV covers the Access report system, a portion of the software entirely dedicated to both getting your information onto the printed page and driving you nuts in the process.

Part V: Wizards, Forms, and Other Mystical Stuff

At some point, technology approaches magic (one look at the control panel for a modern microwave oven is proof of that). This part explores some of the mystical areas in Access, helping you do stuff faster, seek assistance from the Wizards, and even venture into a bit of programming.

Part VI: The Part of Tens

The words *". . .For Dummies* book" immediately bring to mind the snappy, irreverent Part of Tens. This section dumps a load of tips and cool ideas onto, and hopefully *into,* your head. There's a little bit of everything here, including time-saving tips and the solutions to the most common problems awaiting you in Access 95.

Appendix: Installing Access 95

Since none of this really works well unless you actually have Access 95 loaded on your computer, the Appendix explains precisely how to accomplish this. Don't worry, though — this section gingerly walks you through the whole process.

What the Funny Text Means

Every now and then, you need to tell Access 95 to do something or other. Likewise, there are moments when the program wants to toss its own comments and messages back to you (so be nice — communication is a two-way street). To easily show the difference between a human-to-computer message and vice-versa, I format the commands differently. Here are examples of each kind of message as they appear in the book.

This is something you type to the computer.

```
This is how the computer responds to your command.
```

Since this *is* a Windows 95 program, you won't just be typing all day — you'll also be mousing around quite a lot. Although I don't use a cool font for mouse actions, I *do* assume that you already know the basics. Here are the mouse movements necessary to make Access 95 (and any other Windows 95 program) work:

Click	Position the tip of the mouse pointer (the end of the arrow) on the menu item, button, check box, or whatever else you happen to be aiming at, then quickly press and release the left mouse button.
Double-click	Position the mouse pointer as if you're going to click, but fool it at the last minute by clicking twice in rapid succession.
Click and Drag (Highlight)	Put the tip of the mouse pointer at the place you want to start highlighting, then press and hold the left mouse button. While holding the mouse button down, drag the pointer across whatever you want to highlight. When you reach the end of what you're highlighting, release the mouse button.
Right-click	This works just like clicking, except you're exercising the right mouse button instead of the left mouse button.

Of course, the Access 95 menu comes in handy too. When I want you to pick something from the menu bar, the instruction looks like this:

Select File➪Open Database from the main menu.

The underlined letters are shortcut keys, so that those of you who think mice *should* be in holes can use the keyboard to control Access 95. To use the keyboard shortcut, hold down the Alt key and press the underlined letters. In the example above, the keyboard shortcut is Alt+F, O. Don't type the comma — it's just trying to make the command easier to read.

If you aren't familiar with all these rodent gymnastics or if you want to learn more about Windows 95 in general, pick up a copy of *Windows 95 For Dummies* by Andy Rathbone (IDG Books Worldwide).

Finding Points of Interest

When something in here is particularly valuable, I go out of my way to make sure it stands out. That's what these cool icons are for. They mark text that (for one reason or another) *really* needs your attention. Here's a quick layout of the ones waiting for you in this book and what they mean:

Notes are things I just want to make sure you see, little tidbits that might otherwise vanish into the text.

Tips are *really* helpful words of wisdom that promise to save you time, energy, and perhaps some hair. Whenever you see a tip, take a second to check it out.

Some things are too important to forget, so the Remember icon points them out. These are important steps in a process, points that you don't want to miss.

Sometimes I give in to my dark, nerdy side and slip some technical twaddle into the book. The Technical Stuff icon protects you from it by making it easy to avoid. If you're in an adventuresome mood, check out the technical stuff anyway. It might be interesting.

The Warning icon says it all: *this information could be hazardous to your data's health.* Pay attention to these icons and follow their instructions to keep your databases happy and intact.

Setting Sail on the Voyage

That sums up the preliminaries — there's nothing left to hold you back from the wonders of Access 95. Cleave tightly to *Access For Windows 95 For Dummies*, consign the Microsoft manuals to a suitable dark hole, and dive into Access 95.

- ✔ If you're brand new to the program and don't know which way to turn, start with the general overview in Chapter 1.

- ✔ Those about to design a database, I salute you — and recommend flipping through Chapter 4 for some helpful design and development tips.

- ✔ Looking for something specific? Try the Table of Contents or the Index, or just flip through the book until you find something interesting.

- ✔ For the latest weather forecast in Indianapolis, check out the Yellow Pages for a list of numbers.

Part I

Which Came First: The Data or the Base?

"SOFTWARE SUPPORT SAYS WHATEVER WE DO, DON'T ANYONE START TO RUN."

In this part . . .

*E*verything starts somewhere. It's that way with nature, with science, and with meatballs that roll down your tie. It's only fitting to start the book with a look at where *databases* start, since all the best databases begin as a glimmer in someone's mind.

This part opens with a heretical look at problem-solving, then moves along to cover the new Access 95 program itself. A little later, it reveals the secrets of good data organization and goes on to tell you where to find help when the world of Access 95 has you down.

All in all, this is a pretty good place to start — whether you're new to databases in general or just Access 95 in particular. Either way, welcome aboard!

Chapter 1
The 37-Minute Overview

• •

In This Chapter

▶ Starting the program

▶ Opening a database that's already there

▶ A good database is more than tables

▶ Finding a record

▶ Changing a record

▶ Printing a report

▶ Asking for help

▶ Saving your changes

▶ Getting out when you're done

• •

*I*t's confession time. This chapter will probably take you longer than 37 minutes to go through, if you go through the whole thing. Then again, it might take *less* time than that. Either way, the chapter *does* give you a good overview of Access 95 from start to finish (and I mean that literally).

Since the best way to get into Access 95 is to literally *get into* it, this chapter leads you on a wild, galloping tour of the software, covering the highlights of things you and Access 95 probably do together on a daily basis. It's something of a "Day in the life" thing, designed to show you the important stuff while pointing you to other areas of the book for more information.

If you're new to Access 95, this chapter is a good place to start. If you're already familiar with the older versions of Access, you probably should skip through here anyway to see how things have changed. Enjoy the trip!

Computers are optional

If you truly love your computer and think that it really *can* solve every problem you encounter, I suggest skipping this sidebar. You won't like what I have to say.

Ready for the heresy? Computers are *optional.* There's no rule that says you have to involve a computer in your solution. It's perfectly okay, and often preferable, to solve your problem *without* using a computer.

Remember: the goal of this whole process *isn't* to find a clever way to solve a problem with a computer; it's to find a clever way to solve your problem — period. If the solution involves the computer, that's fine. If it doesn't, that's fine too. Either way, you've solved your problem.

And even if you do want to use a computer, you aren't limited to an Access 95-based solution. Maybe you only need an electronic stack of index cards like Windows Cardfile (provided you still have a copy of the program left over from Windows 3.1 or Windows for Workgroups). Or perhaps there's a special program available that's designed to solve *exactly* your problem (like an accounting package or inventory management system). If there is, try it. Why reinvent the wheel if you don't have to?

In the Beginning, There Was Access 95 (But It Wasn't Running Yet)

The machine is quiet, the screen sits dark and devoid of image, and you aren't getting much work done. Nice as it is, the situation can't go on forever — it's time to start Access 95.

You can't run the software if it isn't installed. If Access 95 is still sitting on your desk, encased in plastic wrap, flip to the installation Appendix at the back of this book for help loading the program. When you're done, come back here and carry on.

Unlike in the old days (way back in the 1980s) when waking up your computer and running a database program could be terribly complicated, starting Access 95 is simple. Here are the steps:

1. **Mentally prepare yourself for the task at hand.**

   If it's before lunch, have a cup of coffee. After lunch, try chocolate.

2. **Turn on the computer, monitor, printer, and any other devices that look interesting.**

   With luck, your computer hums, beeps, and generally comes to life. Shortly after that, Windows 95 should start automatically. When it's loaded and you're ready to go, your screen should look something like Figure 1-1.

If you flip the power switch on the computer and nothing happens, your computer may be attached to a power strip or uninterruptible power supply (also known as *UPS,* just like the shipping company). In that case, turn on the power strip or UPS itself and the computer should start just fine.

3. Click the Start button and then click Programs on the pop-up menu.

So far, so good, but now comes the tricky part: finding Access 95 itself.

4. If there's an option for Access 95 on the Programs menu (see Figure 1-2), click that option to start the program.

Otherwise, look for Access 95 in the Microsoft Office menu (shown in Figure 1-3).

When you start the program, the Microsoft advertisement — er, logo — screen appears, followed shortly by the friendly dialog box in Figure 1-4. If that's what you see on screen, Access is successfully running, so go on to the next section.

If you either can't find the Access 95 icon or the program won't start, invest in a box of brownies and use them to bribe your favorite computer guru to help.

Figure 1-1:
Windows 95
is alive
and well.

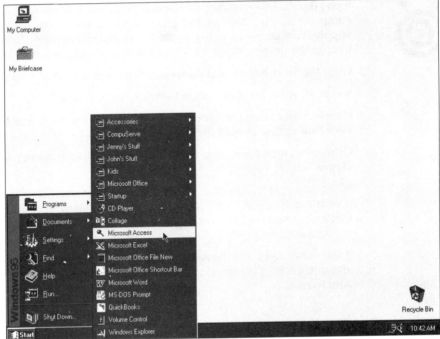

Figure 1-2:
For a smart program, Access 95 doesn't hide very well.

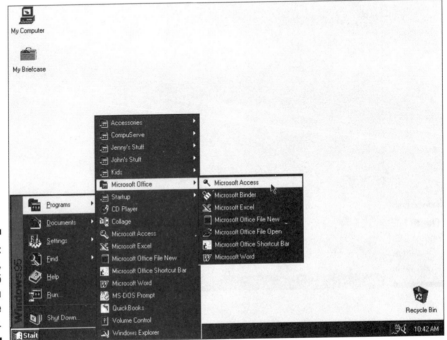

Figure 1-3:
Sometimes, Access 95 makes you look a little harder.

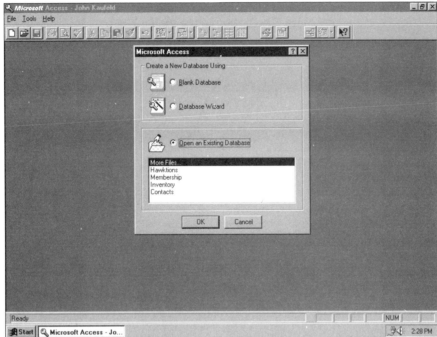

Figure 1-4:
Success at
last —
Access 95 is
running.

Opening an Existing Database

It's nice that the program is alive and kicking, but that alone isn't the ultimate goal. After all, Access 95 without a database file is like a CD player without a CD: nice to look at, but you can't dance to it. Loading your database is next on the hit list.

Database files fall in two distinct categories: those that already exist and those that don't. The odds are that you're working with a database someone created for you. If so, read on — this section is for you. If you want to *create* a new database from scratch, flip ahead to Chapter 4 for help.

If you just now started Access 95 and your screen looks like Figure 1-4, here's the quick way to open a database:

1. **If the database you want to use is listed at the bottom of the dialog box, double-click on the database name. If the database you're looking for isn't on the list, go to the next step.**

   Your database is now open and ready for action. Go on to the next section for more about what's what with your database file.

2. To see a list of the databases in the current directory folder, double-click on the More Files option in the dialog box.

The Open dialog box appears, looking much like Figure 1-5.

Figure 1-5:
The Open
dialog box,
in all its
glory.

3. Double-click on the database you're interested in.

After a moment, the database loads into Access and you're ready to work.

If the database you want to use isn't listed in the dialog box, it's probably in yet another directory folder. Skip ahead to Chapter 6 for help tracking the database around your hard disk or network.

If you've already printed some reports, checked out a form or two, or did something else in Access and want to open another database, use these steps:

1. Select File⇨Open Database from the main menu or click the Open Database button on the Toolbar.

Either way, the Open dialog box (still appearing for your viewing pleasure in Figure 1-5) pops onto the screen.

2. Double-click on the name of the database you want to use.

If the database *still* isn't listed, you may need to go on a quick hunt for the little fellow. Skip ahead to Chapter 6 for help with the Open dialog box's database search functions.

What's All This Other Stuff?

When a database opens, it usually appears on screen looking like Figure 1-6. The tabs across the top of the window display the various things in your database: tables, queries, forms, and so on. In Figure 1-6, the window shows the three tables in the Hawktions database.

Figure 1-6:
A normal database appears, looking, um, normal.

Now that the database is open, you can fiddle with the parts inside:

- ✔ To open a table, click on the tab marked Tables, then double-click on the table you want to see.

- ✔ To run a report, query, or form, click on the appropriate tab, then double-click on the item you want to work with.

- ✔ When you get tired of this database, close it by clicking in the X box in the upper-right corner of the window or by selecting File⇨Close from the main menu. If you're a keyboard fan, Ctrl+W does the dirty deed without resorting to the mouse.

- ✔ If you want to know more about working with Access 95's cool interface (and all the wonderful ways you can play in it), check out Chapter 2.

If some kind soul invested the time to make your life a little easier, you may instead see a startup screen (or *switchboard)* that resembles Figure 1-7. Don't panic — this is a good thing. The only downside is that your switchboard may be unique to your company, so I can't tell you anything about the options on it. Sorry, but I quit doing the psychic thing a while back.

However, you're in luck if it has options like the one in Figure 1-7. In that case, I *can* help you out because that form was created by the Database Wizard (and he's very consistent). Look in the Database Wizard section of Chapter 21 for more information about the form's options and how the whole thing came into being.

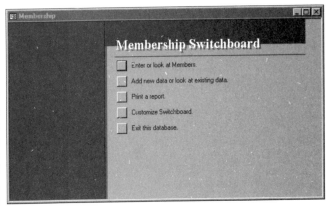

Figure 1-7:
A database
fronted by a
fancy
switchboard
screen.

Finding Candy amongst the Grass Clippings

I don't understand what the big deal is about getting kids to eat stuff. If you want a preschooler to eat something, just let them take it outside and drop it into the yard first, preferably right after you cut the lawn with a mulching mower. Covering the food with freshly cut grass seems to make it all the more interesting. (No, I don't understand that either.)

Finding records in your table is a little like whittling through sticky grass in search of toddler candy. Luckily, Access 95 makes records a whole lot easier (and infinitely less messy) to find. Here's one way to do it:

1. **Open the table you want to search.**

   If you don't know how, refer to the previous section.

2. **Click in the field you want to search.**

3. **Select Edit⇨Find from the main menu or click the Find toolbar button.**

   This brings up the Find dialog box (see Figure 1-8).

   Access 95 displays the name of the field that you're searching in the dialog box's title bar. If the title bar is proudly displaying the *wrong* field name, press Esc or click Cancel to make the Find dialog box go away, then try Step 2 again.

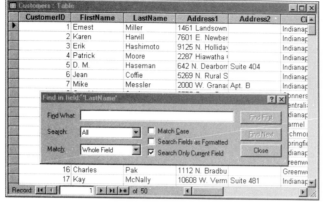

Figure 1-8:
The Find
dialog box
finally
shows up.

4. Type whatever it is you're looking for in the Find What text box (see Figure 1-9) and then press Enter or click the Find Next button.

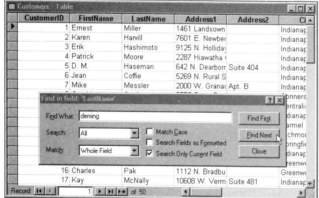

Figure 1-9:
Ready to
seek out a
record.

The search begins — and is probably over before you know it.

If the program finds a matching record, Access 95 highlights the data for you (see Figure 1-10).

If no record matches your criteria, a big, officious dialog box informs you that `The search item was not found.` If this happens, click OK and smile as the dialog box disappears; then double-check what you typed in the Find What text box. The odds are that you accidentally mistyped the entry. If so, fix it and try the search again. If you *still* can't find the record, either look in Chapter 10 for more details about the Find dialog box or grab a nearby guru and seek personal guidance.

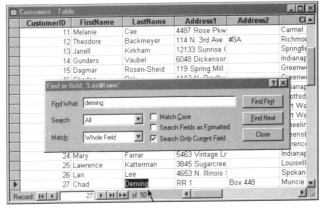

Figure 1-10:
Customer
Deming is
found —
hooray!

5. **When you're done with Find, close the dialog box by clicking Close or pressing Esc.**

   There are a lot more tricks you can do with the Find command, so be sure to look in Chapter 10 when you're ready to impress the coworkers.

There are also some tricky ways to find records that involve the right mouse button, but I'm saving those for Chapter 10.

Making a Few Changes

Unfortunately for the fruit growers and dairy farmers, life isn't always peaches and cream. Your customers move, the phone company changes an area code, or the digital gremlins mess up your typing skills. Whatever the cause, it's your job to fix the problem. Lucky you.

Changing the stuff in your tables isn't hard. In fact, it's almost too easy. The precise steps are outlined below. Keep in mind that your changes are *automatically* saved. When you finish working on the record, the new information is written to the database *right then*. If you make a mistake, *immediately* press Ctrl+Z to undo your changes — don't put it off until later.

Here's a quick word from the Society of the Perpetually Nervous: be *very* careful when changing the records in your database. It's easy to make changes, but it's tough to recover from them. Access 95 will only help you undo the *last thing you changed*.

1. **View the table on-screen as a data sheet or in a form.**

   Either way, your data is hanging out on the monitor and looking cool.

2. Click in the field you want to change.

A flashing toothpick cursor appears in the field, and the cursor changes to an I-beam.

3. Perform whatever repairs the field needs.

All of the standard editing keys (Home, End, Backspace, and Delete) work when you're changing an entry in Access 95. See Chapter 6 for the key-by-key details.

4. When the field is *just right*, press Return to save the changes.

As soon as you press Return, the data is saved — and I do mean *saved*. If you immediately decide that you like the old data better, press Ctrl+Z or select Edit⇨Undo Current Field/Record from the main menu.

Reporting the Results

Capturing all those wonderful details in your tables is nice, but it's even *nicer* to see those records fill a printed page. That's where the Access 95 report system comes in.

Making your database look wonderful on paper is a cinch with Access 95. The program has all kinds of report options, plus a reasonably strong Report Wizard to walk you through the hard stuff. Check out Part IV for more about all the really cool report stuff.

Since printing a report is one of the most common things people do with Access 95 (who said computers would bring on the paperless office?), here's how to do it:

1. If your database display looks like Figure 1-11, click the Reports tab.

If you're working with a custom form or a custom-built Access application that's unique to your company, click on the Reports option (or whatever option sounds like that) and follow the system's instructions. Sorry I can't be more help!

2. Right-click on the report you want to print.

A menu pops up where the mouse pointer is on-screen.

3. Select Print on the pop-up menu (see Figure 1-12).

Access 95 puts a little dialog box in the middle of the screen to tell you how the print job is going. When the print job is done, the dialog box vanishes without a trace.

If you change your mind while the report is printing, click Cancel on the so-how's-the-print-job-going dialog box to stop the process.

Figure 1-11:
One click
lists all the
current
reports.

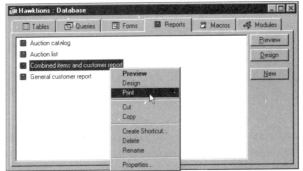

Figure 1-12:
Voilá — an
instant Print
menu!

Saving Your Hard Work

Actually, there's nothing much to say here — Access 95 saves your work for
you. This is both good and, well, not so good.

It's good because it's one less detail left laying around to clutter up your life. It's
less than good because Access 95 doesn't pay attention to what it's saving — it
just saves everything that's there. If you accidentally wipe out 237 records and
then make a couple errant clicks, it's *good-bye records, hello backups.*

I said it in the previous section, but it bears saying again. When you're changing
the records in your tables, *please* be careful. It takes only a second to mess up a
record. Don't let this happen to you.

Help is always just a few clicks away

No matter where you are in Access 95, help is always nearby. Chapter 3 covers all of your help options in gory detail, but here's one to get you started.

If you're stumped for what to do next, press the F1 key at the top of your keyboard. This is the Windows universal *help me* key. It brings up a dialog box that's jam-packed with help topics ranging from an overview of the newest, coolest things about Access 95 to phenomenally trivial explorations of macros.

Unless you're in a mood to browse, click the Find tab at the top of the window and search for your topic of interest. You can also try your luck with the Answer Wizard, who listens to your questions and comes up with the darndest answers to them.

The Great Backup Lecture

I know you've probably heard this before, but the PC support nerd in me won't let the chapter close without a few words about backing up your databases. Even though I joke about it, doing regular backups is a *vital* part of using a computer with Access 95 (or any program, for that matter).

Why is it so important? Take a minute and imagine life without your computer. Don't reminisce about business in the Good Old Days of the 1970s — think about what would happen if you walked in one morning and found *no* computer awaiting your arrival. None. Zippo. The desk is empty — no business letters, no receivables, no customer list, no nothing.

Unless you want to look at your business, raise your hand, and wave good-bye, you need a formal backup plan. Even if it's just you and your computer, write down some notes about how your backup process works. Here are some specific things to include:

- ✔ How often is the computer backed up? A better way to ask this question is "How much data can you afford to lose?" If your information changes daily (like an accounting system, for instance), you need to make backups every day or two. If you mainly play adventure games on your machine and use Access 95 as infrequently as possible, back it up every week or two. There's no universal answer that's right for everyone.

- ✔ Where are the backup disks or tapes stored? If the backups are stored right next to the computer, they'll be conveniently destroyed along with the computer if there's a fire. Keep your backups in another building if possible, or at least in another room if you have no other options.

> ✔ How do you back up the data? Write down a step-by-step procedure, along with a way to figure out what tape or disk set to use in the backup process.
>
> ✔ How do you *restore* the data? Again, make it a step-by-step process. Your mind won't be particularly clear if you have to do this, so make the steps simple and understandable.
>
> ✔ The nerd's almost done, so don't give up yet.

Having a procedure is good; actually *doing* the backups is better. After you settle into the backup routine, try restoring your data once to make sure it works. If the program has a problem putting the data back onto your disk, it's *much* better to find out before the disk dies than afterward. Set aside a couple hours of your copious free time and make sure your efforts will pay off on that fateful day when the disk drive dies. You'll thank me later.

Making a Graceful Exit

When you're done, you're done — but remember to give Access 95 a break, too. When it's time to shut down for the day, do it the right way:

1. **If you have a database open, select File⇨Close from the menu bar or click the X button in the upper-right corner of the database's window.**

   Technically, you don't need to do this, but I'm old-fashioned enough to not trust my program to close everything by itself without screwing something up. When it's possible (and doesn't make me look *too* much like a nerd), I close my files manually before shutting down the program.

2. **Close Access 95 by selecting File⇨Exit from the menu bar.**

   Nighty-night Access!

Go ahead and shut down Windows 95 as well if you're done for the night. To do that, click Start, then click Shut Down. When Windows asks if you're serious about this shut-down thing, click Yes. Once Windows 95 gets done doing whatever it is that software does just before bedtime, turn off your computer and make your escape to freedom.

Chapter 2

Finding Your Way around Like a Native

*C*ruising around an unfamiliar city is both exciting and frustrating. Seeing the sights, recognizing famous landmarks, and discovering new places to exercise your credit card make it fun. Finding yourself lost deep within a neighborhood that's *in transition* makes it, ah, exciting. Being unable to find your way back in either case makes it frustrating.

Driving your mouse through Access 95 if you're familiar with previous versions of Access is much the same. You're on unfamiliar territory — where'd they move that menu item to? It used to be right, um... geez, the whole *menu* is gone.

I know the feeling. There's nothing worse than having a lot of work to accomplish and enjoying the "help" of a new program. This chapter helps you out of that trap by taking you on a tour of the sights and such of Access 95. It covers the common things you see and deal with on-screen, from the main window to the toolbar and beyond. Kick back and enjoy the jaunt — it's a great way to get comfortable with Access 95.

Making Sense of the Sights

Because Access 95 is, after all, a Windows 95 program, the first stop on this merry visual jaunt is the program's main window. Figure 2-1 shows Access 95 in a common pose, displaying a database window (which is covered later in this chapter).

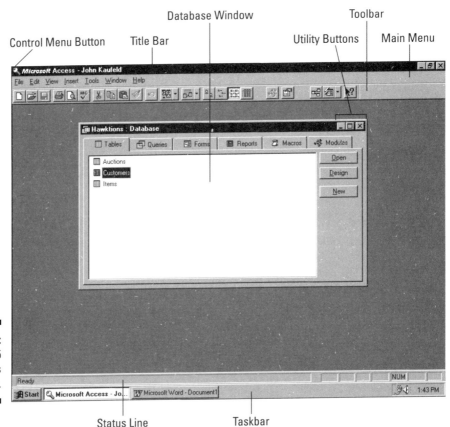

Figure 2-1:
Access 95
in all of its
glory.

Status Line   Taskbar

You need to know about eight parts of the main Access 95 window. Each part is briefly described. If you're *really* new to Windows 95, consider picking up a copy of *Windows 95 For Dummies* (IDG Books Worldwide) by Andy Rathbone. It'll make your life with Windows 95 a *lot* easier, I promise.

Control Menu Button: Click on the Access "key" to open the Control Menu. Frankly, this menu does a lot of nerd stuff, but you *can* use it to make Access 95 go away. In Windows 3.1, the button's picture was a box with a horizontal bar in it. These days, it looks a lot spiffier.

Title Bar: Every window comes complete with a space along the top for the title. This space has a second purpose too: It changes color to let you know which program is currently in charge of Windows.

Main Menu: Between the Title Bar and the Toolbar sits the Main Menu, Keeper of the Digital Peace. Aside from preventing fights between the bars, it's also your main stopping point for Access 95 commands and functions.

Toolbar: Think of the Toolbar as an electronic version of Lon Chaney, the Man of 1,000 Faces. Just about every time you do something in Access 95, the Toolbar does a quick change. There's more about this slippery character later in the chapter.

Utility Buttons: These three buttons appear on every window. From left to right, these buttons reduce the current program to a button on the Taskbar, make the current program either fit in a window or take up the whole screen (one button, two tasks — pretty cool, eh?), and close the current window.

Status Line: Access 95 is a talkative system, with words of wisdom to share about every little thing. Whenever it wants to tell you something, the message appears on the Status Line. On the far right of the Status Line are indicators for keyboard settings such as Caps Lock. In Figure 2-1, the NUM indicator appears down there, telling me that my Number Lock is turned on.

Database Window: In the midst of this maelstrom sits a serene database window, explained in the next section.

Taskbar: Across the bottom of the screen is the Windows 95 Taskbar, Microsoft's quick-and-easy tool for switching between programs. Each running program has a button down here. To use another program, just click on its button.

Windows Shopping for Fun and Understanding

There's more to Access 95 than the big picture window. The program is chock full of windows for every need and occasion. This section looks at four of the most common ones: the database window, datasheet window, form window, and query (you guessed it) window.

For the details of how these windows work, what to do with them, and why you should even care, keep trekking through the book. Databases and datasheets are in Part II, queries in Part III, and forms have a supporting role in Part V.

The database window

Most of the time when you open a database, it appears in a window like Figure 2-2. This window gives you access to all the cool stuff in your database, provides tools to change things or create new items, and generally helps you manage your database stuff. And it looks cool. Who could ask for more?

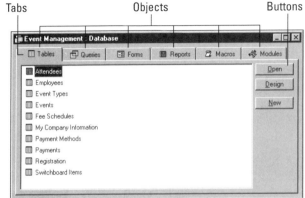

Figure 2-2:
Well, this is
another fine
database
that I've
gotten
myself into.

Your database *might* also start up looking like Figure 2-3. Don't let the pretty face fool you, though — this is just a fancier front hung onto Figure 2-2's database. Seeing something like this is a clue that you're working with a formal Access 95 application. It might be something created with a Wizard (like the one in Figure 2-3), or perhaps one of your in-house nerds whipped it up just for you. This special form is called a *switchboard.* Check out Chapter 21 for some more about using these in your tables.

Turning back to the database window, the *tabs* across the top of the window switch between lists of the *objects* (tables, queries, reports, and so on) that make up the database. Along the right side are three *buttons* for working with the database's objects: Open displays the current object, Design lets you change the object, and New creates a new object.

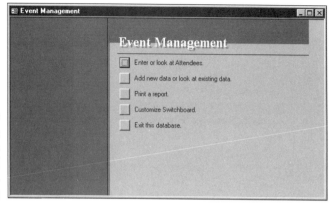

Figure 2-3:
A wizard-
created
switchboard.

The datasheet window

Is it a table or a spreadsheet? Only its owner knows for sure! Such are the traumas of the modern database. Being mistaken for a spreadsheet, for goodness sake! What's the world coming to?

Looking at Figure 2-4, it's easy to see why people might confuse the two. Yes, that's a *table*. Looks kinda like a spreadsheet, doesn't it? In *datasheet view,* an Access 95 table appears (and arguably acts) like a simple spreadsheet. The resemblance is only skin-deep, though — it's really a very different animal.

The datasheet window shows the *table name* across its top, just as it should. Right under that, the table's *fields* are arrayed across the window. The table's *records* are laid out in rows. Don't worry if you're not exactly sure about the difference between a record and a field. Chapter 4 has all the details about that.

On the right side and lower-right corner are a pair of *scroll bars,* which make moving through the table a real breeze. The *navigation buttons* are hanging out in the window's lower-left side. These buttons are a lot like the controls on a compact disc player or VCR (videocassette recorder). The buttons that have arrows pointing to a bar take you to the first or last record of the table. The arrow-only buttons move you to the next or previous record. Clicking on the arrow and asterisk button adds a new record to the table.

The form window

Form view is the other popular way to look at Access 95 tables. With forms, the data looks more, well, traditional — none of that sissy spreadsheet-style stuff. A form usually shows the data in a table at the blinding rate of one record per screen, the same way that the nerds of the 1970s worked with their data using million-dollar computers that had all the intelligence of today's microwaves.

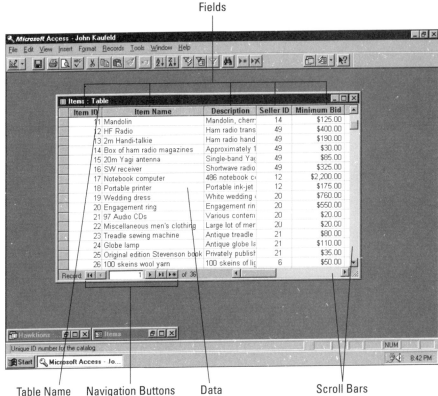

Fields

Figure 2-4:
The Items
table
dressed in
spreadsheet
drag.

Table Name   Navigation Buttons   Data   Scroll Bars

Figure 2-5 is a very simple but classic example of an Access 95 form. Along the top is the ever-anticipated *title bar*. The table's *fields* take up the middle of the form. In the lower-left corner are the same *navigation buttons* you saw and fiddled with in the datasheet window.

If forms really tweak your interest, check out Chapter 21 for more information.

The query window

The heart of any database program is its ability to search for information. In Access 95, its heart is the query system. And sitting at the heart of the query system is the *query window,* lovingly reproduced in Figure 2-6.

Fields   Title Bar

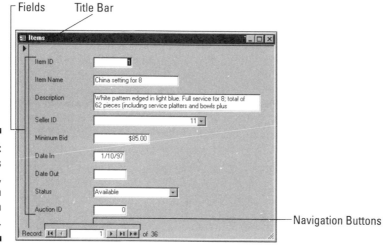

Figure 2-5:
The Items
database,
appearing in
a Form
near you.

Navigation Buttons

Title Bar   Tables

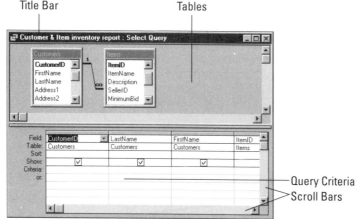

Figure 2-6:
The digital
Holmes
at your
service.

Query Criteria
Scroll Bars

The top of the window displays the *title bar,* showing the query's given name. The window's top half shows the *tables* involved in the query. If the query uses more than one table, this section also shows how the tables are linked together (or *joined*). The lower half displays the *query criteria* — the instructions that make the query work. Because all of this stuff can get large and complicated, the window has several *scroll bars* to help you see everything clearly.

When you run a query, Access 95 usually displays the results in a datasheet.

Belly up to the Toolbar, Folks!

Toolbars are the Windows equivalent of sliced bread — they're *that* useful. Access 95 has a bunch of them, too. You won't ever find yourself without a toolbar around to help.

So what *is* a toolbar? It's that row of cool buttons just below the menu at the top of the screen. Figure 2-7 shows the Database toolbar in action (well, as much action as any inanimate object ever shows).

Figure 2-7: The Database toolbar, just sitting there.

The toolbars give you single-click access to the best features of Access 95. The engineers designed the toolbars to contain the most common functions you need when working with your data. The Datasheet toolbar, for example, includes three buttons that control the Filter tools (tools that help you quickly find things in your database). Instead of working your way through a menu to find them, they're out in the open, just a mouse click away.

Because there's a toolbar for literally every occasion, I describe the toolbars throughout the book. Don't worry if you can't remember what all of the buttons do — neither can I. If you're button-challenged too, check out the sidebar for a useful word about *ToolTips,* Access 95's built-in toolbar button reminder system.

Quick — what does that button do?

There are 19 different toolbars in Access 95. (Okay, it's a nerd statistic, but I'm building up to a point — trust me.) Each toolbar has, um, lots of buttons on it. There's no way that anyone, not even the programmers, can remember what all of the buttons do. Besides, who'd want to try?

Unfortunately, toolbars are pretty useless if you don't know what the buttons do. To resolve this problem, Microsoft came up with *ToolTips.* These are little pop-up descriptions that appear when you point the mouse at a toolbar button.

To see a button's ToolTip, just aim the mouse pointer at the button in question. Hold the pointer

there for a second and {poof!} the ToolTip appears. If you do this and nothing happens, your ToolTips might be turned off. To turn them on, right-click anywhere on the toolbar, and then select Toolbars from the pop-up menu. Make sure there's a check mark next to Show ToolTips. Click on Close to make the dialog box vanish.

If the ToolTip isn't enough to jog your memory, just look at the Status Bar as you point at the mysterious toolbar button. Access 95 displays a longer explanation of the button's purpose down there.

Menus, Menus Everywhere (and Keystrokes that Work as Well)

Truth be told, there isn't a lot to say about the Access 95 menus. The main thing that you're sure to notice is that they change every time you do something new. Gone are the days of *one program, one menu.* Now we have *context-sensitive* menus that show different options depending on what you're doing at the moment.

Some things never change, though. Here's a brief rundown of generic menu truisms:

✔ If your mouse dies, you can get to the menu items from the keyboard. Just hold down the Alt key and press the underlined letter of the menu item you want. For instance, press Alt+F to open the File menu.

✔ Some menu items have a specific key assigned to them. The Copy command (Edit➪Copy on the menu) also works without the menu by pressing Ctrl+C. If an item has a *keyboard equivalent,* it's listed right next to the item in the pull-down menu.

✔ If you can't remember what a menu item does, pull down the menu by clicking once on the menu name (File, Edit, and so on) and then move the mouse pointer to the menu item. Check the Status Bar for a brief synopsis of what the option does.

Playing with the Other Mouse Button

After surviving years of neglect and general indifference, the right mouse button comes into its own with Windows 95. Finally, there's something for it to do. Right mouse buttons of the world, rejoice!

In Access 95 (just like its other Windows 95 counterparts), the right mouse button pops up a list of things you can do with the current on-screen item. In Figure 2-8, I right-clicked on the Customers table. Access 95 is right there, offering a list of common things to do with tables. Instead of working through the main menu to copy the current table, for instance, I can right click and select Copy from the pop-up menu. Talk about a time-saver!

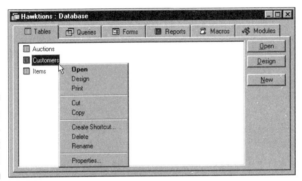

Figure 2-8:
Too cool —
an instant
menu!

Experiment with the right mouse button. Try right-clicking on everything in sight — see what happens. Don't worry about messing up your system because you can't do any lasting harm with the mouse. See what you can find!

Chapter 3

Calling the Online St. Bernard and Other Forms of Help

*I*t's easy to get in over your head sometimes. For instance, mountains are *much* taller after you start climbing than they were when you looked up from the ground. Plus, your equipment *never* seems to fail when you're packing it. Instead, it waits until you're in the middle of nowhere, dangling precariously from the crumbling edge of a craggy peak. Then — and only then — it remembers an innate fear of heights and has heart failure.

That's why God invented St. Bernards. When you're lost in the alpine wilderness, cold, wet, and alone, it's reassuring to know that a St. Bernard will be along soon. I'm a little unclear about precisely what the dog will *do* when it finds you, but at that point I'd probably settle for the companionship.

Access 95 has its own built-in St. Bernard, although on-screen it looks a lot more like a few dialog boxes than a husky canine. This chapter explores several different ways to find answers to your Access 95 questions. Knowing where to look for information is as important as knowing the information itself, so browse through here and learn about your options.

Watch where you step — St. Bernards are kinda big, and, well... I think you know what I mean.

When in Doubt, Press F1

No matter where you are in Access 95, help is available. It may not be obvious, but it's there, waiting for your call. Just press F1, and the help window pops into action (Figure 3-1).

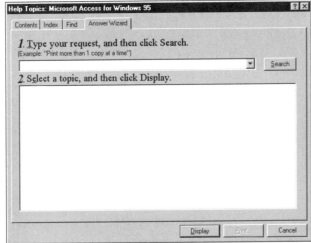

Figure 3-1:
The Help
system
reports
for duty.

The four tabs across the top of the window give you different ways to find answers. There's a method here for everyone, regardless of how you like to do research. The following sections explore each of the tabs: Contents, Index, Find, and Answer Wizard. I cover the Answer Wizard first since it's the first option you see (and because I like lists to be in alphabetical order).

Answer Wizard

The *Answer Wizard* starts out on top, since it's the newest (and by far the easiest) way to chat with the help system. The key word in that sentence is *chat,* because that describes how you interact with this electronic marvel. Instead of *you* trying to figure out how the programmers would describe your problem, the Answer Wizard *thinks about* your question and displays topics that it thinks are relevant. Here's how to use it:

1. **Click the Answer Wizard tab.**

   The Answer Wizard form appears.

2. **In the box at the top of the window, type your question in plain language, just like Figure 3-2.**

You read it right — in *plain language*. Can you believe it? A program that actually *understands* you. Who knows where this dangerous trend might lead?

Figure 3-2:
No computerese, no jargon — just a simple question.

3. Click Search or press Enter when you're done typing.

The Answer Wizard does its wizard thing and displays a list of help documents that it thinks will answer your question (see Figure 3-3).

Figure 3-3:
There's my answer.

4. Double-click the help document to see it.

If you want to inquire more of the Answer Wizard after reading the help document, click the Help Topics button at the top of the document window.

Contents

The *Contents tab* is for casual browsers or people who enjoy digging around in a book's Table of Contents in search of something. Here's how to use it:

1. Click the Contents tab.

The help window lists the available master help topics, complete with little book icons next to each one.

The book icon means this entry leads to other help topics or specific help documents.

2. Find a help topic that looks interesting and double-click it.

The system opens the help topic, changes the closed book icon to an open book (too cute!), and shows you either another list of topics or specific help documents (see Figure 3-4).

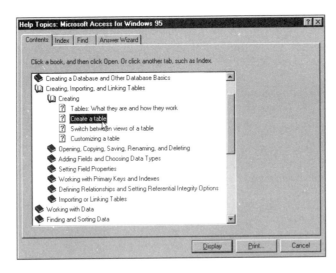

Figure 3-4:
There's the
information
I want.

The help documents are marked with the question-mark-on-a-page icon (but you probably figured that out on your own).

If you choose the wrong topic, double-click on the topic name again to make it go away.

3. **Repeat Step 2 until you find what you're looking for.**

   After you're done reading the help document, click Help <u>T</u>opics to see the Contents page again.

Find

Last of all is the *Find tab.* Arguably, this is a good place for it. Compared to the other options (especially the Answer Wizard), Find is absolutely archaic. But if your frustration level is a little low for the day and you want to raise it a notch or two, here's how to do it:

1. **Click the Find tab.**

   As you expect, the Find page appears on-screen.

   If this is the first time you've ever used Find, the help system will tell you that it has to create a word list before you can do the search. Just patiently follow along with the prompts and soon you'll be ready for Step 2. Didn't I warn you this would be frustrating?

2. **In the box at the top of the window, type a couple of key words that describe what you're looking for.**

   As you type, the Find system searches for topics that match your entry and displays a list of possible matches in the big window at the bottom of the screen. Unfortunately, Find has no intelligence whatsoever, so proceed on to Step 3 to go answer-wading.

3. **Scroll through the list at the bottom of the window until you find something that looks like your topic.**

   When (and if) you find a topic of interest (see Figure 3-5), double-click on the topic to see the help document.

   Better yet, why not click the Answer Wizard or Index tab and look for your answer that way?

Index

If you prefer diving into the index rather than rattling through the table of contents, click the *Index tab.* It works just like the index of a book, except it's automated. Here's how to use it:

1. **Click the Index tab.**

   The screen changes to show the Index page.

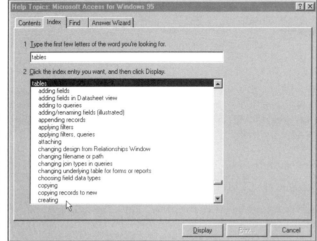

Figure 3-5:
I finally
found my
topic (and
I'm not sure
Find helped
at all).

2. Type the term you're looking for in the box at the top of the window.

As you type, the list at the bottom of the window highlights the best match it can find. Since this is organized just like a book index, start with the most general part of what you're looking for, then look for specific topics when you get there (see Figure 3-6 for an example).

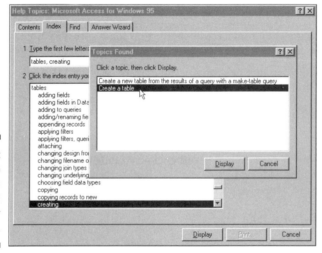

Figure 3-6:
I want to
create a
table, so I
looked for
Tables.

3. **When you find the topic you're looking for, double-click to see the help document.**

   If a couple of items match your topic, the help system displays a dialog box like Figure 3-7. If that happens, double-click on your choice to see it.

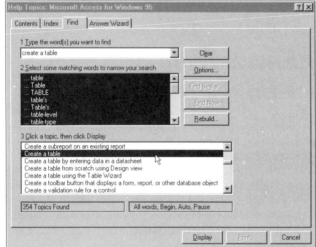

Figure 3-7:
I'll take what's behind door number two.

To get back to the Index page from a help document, click the Help Topics button on the topic screen.

The Whatzis Toolbar Button

 Whatzis isn't the technical term for this button, but it should be (those programmers just aren't clever about naming things). I'm talking about the button on the right side of the toolbar with a mouse pointer and question mark on it. This is your *Whatzis* button — your tool for quickly finding out what any button or menu item in Access 95 does.

Not only is the Whatzis button informative, it's easy to use. Here's how to use it:

1. **Click the Whatzis button on the toolbar.**

   The button clicks in to let you know that it's *on*. The big change is the mouse pointer itself, which suddenly sports a large question mark.

2. **Select the menu or click the button you want to know more about.**

   Access 95 displays a help screen with the name of the item and a brief description of what it does.

3. **Click once more to make the helpful little help screen go away.**

   Quick and easy answers for those brain-blank moments of life — it just doesn't get better than this.

Your Modem Knows More than You May Think

There's gold in those on-line services! If you have access (pardon the pun) to the Internet or an account on America Online, CompuServe, GEnie, or Prodigy, then a world of answers waits at your modem.

Microsoft maintains official support areas on the major on-line services, plus a very complete World Wide Web page for the Internet crowd. A host of informal question and answer areas cover Microsoft products as well. Table 3-1 explains how to find the support areas on each system.

Table 3-1	Microsoft Support Areas Available On-line	
System	*Access Command*	*Notes*
America Online	keyword `PCApplications`	Look for *MS Access Q&A* in the message boards under Database Use and Development
CompuServe	go `MSACCESS`	This whole area is devoted to Access; lots of good stuff
GEnie	move to page `505`	Includes the Microsoft Roundtable and knowledge base
Prodigy	jump `MICROSOFT`	Offers support forums and the knowledge base
Newsgroup	`comp.databases.ms-access`	Requires access to the Internet newsgroups
World Wide Web	`http://www.microsoft.com/Support/`	Requires access to the Web

If you have an Internet e-mail address and enjoy having your mailbox full, you can sign up for the Access mailing list. See the sidebar "Drinking at the never-empty well of a mailing list" for more details.

A slew of . . .*For Dummies* books are available to help you navigate the on-line world. Among them, there's *America Online For Dummies,* 2nd Edition (written by yours truly), *CompuServe For Dummies* (by Wallace Wang), and *The Internet For Dummies,* 2nd Edition (from John Levine). Of course, these fine books are brought to you by IDG Books Worldwide, the sponsor of today's program.

It's on the Tip of My Fax

Here's the easiest, most inexpensive way to get information about Access 95 (or any Microsoft product for that matter). It's toll-free, quick, and relatively painless. What is it? (Drumroll please!) It's FastTips, the automated Microsoft information system.

FastTips offers recorded answers to common questions and documents from Microsoft's support library. To use the *answers to common questions* part of the system, you need a touch-tone phone. To receive documents, you also need a fax machine.

The system is available 24 hours a day, 7 days a week. It even works on weekends and holidays, just like you sometimes do. That's why it's such a great thing to know about — it's available at those odd times of the day and night when you have a deadline looming and nowhere to turn for help.

Drinking at the never-empty well of a mailing list

If your company has Internet e-mail, consider signing up for the Access mailing list. This is a never-ending discussion of Access at all levels, from novice to nerd. Aside from filling your mailbox with important-looking messages, the list gives you a way to get answers fast at any time.

To join the mailing list, send a message to LISTSERV@peach.ease.lsoft.com. The subject can be anything (the computer on the other end doesn't care). In the body of the message, type SUBSCRIBE ACCESS-L followed by your real name, *not* your e-mail address. The mailing list computer automatically picks up your e-mail address from the message itself.

After you subscribe, your first message explains how the list works, how to send messages to it, and how to get off of it when you decide you've had enough. Give it a try — mailing lists are great tools!

Here's how to reach FastTips:

1. Get some paper and a pencil, then take a few deep breaths to relax.

You're about to tangle with a menu-driven voice response system, so it's important to be in the proper frame of mind for the experience.

Make sure you have the fax number handy if you're requesting documents.

2. Find a touch-tone phone and press 1-800-936-4100.

If you're planning to request faxed documents, you *don't* have to call from the fax machine; just know the fax number.

3. Listen patiently to the first menu and then select the option for Access.

As of this writing, Access is option 4 on the main menu, but such things change with time. If they *did* change the menu item, write the new number into this book so that you have it the next time you call.

4. Follow the menu prompts to find the information you want.

The first time you call, request a map and catalog. There are formal options on the menu for just this purpose. Navigating FastTips is just like driving to Cleveland, except without the car. The trip is easier if you know where you're going and what you're looking for. Before trying to do big things with FastTips, get a system map and catalog to review.

If you request a fax, don't worry if the fax doesn't arrive for 10 to 15 minutes. If the system is particularly busy, it might take a little longer. Be patient — use the time for a stretch break.

Talking to a Human

Sometimes, you've had it up to *here* with computers and automation in general. At that point, you just want to talk to a human — any human — who can help solve your problem. Microsoft provides a variety of phone numbers for just such occasions.

✔ To reach Access 95 phone support, call 206-635-7050 from the United States. Live human beings are available from 6:00 a.m. to 6:00 p.m. Pacific Time, Monday through Friday (except holidays). You pay for the phone call, but the answers are free.

✔ In Canada, the free support number is 905-568-3503. It's staffed from 8:00 a.m. to 8:00 p.m. Eastern Time, Monday through Friday.

If you'd rather exercise your charge card, call 800-936-5700. This number uses a flat $25 per incident charge. If you're in Canada, haul out your credit card and call 800-668-7975. Your only choice is the flat $25 per incident fee — sorry, but that's how these things go. The nice thing about paying for support is that these numbers are staffed 24 hours a day. I guess you really *do* get what you pay for.

When you pay for support, Microsoft charges you per support incident, not per phone call. Microsoft defines an *incident* as *all of the calls related to the same problem* or something like that. The bottom line is that if you have to call several times trying to get the same problem solved, you only pay for one call.

✔ If you have a light fluffy product question (like "What's the current version number of Microsoft Access and what's the weather like in Redmond, Washington?"), call Microsoft Sales at 800-426-9400. These folks are at the phones, waiting for your call, from 6:30 a.m. to 5:30 p.m. Pacific Time, Monday through Friday.

✔ If you are deaf or hearing-impaired and have a TDD or TT modem, call 206-635-4948 between 6:00 a.m. and 6:00 p.m. Pacific Time, Monday through Friday. This number works for all Microsoft products (Word, Excel, PowerPoint, and the others).

Part II
Truly Tempting Tables

The 5th Wave   By Rich Tennant

"THE ARTIST WAS ALSO A PROGRAMMER AND EVIDENTLY PRODUCED SEVERAL VARIATIONS ON THIS THEME."

In this part . . .

Now that you have Access 95, your life is all about storing, managing, organizing, and reorganizing data. (By the way, welcome to your new life. I hope you enjoy your stay here.) Because data hangs out in tables, you need to know how to do the whole table thing if you have *any* hope of making your data do tricks.

This part eases you into the role of Commander of All Tables You Survey by covering the basics. It takes you from creating tables, through using tables, and on into maintaining and repairing tables. Heck, if you're not careful you may find yourself attacking the dining room table by the end of Chapter 9.

Chapter 4

Designing and Building a Home for Your Data

· ·

In This Chapter

▶ Fields, fields everywhere

▶ Sample fields to simplify your day

▶ Flat files and relational databases revealed

▶ Designing your tables

▶ Creating the database

▶ Building a table with the Table Wizard

▶ Assembling a table by hand

· ·

*T*his may be the single most important chapter in this book. Why? Because really useful databases grow from carefully considered plans. The problem is that nobody ever explains stuff like how to successfully string a bunch of fields together and make a table out of them. For some unknown reason, *they* think you already know how to do it — that it's instinct, like the birds flying south for the winter or my wife finding the best sales in the mall.

If you didn't pop from the womb muttering "phone numbers and postal codes are treated as text even though they're numbers," then this chapter is for you. The following pages divulge the secrets of fields, tables, and databases in Technicolor glory. The chapter covers the terms you need to know, tips for choosing fields and designing tables, and details on how to put together cool tables and great databases.

Sometimes the stuff in here isn't pretty. This information takes you to the very edge of nerddom, so tread carefully (and shoot lots of pictures — the nerdlets are just *too* cute in their little taped-together glasses!).

Database Terms to Know and Tolerate

Wait! Don't skip this section just because it's about terminology. I promise to keep the techno-weenie content of this book to a minimum, but there are a few magic nerd words you simply *must* know before your foray into database development.

If you just felt faint because you didn't realize that you are developing a database, just put the book down for a moment, take a few deep breaths, and remember that it's *only* a computer, not something really important like kids, kites, or chocolate mousse.

The few terms you need to know are listed below. There's a brief explanation of each one, plus a translation guide for people migrating to Access 95 from the other major Windows databases: dBASE, Microsoft FoxPro, and Paradox. They're listed from smallest to largest, like a backwards version of that "flea on the wart on the frog on the bump on the log in the hole in the bottom of the sea" song that my kids sing incessantly some days. The definitions kinda build on each other, so it makes the most sense if you start with *data* and work your way down to *database*.

If you're switching over to Access 95 from one of the other Windows database programs, there's a table on the Cheat Sheet that translates all of the major terms from what those *other* programs use to the equally odd Access 95 names.

Data (your stuff)

Data is the stuff that Access stores, shuffles, and stacks for you. Data hangs out in *fields*. Every time some company calls and asks for *Your Name (last name first)*, you're providing data. Depending on how the fields are designed, *Your Name* might be one piece of data (your whole name, last name first) or three pieces (last name, first name, and middle initial). If you tack Junior or something else onto the end, it might even be more.

✔ dBASE, FoxPro, and Paradox all agree that data should, in fact, be called *data.* Don't expect this degree of cooperation to continue much beyond the term *record,* because that's where it ends.

✔ Database programs view data differently than you and I do. If you see 16773, you know it's a number — it's an intuitive thing. Access 95 and the other database programs see 16773 as either a number or a group of characters, depending on what type of *field* it's stored in. There's more about this peculiar behavior in "Frolicking through the Fields" later in the chapter. Please make sure you're comfortable with it because this little oddity can *really* throw you for a loop sometimes.

Fields (homes for your stuff)

If you read the section about data, you already know what a *field* is — it's the place that your data lives. One field holds one piece of data. If you're storing information about a baseball card collection, possible fields would include Player Name, Position, Year, Team, Manufacturer, Condition, and so on. Each one of those items is a unique *field*.

- ✔ As with the term *data,* dBASE, FoxPro, and Paradox all agree about what a *field* is.

- ✔ The programs begin to disagree when you talk about the types of fields available. Just because you *always used to do it this way in Paradox* doesn't mean the same method works in Access 95. For more details, flip ahead to "Frolicking in the Fields," just a couple pages away in this chapter.

Records (the homes on one block)

Having fields is a good start, but if you stopped there, how would you know which last name went with which first name? Something needs to keep those unruly fields in order — something like a *record.* All of the fields for one baseball card, one accounting entry, or one of whatever it is you're tracking with Access 95 are collectively known as a *record.* If you have two baseball cards in your collection, then there would be two records of information about the cards.

- ✔ In one final burst of similarity, dBASE, FoxPro, and Paradox concur on the term *record* (but the party ends here).

- ✔ Each record in a *table* has the exact same fields, but probably different data inside those fields. By the way, I snuck *table* into the last sentence because that's the next term you need to know (plus I like the challenge of writing sneaky prose).

Table (the blocks of a neighborhood)

Put simply (for what better way to put it?), a *table* is a collection of *records* that describe similar data. The key phrase to remember in that last sentence is *similar data.* All of the records in a single table contain similar data. The information about that baseball card collection might fit into a single table. So would the accounting data. However, a single table would *not* handle both baseball cards *and* accounting entries. Combining the two is a novel concept (and might even make accounting fun), but it's not going to work in Access 95.

✔ Paradox and FoxPro agree with Access 95 about the what a table is. Isn't that nice?

✔ dBASE has its own ideas about this *table* thing. It prefers the term *database file*.

✔ Did you notice that I said the baseball card collection *might* fit in one table? I'm not hedging my bet because I think that the table can't physically hold entries about all of your cards. No, it's because you might use a few *related* tables to hold the data. That's all you need to know for now, but this is an important topic to understand. Be sure to peek at "Flat Files versus Relational Databases: Let the Contest Begin!" later in this chapter for the whole scoop.

✔ By the way, if a collection of records is called a table, what do you call a collection of compact discs? An ottoman?

Database (a community of neighborhoods)

An Access 95 *database* (or *database file* — the terms are interchangeable) is a collection of everything relating to a particular set of information. The database contains all of the tables, queries, reports, forms, and other things that Access 95 helps you create to manage and work with your stuff. Instead of storing all of those items *individually* on the disk drive, where they can become lost, misplaced, or accidentally erased, they're grouped into a single collective file.

✔ dBASE and FoxPro call this a *catalog*. Conceptually, catalogs are like databases, except that the catalog is a separate file that just lists files that you say are related. In Access 95, a database file actually *contains* the tables, reports, and such, so it's doing much more than merely organizing them for you.

✔ Paradox doesn't have anything like an Access 95 database file. The closest you could come would be a subdirectory that contained all of the tables, queries, reports, and forms.

Frolicking through the Fields

A *field* is the place where your data lives; one field holds one piece of data. If you're storing information about a book collection, possible fields would include Title, Author, Copyright Date, Publisher, Edition, Price, and so on. Each one of those items is a unique *field*.

Because there are so many different kinds of stuff in the world, Access 95 offers a variety of field types for, well, stuff storage. In fact, Access 95 puts eight different field types at your disposal. At first blush, this may not seem like a lot of flexibility, but believe me — it is. Thanks to the field options, you can customize the fields to precisely suit your needs.

A lot of options are available for each field. You can request an entry, test the data to see if it's what you're looking for, and automatically format it just the way you want. Everything you need to know about this cool stuff awaits your attention in Chapter 7.

All of the field types are listed below. They're in the same order as they appear on-screen in Access 95. Don't worry if you can't figure out why *anyone* would want to use one type or another. Just focus on the ones you need, make a mental note about the others, and go on with your work.

Text: This field stores text — letters, numbers, and any combination thereof — up to 255 characters. The thing you need to remember is that numbers in a text field *aren't* numbers any more; they're just a bunch of digits hanging out together in a field. Be careful of this when you design the tables in your database.

Memo: This is a really *big* text field. It's great for general notes, detailed descriptions, and anything else that requires a lot of space. Memo fields hold up to 64,000 characters of information — that's almost 18 pages of text.

Number: As you probably guessed, this field holds real for-sure numbers. You can add, subtract, and calculate your way to fame and fortune with these fields. *Currency* fields are a specific kind of number field. If you're working with dollars and cents (or pounds and pence), use a currency field. For your other numeric needs, try a number field.

Date/Time: Time waits for no one (and if you're too late, your dates won't, either). Use a Date/Time field to track the whens of life. These fields store time, date, or a combination of the two, depending on which format you use. Pretty versatile, eh?

Currency: In an Access 95 database, the bucks stop here. For that matter, so do the lira, marks, and yen. Use this field to track money, prices, invoice amounts, and so on. If you're in the mood for some *other* kind of number, check out the *number* field.

AutoNumber: If I have to name one thing that makes Access 95 a truly cool product, this is it. The AutoNumber field does just what it says: it fills itself with an automatically generated number every time you make a new record. Just think — when you add a customer to your table, Access 95 generates the customer number *automatically!* This field type is an absolute boon for people like you and me because making an automatically numbered field used to require a programming degree. With Access 95, it just takes a mouse click.

Yes/No: When you need a simple *yes* or *no,* this is the field to use. Depending on the format you choose, this field type holds Yes/No, True/False, and On/Off.

OLE object: You probably won't ever use this type of field. It falls under the heading of *technoweenie features in Access 95.* OLE (pronounced O-Lay) stands for Object Linking and Embedding, a very powerful, very nerdy technology. If you simply *must* learn more about the OLE object field, consult Access 95's help system or pick up a copy of the *Access for Windows 95 Bible* from IDG Books Worldwide.

Text fields have one more setting you need to know about: size. When you create a text field, Access 95 wants to know how many characters the field holds. That's the field *size.* If you create a field called First Name that's size 6, *Joseph* fits into it, but not *Jennifer.* A good rule of thumb is to make the field a little larger than you think you'll actually need. It's easy to make the field even larger if you need to, but it's very dangerous to make it smaller. By the way, performing surgery on fields is covered in Chapter 9.

A Smattering of Fields to Get You Started

To give you a head start in the database race, Table 4-1 lists some common fields already starring in databases around the world. Some oldies-but-goodies are in here, plus some examples especially for the computer-oriented 1990s.

All of these are *text* fields, even the ones like Fax Number. That's because most data — most of the stuff you want to pack your database with — is *text* when you get down to the details.

Playing the (field) name game

Of all the Windows database programs out there, I think Access 95 has the simplest field-naming rules. Just remember three things and your field names will be perfect every time.

First, *start with a letter or number.* After the first character, you're free to use any letter or number. You can include spaces in field names, too!

Second, *make the name short and easy to understand.* You actually have up to 64 characters for a field name, but don't even *think* about using all of that space. But don't get stingy and create names like N1 or AZ773 unless they mean something particular to your company or organization.

Finally, *just use letters, numbers, and an occasional space in your field names.* Although Access 95 lets you include all kinds of crazy punctuation marks in field names, don't do it. Keep it simple so that the solution you develop with Access 95 doesn't turn into a problem on its own.

✔ Here's an easy rule of thumb about when to put a number into a text field instead of a number field. Ask yourself, "Will I ever do *math* with this number?" If so, it goes in a number field. Otherwise, stuff it into a text field.

✔ The Table Wizard is packed with ready-made fields for your tables. Look ahead to "Creating Tables at the Wave of a Wand" later in this chapter for more information.

Table 4-1	A Field for Every Occasion		
Name	*Type*	*Size*	*Notes*
Title	Text	4	Mr., Ms., Mrs., Mme., Sir
First Name	Text	15	person's first name
Middle Initial	Text	4	person's middle initial; allows for two initials and punctuation
Last Name	Text	20	person's last name
Job	Text	25	job title or position
Company	Text	25	company name
Address 1, Address 2	Text	30	include two fields for address since some corporate locations are pretty complicated these days
City	Text	20	city name
State, Province	Text	4	state or province; apply the name appropriately for the data you're storing
Zip Code, Postal Code	Text	10	zip or postal code; note that this is stored as text characters, not a number
Country	Text	15	not needed if you only work within a single country
Office Phone	Text	12	voice telephone number; increase the size to 17 for an extension
Fax Number	Text	12	fax number
Home Phone	Text	12	home telephone number (only necessary for people with lives)

(continued)

Table 4-1 *(continued)*

Name	Type	Size	Notes
Cellular Phone	Text	12	cell or car phone
America Online	Text	10	screen name on America Online
CompuServe	Text	12	user ID on CompuServe; even though it's all numeric, treat the number as text for storage purposes
Prodigy	Text	8	Prodigy user ID
E-mail address	Text	30	Internet e-mail address
Telex	Text	12	standard Telex number; use size 22 to include answerback service
SSN	Text	11	U.S. Social Security Number, including dashes

Flat Files versus Relational Databases: Let the Contest Begin!

Unlike ice cream, cars, and summer days, the tables in your database come in only two basic flavors: *flat* and *relational*. These two escapees from the *Nerd Term of the Month Club* explain how information is stored in the tables of your database. And *you* get to choose which one your new database will use!

In a *flat* system (also known as *flat file*), all of the data is lumped together into a single table. The phone directory is a good example of a flat file. Names, addresses, and phone numbers (data) are crammed into a single place (the database). There is some duplication — if one person has three phone lines at home, her name and address are listed three times in the directory — but things work just fine overall.

A *relational* system (or *relational database*) works very hard to use as little storage space as possible by cutting down on the redundant data. In the phone book example, one table might contain customer name and address informa-tion, while another holds the actual phone numbers.

The key to this advanced technology is called just that: the *key field* (or *linking field)*. Both tables contain this field. The key field's data links together matching records from different tables, just like the claim stub you receive when you drop off film for processing. To join up with your film again, you present the claim number. That's why big department stores always ask for your account number, then jovially call you by name — like they were just kidding about the whole number thing in the first place.

There are pluses and minuses to both the flat file and relational approaches:

✔ Flat systems are easy to build and maintain. They're great for simple things like mailing lists, phone directories, and video collections. Flat systems are simple solutions for simple problems.

✔ Relational systems really shine in *big* business problems like invoicing, accounting, or inventory. If you have a small problem to solve (like a mailing list or membership database), a relational approach may be more solution than you need.

✔ Anyone can create a very workable flat database system — and I *do* mean anyone. Developing a solid relational database takes skill and practice (and, in some countries, a nerd license).

Your company probably has a lot of information stored in relational database systems. It's important for you to understand how to *use* relational systems, so that's covered just about everywhere you turn in this book. Specifically, check out Chapter 5 to find out about dealing with the relationships between tables.

On the other hand, I don't recommend that you set off to *build* a relational database system by yourself. If you're *sure* you need one, let the Database Wizard or a friendly guru help you bring it to life. There's a lot to understand about how fields work together to form relations (cross Biology 101 with your first Computer Science class and you get the picture). Get some help the first time, then try it on your own later.

The following section explores the steps you use to design your database's tables, which is the next step toward creating your database. Here's one final note before I send you careening down the path toward your database: even though Access 95 is a relational database program, it does flat systems quite nicely. Don't worry — whichever way you go, you bought the right program!

Great Tables Start with Great Designs

You're *almost* ready to start up the computer and run Access 95. Almost, but not quite. There's one more step: designing the tables for your database. I know this seems like a lot of paperwork, but it's absolutely necessary to build good databases. When I create systems for my clients, this is exactly how I do it.

1. **Get out a clean pad of paper and something to write with.**

   Despite the wonders of a computer, some things still work best on paper. Besides, if the database design isn't going well, you can always doodle.

2. **Write brief descriptions of the reports, lists, and other things you want to come *out* of the system.**

   It seems kinda backward, but these reports and such are the *real* reason you're creating the database. If you can't get the information that you need out of the system, why have the system at all?

3. **On another sheet of paper, sketch the outputs you listed in Step 2.**

   You needn't go into a lot of design work at this point — that's not the goal. You're figuring out what information you need to build the outputs (reports, lists, mailing labels, and everything else). Just get a rough idea of what you want the most important reports to look like, then write down the data that's on them. This list is the road map to your database's fields. Now you know where you're going!

4. **Add more detail to the field list, including name, field type, and size (for text fields).**

   You still need to do this step even if you're planning to use the Database Wizard or Table Wizard when you build the table.

5. **Organize the fields into one or more tables.**

   Look for fields that naturally go together, like name, address, and phone number. If there are a lot of fields or if you run out of ideas for putting them together, get help from your friendly guru.

The last step is the hardest one, but it gets easier with experience. To get some experience, create some sample databases with the Database Wizard and look at how they fit together. Pick a topic you know about (accounting, event scheduling, or — if you're like me — compact disc collecting) and see how the pros at Microsoft did it.

It's Finally Time to Build the Database

After reading page after page, writing reams of notes, and sucking down two or three cans of pop, the moment is here — it's time to build the database! Here's where you create the master holding file for your tables, reports, forms, and other stuff. Plus, if you use a Database Wizard, this step *also* creates the tables, reports, and forms for you — it's one-stop shopping!

If you used to work with some *other* database program, you may have learned that the term *database* meant "where you store the data." In Access 95, that's called a *table*. Tables live inside databases, along with all the other sundry stuff you create to get the job done.

Without further adieu, here's how to create a database in Access 95:

1. **Start Access 95 if it's not already running.**

   I know, I know — I *have* to say it; it's an author thing.

2. **Select File⇨New Database from the main menu (see Figure 4-1) or click the New Database toolbar button.**

   The New Database window appears on-screen, displaying a fine array of Database Wizards to assist you.

Figure 4-1:
It only takes
a quick click
to create a
database.

If you just started Access 95, your screen looks more like Figure 4-2. In that case, click the Database Wizard radio button to enlist the wizard's help, then click OK to bring up the New Database window.

To create a new database by hand, click the Blank Database radio button, then click OK. Continue with Step 4 below.

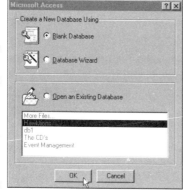

Figure 4-2:
If you just
started
Access 95,
making
a new
database is
even easier.

3. **Scroll through the list until you find a Database Wizard that sounds close to what you want to do. When you find one, double-click on it.**

   To create a database by hand, double-click the Blank Database icon in the upper-left corner of the screen.

   Either way, the File New Database dialog box appears.

4. **Type a name for your database, then click Create (see Figure 4-3).**

   To store the database somewhere other than the default location (usually the My Documents folder), choose a different folder by clicking the down arrow next to Save in and working through the directory tree until you find the one you're looking for.

Figure 4-3:
One new
database,
coming
right up!

Are you getting a headache from all this talk of folders, directory trees, and such? *Windows 95 For Dummies* by Andy Rathbone (IDG Books Worldwide) is the perfect remedy. Read once before bedtime and throughout the day as needed.

If a dialog box pops up and asks if you want to replace an existing file, Access 95 is saying that a database with the name you entered is already on the disk. If this is news to you, click No, and then come up with a different name for your new database. On the other hand, if you *intended* to replace that old database with a new one, click Yes and proceed.

5. **The Wizard displays a brief this-is-what-I'm-up-to window. Skim over what the little fellow says, then click Next to continue.**

   If you chose the Blank Database option, you see a blank database (see Figure 4-4). To create tables for your new database, skip ahead to the next section in this chapter.

Figure 4-4:
Yup — it's
blank
alright.

6. **On the Fields dialog box (see Figure 4-5), you can add or remove standard fields from the standard database that the wizard is building for you. Unless you're particularly moved to change something, click Next.**

One cool feature of this dialog box is the *sample data check box.* It's on the window's lower-left side. To have Access 95 generate some sample data for your table, click here. This is really helpful if you're planning to quickly test some reports. You don't *have* to click this, but it makes a lot of sense.

7. **Now that the hard part is done, the wizard wants your opinion on some aesthetic questions. On these two pages, single-click to see what an option looks like; click Next to make your choice.**

First, the wizard wants you to choose a style for the database's on-screen displays. Single-click on the options to see what's available, then double-click on the one you like.

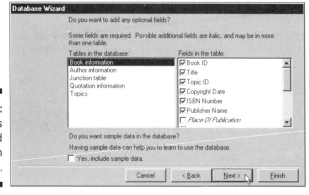

Figure 4-5:
The fields
look good
and fresh
to me.

Although my wife will accuse me of being bland again, I recommend sticking with the standard *Win95* option. The others are pretty, but they take more time to load. Stick with the simple stuff and you'll go far faster.

Next, consider the font and style for your report. I have no cool recommendations for you here — pick something you like and hit the Next button.

8. **As you head for home, the wizard wants a general title for the database forms and reports. The wizard kindly offers his own name, but you're free to change it by simply typing something new in the box at the top of the window. Click Next when you're done.**

If you're really into graphics, click the check box that puts a picture on your database's reports and main window. Click the Picture button to choose the graphic you want to include.

9. **Click Finish to build the database.**

The wizard clunks and thunks for a while, giving you constant updates on how it's doing (see Figure 4-6).

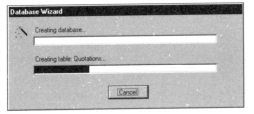

Figure 4-6: The wizard at work — your database is moments away.

Then (miraculously) it's done — your finished database appears on screen, much like Figure 4-7.

Now that the database is ready, flip through Chapters 6 and 7 for information on entering data, customizing the tables, and getting comfy with your new addition.

Creating Tables at the Wave of a Wand

Adding a new table to an existing database is easy with the Access 95 Table Wizard. The Table Wizard offers a variety of ready-made fields to choose from, plus it does all the dirty work of table creation behind the scenes, so you can focus on important stuff (like wondering when you can go home for the day).

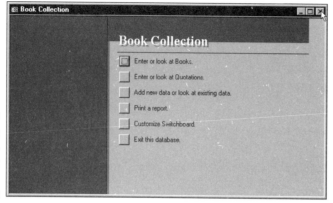

Figure 4-7:
Whoa —
instant
database!

With the Table Wizard, you don't so much *build* a table as *assemble* it. The wizard brings lots of pieces and parts — you pick out what you want and go from there.

This approach is helpful when you're completely new at building tables. Instead of worrying about details like field types and sizes, you get to worry about bigger stuff, like field names and purposes. But after building a few tables, you probably won't use the Table Wizard any more. Instead of helping, he'll start getting in the way because you already know what fields you want and how to make them.

As of this writing, the Table Wizard has some *very* rough edges. Hopefully, Those That Write Software will smooth things out before you actually get your hands on Access 95. Since I can't be sure that they really *will* fix the problems, though, the steps below include notes to protect your digital knees from scrapes and scratches on the trouble spots.

Without further ado, here's how to ask the wizard to help you build a table:

1. **Open the database file that needs a new table. Select File ⇨Open from the main menu or click the Open Database button on the Toolbar.**

   The database pops into its on-screen window.

   If you see a fancy form like Figure 4-8 instead of the database window, click the X button to close the form and then click the Restore button (third from the right) on the database window in the lower-left corner of the screen. *Now* your database window is ready and waiting.

Figure 4-8:
Get rid of the
switchboard
and then
view the
database.

2. **Click the Tables tab and then click <u>N</u>ew to start the creation process.**

   Doing this tells Access 95 that you want to add a table to the database. If
   you forget to click the Tables tab first, Access 95 may think you want to
   add a report, form, or goodness only knows *what* else to your database.

3. **In the New Table dialog box, double-click the Table Wizard entry.**

   Your disk drive probably sounds like it's lost its mind right now, but that's
   just part of waking up the wizard and getting him ready for the show.
   Pretty soon (in less than a minute), the Table Wizard dialog box of
   Figure 4-9 pops into view.

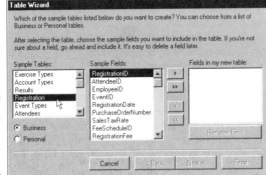

Figure 4-9:
All hail the
mighty Table
Wizard!

4. **Click on a sample table to display the available fields.**

   Remember those "rough spots" I mentioned? The Sample Tables list is the
   biggest one — it's a *mess*. The tables are jumbled together in no particular
   order, plus there aren't any descriptions of the fields and what they do. If
   you look up the term *user friendly* in the dictionary, this dialog box would
   not be listed as an example. Check out the "Highlights from the sample
   tables" sidebar to help make sense of this seething data morass.

5. **The Table Wizard offers you all kinds of ready-made fields to assemble into a table. Double-click on the fields you want for the table.**

When you double-click, the field name hops into the Fields in my new table column. Choose the fields in the order you want them to appear in the new table. Don't worry if you get one or two out of order — it's easy to fix that later (Chapter 9 tells you how).

If you like *all* of the fields from a particular table, click the >> button. That copies the table's entire set of fields.

To remove a field you chose by accident, click the < button. To remove *all* of the fields and start over with a clean slate, click the << button.

If you're not happy with the current name of a field in your new table, click on the field name, then click Rename Field. Type the new field name into the dialog box and click OK to make the change. Too easy, eh?

6. **Repeat Steps 4 and 5 until your table is populated with fields (see Figure 4-10). When you're done picking fields, click <u>N</u>ext to continue.**

So far, so good — now you're down to the simple stuff. On-screen, the field information runs off to hide as the wizard needs to know some general stuff about the table.

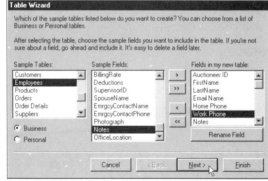

Figure 4-10: After reworking the fields a bit, it's time to move on.

7. **Type a name for the table, then click <u>N</u>ext when you're done.**

The table name information vanishes, replaced with the table relationship screen.

Leave the primary key settings alone for now. You can mess with those later (see Chapter 5).

8. **Access 95 wants to know if this table is related to any of the other tables in the database. If it is, click the Relationships button and explain how the tables are involved with each other. Click Next when you're done.**

The Table Wizard is pretty intelligent about this relationship stuff. It checks for fields that might link this new table to the existing ones in your database. The wizard reports its findings in this dialog box.

If you *thought* there would be a relationship but the wizard couldn't find one, click the related table's entry in the dialog box, then click Relationships. Follow the on-screen prompts to explain how the link works.

There's more about table relationships in Chapter 5. Look there if you're a little foggy about the how's and why's of linking tables together.

9. **You're *really* done — click Finish to complete the task and build the new table.**

Whew! You did it. The table proudly takes its place in your database (see Figure 4-11).

Figure 4-11:
There's the new table — this thing really worked!

Building Tables by Hand, Just Like in the Old Days

Although automation is a generally great thing, at times it just plain gets in the way. For instance, I appreciate the fact that with the right automatic gizmo, I can clap my hands and turn off the television. This becomes a problem when I start keeping time with my favorite song and accidentally drive the TV insane.

Likewise, the Table Wizard makes life easy at first, but soon you know more about what you want than it does. Don't worry — when you're ready for independence, Access 95 is there with a straight-forward way to build tables by hand.

Highlights from the sample tables

In hopes of making the Table Wizard a little more useful, here are some brief descriptions of the sample tables. This doesn't cover all the sample tables — just the ones that I think are most useful.

Many of these tables link together to form relational databases. For instance, Calls, Contacts, Contact Types, and To Do's work together as a single system. Don't bother trying to put the individual pieces together with the Table Wizard. Use the Database Wizard instead — it's a *lot* easier!

Attendees: general mailing list information (name, address, and so on) geared toward seminar attendees.

Calls: rudimentary customer contact database.

Clients: customer mailing list information.

Contacts: very full-featured customer information table; stores details about your customers.

Customers: you guessed it — a customer information list, complete with a field for e-mail address.

Employees: solid employee information table; good example of the detail you can include in a single table.

Events: great for meeting planners or trainers setting up their own room information.

Orders: tracks customer order data.

Order Details: covers the line items for each order.

Products: general product information for a catalog and sales system.

Registration: fields for checking in people at seminars, training courses, or other events requiring pre-registration.

Reservations: handles event reservations and pre-paid fees.

To Do's: tracks to-do items.

Actually, there are *two* easy ways to build a table without the Table Wizard. The easiest is *Datasheet view,* where Access 95 displays a blank datasheet and you start typing in data. Once you're done entering data, Access 95 looks at your entries and assigns field types based on what it sees there. The only problem with this method is that you often have to manually tweak the field types because Access 95 misinterpreted the data it found. The bottom line: for anything more complicated than a *really* simple table, Datasheet view creation is a nice thought, but it will drive you nuts in the end.

The formal, almost nerd-like way to build new databases is with *Design view.* In this mode, you have full control over the new table's fields. Don't get all weirded out because the screen looks complicated — just go slow, follow my steps, and everything will be fine.

To create a new table by hand, cruise through these steps:

1. **Select <u>F</u>ile⇨<u>O</u>pen from the main menu; then double-click on the data-base that needs a new table.**

   The database file appears on-screen. If a cool-looking form appears in its place, click the X button in the form's upper-right corner to make the form go away; then click the Restore button on the database window to bring the database front and center on the screen.

    You can also click the Open Database button on the toolbar, but that's old news by now.

2. **Click the Tables tab and then click <u>N</u>ew.**

   The New Table dialog box appears, mysteriously suspended above the database file in mid-screen. And to think that your friends said computers were boring!

   If Access 95 thinks you want to create a report, form, or other odd electronic accouterment, click Cancel and then make sure that you clicked the Table tab before hitting the <u>N</u>ew button.

3. **Double-click on the Design View option.**

   Access 95 displays a blank table design form that looks a whole heckuva lot like Figure 4-12.

    Remember the note earlier about creating tables in Datasheet view? Double-click the Datasheet View option in this list if that's how you want to build your table. Also, refer to Chapter 8 for lots of cool tips about working with a datasheet.

4. **Type in the field name and then press Tab to move on.**

   The cursor moves to the Data Type column. See — this manual stuff isn't so bad, is it?

5. **Click the down arrow to list all available field types. Click again on the field type you want (see Figure 4-13). Press Tab to continue.**

   The cursor moves into the Description field.

    If you create a Text field, you also need to adjust the field size (the default size is 50, which is too much field for almost anyone). Click in the Field Size box in the lower-left side of the screen before tabbing elsewhere; then type the correct field size.

6. **Type a clear, concise description of what this field contains. Press Tab once more to move the cursor back into the Field Name column.**

   This step is *really* important! The Description information appears in the status line at the bottom of the screen — it's automatic help text. *Please* take the time to write a quick description so your tables will be just that much *easier* to use.

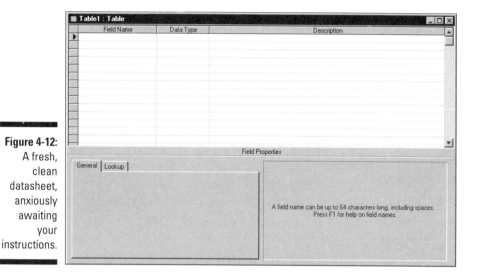

Figure 4-12:
A fresh,
clean
datasheet,
anxiously
awaiting
your
instructions.

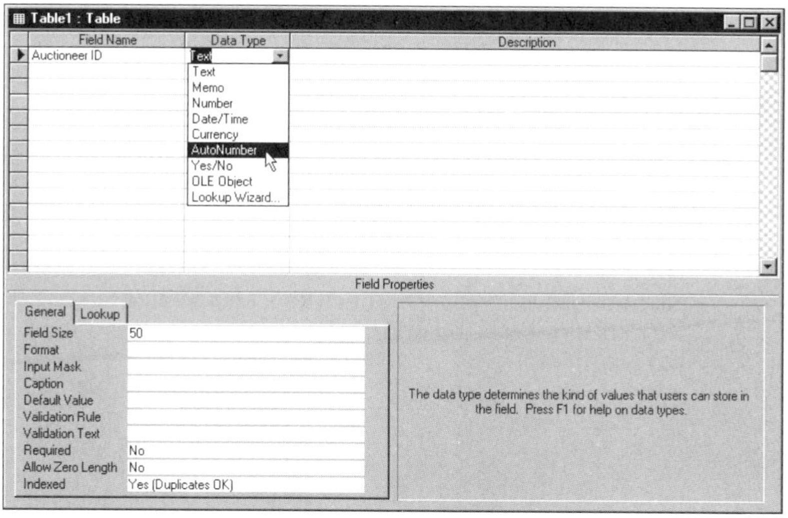

Figure 4-13:
You can
select from
all available
field (data)
types.

7. **Repeat Steps 4 through 6 until all the fields are in place (see Figure 4-14).**

What a feeling of achievement! Your new table is almost ready to work.

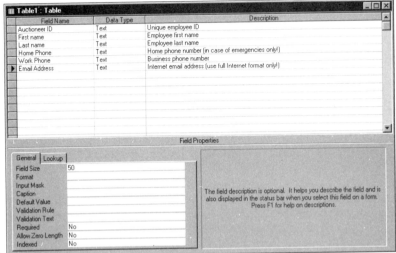

Figure 4-14:
The fields
are in
place... time
to give it the
stress test!

8. **Select File⇨Save to write the new table to your disk drive or else click the Save button on the Toolbar. In the dialog box, type in the name you want to use for the table and press Enter.**

Access 95 may send you a dialog box complaining that There is no primary key defined. This means that your table won't automatically put itself into any kind of order. Click Yes in the dialog box to create a key field, then check out Chapter 5 for more about the whole key field thing.

9. **Enjoy your new table!**

That's not bad for doing the work without automated intervention! Congratulations on a job well done.

Chapter 5

Indexes, Keys, and Relationships: Why You Care

- -

In This Chapter

▶ Speeding up your life with indexes

▶ Getting organized with a primary key

▶ The scoop about relationships

▶ Building relationships between your tables

- -

*E*very year, it's the same things over and over. Do more with less. Work smarter not harder. They're not problems, they're *opportunities for achievement*. Why do I bring up such wonderful thoughts in a fun book like this? Because this chapter is at least a partial cure for the phrases that afflict you.

You need to get more done in less time, right? Check out the index feature in Access 95. It makes your queries fly, your sorts sing, and your hair hold firm in its current position. Are you plagued with *opportunities* because your tables are infested with duplicate data? Ferret out the problems with a well-placed key field.

These tools, plus tips about building useful relationships between tables, await you herein. Don't just stand there — dive in!

Indexing Your Way to Fame, Fortune, and Much Faster Queries

Psst — you with the book. Yeah, you. C'mere for a minute. Want some inside information about your software? I've got a tip on a feature that'll blow you away. It speeds up your queries, makes sorting a snap, and prevents duplicate records in your tables. Pretty cool, eh? Oh, you *are* interested. Okay then — here's the scoop.

The cool, semi-secret feature I'm talking about is an *index*. An index works just like the index in a book. When you want to find something in the book, you can either look for it page by page or just go to the index, discover it's on page 731, and turn right to that page.

An Access 95 index works the same way, but instead of listing page numbers, it tracks *record* numbers. When you sort or query a table using an indexed field, most of the work is already done by the index. That's why indexes dramatically speed up queries and sorts — the index lets the query zero in on the information it's looking for without having to sift through the whole table to find it.

Here are a few random thoughts about indexes:

- ✔ Each field in a table can be indexed.

- ✔ Key fields are automatically indexed. (See the next section for more about keys.)

- ✔ Although indexes make lots of things faster, they actually *slow down* some processes. Adding records to a table with several indexes takes a little longer than adding records to an unindexed table. Access 95 is updating the indexes behind the scenes, but it still takes time to do it.

- ✔ Indexes either *allow* duplicate entries in your table or *prevent* them. The choice is yours. How do you choose the right one for your table? Most of the time, you want to *allow* duplicate records. Numbers unique to a particular record should be indexed as *No duplicates* (you don't want two customers to have the same Customer Number). This enlists Access 95's help to make sure that no two records have the same values in the indexed field.

- ✔ To list the table's indexes, open the table in Design view and click the Indexes button on the toolbar.

The programmers at Microsoft made creating an index a pretty straightforward operation. Here's how it works:

1. **With the table open in Design view, click on the name of the field you want to index.**

   The blinking toothpick cursor lands in the field name.

2. **Click on the Indexed box in the General tab of Field Properties.**

   The toothpick cursor, always eager to please, hops into the Indexed box. A down arrow appears on the right end of the box as well.

3. **Click the down arrow at the end of the box to list your index options. Select the kind of index you want from the list (see Figure 5-1).**

   Most of the time, choose Yes (Duplicates OK). In special cases when you want every record to have a unique value in this field (like Customer Numbers in your Customer table), select Yes (No Duplicates).

4. Click the Save toolbar button or select File⇨Save to make the change permanent.

Depending on the size of your table, it may take a few moments of effort to create the index. Don't be surprised if you have to wait a little while before Access 95 is done.

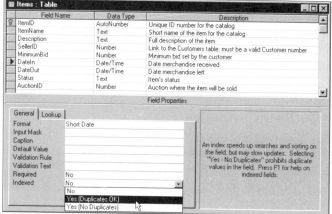

Figure 5-1: Building an index is a one-click operation.

To remove an index, follow the steps above. In Step 3, select No on the pull-down menu. Access 95 wordlessly deletes the field's index.

Primarily Keying up Your Table

A table's *primary key* is a special kind of indexed field. Just about every table you create *should* have a primary key. Why? Because it helps keep your data more organized (and because many nerds pitch a snit if you don't).

You need to know a few things about the primary key before you run off and create one:

- ✔ First, a table can only have *one* primary key. Although you can create indexes for every field, there's only *one* primary key per table.

- ✔ When you create a new table, if you don't designate a primary key Access 95 asks if you want one. If you say yes, the program gleefully creates an AutoNumber field at the beginning of your table and anoints it as the primary key.

- ✔ Most of the time the primary key is a single field, but in special circum-stances two or more fields can share the job. The technical term for that is *multifield key*.

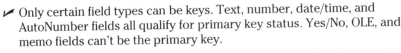

✔ Only certain field types can be keys. Text, number, date/time, and AutoNumber fields all qualify for primary key status. Yes/No, OLE, and memo fields can't be the primary key.

✔ Records are automatically sorted by the primary key. This is part of the organizational thing I mentioned before — it just keeps things neat and tidy in your table.

✔ By default, the values in a key field *must* be unique. If they aren't, how can you hope to find anything?

✔ Unlike many other database programs, Access 95 doesn't care where the key field is, physically, in the table. It can be the first field, the last field, or one somewhere in the middle. The placement choice is all yours.

To nominate a field for the job of primary key, follow these steps:

1. **Open the table in Design view.**

   If you're not familiar with this step, you probably *shouldn't* be messing with the primary key. I recommend spending a little time back in Chapters 1 and 4 before tackling the primary key thing.

2. **Right-click in the button next to the field you've picked for the primary key.**

   One of those cool pop-up menus appears. For some ideas on how to pick the *right* field for a primary key, see the sidebar.

3. **Select Primary Key from the menu (see Figure 5-2).**

   A little key symbol appears in the button. The primary key is set!

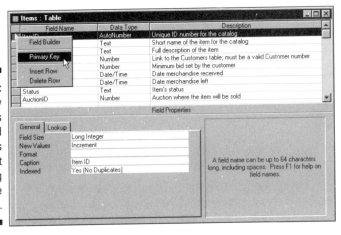

Figure 5-2: The primary key is created (and there was great rejoicing among the records).

Picking the right field is a *key* issue

What makes a good key field? How do you find the right one? Good questions — in fact, they're the two most important questions to ask about a primary key.

The top attribute of a good key field is *uniqueness*. The values in a key field *must* be unique. Access 95 won't tolerate duplicate key values. Each and every entry in the key field must be the only one of its kind.

With the word *unique* firmly imprinted in your mind, it's time to look for a natural key field in your table. Do you have any fields that *always*

contain unique data? Is there a Customer Number, Stock Keeping Unit, Vehicle ID, or some other field that's different in every record?

If you have a natural key, that's great. Use it! If you don't, I recommend adding an AutoNumber field to your table. This field type automatically inserts a new, unique number into each record of your table. It even keeps track of numbers that you delete so it won't try to use them again. You don't have to worry about programming or any special tricks to make the system work. The AutoNumber field takes care of everything.

Divulging the Secrets of a Good Relationship

I introduce the relational thing back in Chapter 4. As a quick recap, databases come in two basic kinds. In a *flat file* system, all the data is lumped into one big file. It's called a flat file because, organizationally speaking, it's flat — like a company with only one job classification.

At the other end of the spectrum are *relational databases*. Here, data is split up among two or more tables. One table may contain customer names and addresses while another records the customer's credit information and payment history. The credit information is tied to the customer data by a *linking field*, which, given the example, is probably a customer number of some sort.

✔ Usually, the linking field is the primary key in one table, but nothing special in the other. For instance, the customer information is probably arranged by customer number, while the credit data is organized by credit card number.

✔ Tables don't mystically start relating to each other just because they're cooped inside the same database file. You explain the relationships to Access 95 and it handles the details. Instructions for doing that very thing are in the next section.

✔ Linking fields should be *identical* — same data type, same size, same everything. If you're in the mood for individuality, this is *not* the place to express it. Lock-step precision goes a whole lot further in the weird world of databases.

When you link two tables together, they form one of four possible relationships. Although this information borders on the technical side, Access 95 is particularly fond of these terms so please take a minute and check them out.

✔ *One-to-One* relationships are the simplest, but they don't happen often. Here, one record in the first table links to *exactly* one record in the second table. Back in the example, if one customer has one (and only one) store credit account, then the customer and credit tables have a one-to-one link.

✔ *One-to-Many* is a much more common relationship. In this relationship, one record in the first table links to *many* records in the second. One sample customer may make many purchases at the store, so one customer record is linked to many sales records in the transaction table.

✔ *Many-to-One* relationships are simply the reverse of *one-to-many*. Look at the relationship from the sales record end this time instead of the customer end. Many sales transactions are linked back to one customer (a customer that *we* want to keep happy).

✔ *Many-to-Many* relationships are very complicated (just like real life). Here, many records in one table link to many records in another. Each store sales clerk sells many products, and each product is sold by many sales clerks. To have any hope of figuring out what's going on, you need a table in the middle to play traffic cop. Sound confusing? Trust me, it is.

On your forays into data management, you probably tangle with the first three relationships often, particularly if you're in a corporate environment. If you're a particularly nice individual, lead a good life, and follow the straight and narrow path, you hopefully won't ever come across a many-to-many relationship. If you *do* fall into one, stock up on junk food and put out the word that you're looking for a hungry technoid who knows Access 95.

Linking Your Tables with the Relationship Builder Thingie

The mechanics of linking tables together in Access 95 are quite visual. There's none of Paradox's informal sneaking around behind your data's back, nor is it a technical mating dance like FoxPro. In Access 95, look at tables, draw lines, and get on with your business. I hate to say this, but it's actually kinda fun.

✔ You can only link tables that are in the same database. Sorry, but that's how life goes in the big city.

✔ Although you can also formally link queries to tables, that's a little outside the range of normalcy. For more about that, check out the *Access For Windows 95 Bible* (IDG Books Worldwide).

When it's time to arrange some formal relationships between your more impassioned tables, here's how to do it:

1. **From the database window, select** <u>T</u>**ools**⇨**Relationships or click the Relationships button on the toolbar.**

   The Relationships window appears, probably looking quite blank at the moment.

   If some tables are already listed in the window, someone (or some-Wizard) has already defined relationships for this database. If you're in a corporate environment, *please* stop at this point and seek assistance from your Information Systems folks before mucking around with this database.

2. **Select** <u>R</u>**elationships**⇨**Show Table from the menu or click the Show Table button on the toolbar.**

   The Show Table dialog box appears on-screen, listing the tables in the current database file.

3. **Click on the first table involved in this would-be relationship, then click** <u>A</u>**dd. Repeat the process with the other tables you want to get involved. When you're done, click** <u>C</u>**lose (just like Figure 5-3).**

   With the tables present in the window, you're ready to start the relation-ships! (Do you feel like a matchmaker yet?)

4. **Decide which two tables you want to start with. In each table's window, scroll through the field list until the linking fields are both visible on-screen (see Figure 5-4).**

   In Access 95, you need to *see* the two linking fields on-screen before you can make a relationship.

5. **Put the mouse pointer on the field you want to link with, then hold the left mouse button down.**

   Did I mention that the same people who developed the old *Twister* game also designed the relationship builder? No? Hmm... that must've slipped my mind. Oh well, carry on — you'll discover that soon enough.

6. **While holding down the mouse button, slide the mouse from one linking field to the other. When the mouse pointer is on top of the second field, release the mouse button.**

   A dialog box detailing the soon-to-be relationship appears.

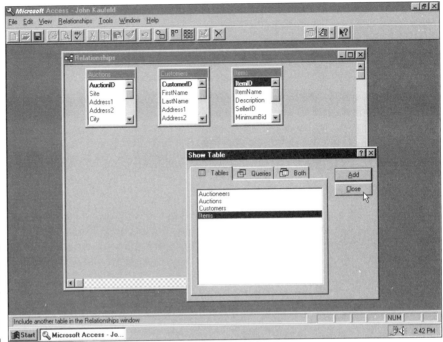

Figure 5-3:
All tables
reporting for
relationship
practice, sir!

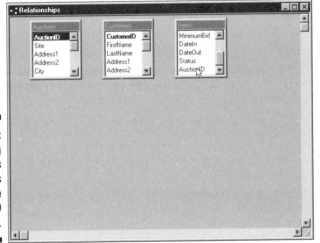

Figure 5-4:
I'm linking
Auctions
and Items
with the
AuctionID
field.

7. **Make sure the table and field names in the dialog box are correct. When you're sure the entries are right, click Create (see Figure 5-5).**

    A line appears to show you that the tables are linked, as you see in Figure 5-6. I moved the Customers table entry out of the way to make things a little clearer in the picture.

    If the table names or field names listed in the dialog box are wrong, just click Cancel and try Step 5 again.

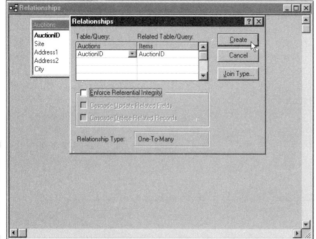

Figure 5-5:
This relationship is off to a good start.

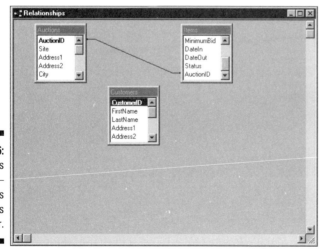

Figure 5-6:
The match is made —
Auctions and Items are together.

8. **To link another pair of tables, go back to Step 4 and begin again.**

   When you're done, the Relationships window may look a little messy, like Figure 5-7. To clean it up, put the mouse pointer on the title bar of a table window and then click and drag the table window to another part of the screen (see Figure 5-8).

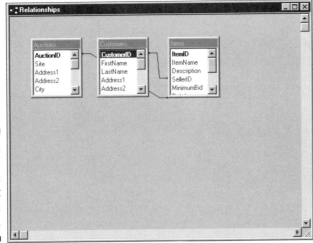

Figure 5-7:
With relationships like this, it could be a soap opera.

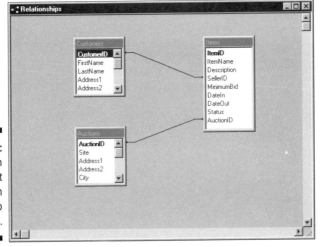

Figure 5-8:
That's much neater, not to mention easier to understand.

This doesn't change the relationship — it just moves the window around. In no time at all, things start looking neat and tidy.

Chapter 6

New Data, Old Data, and Data in Need of Repair

*T*he biggest cost surrounding *everything* in your life is maintenance. No matter what you're talking about — house, car, stereo, television, child, pet, significant other — it *always* costs more to keep it in good working order than it did to acquire the item in the first place.

An exception to the rule is your data. Thanks to the tools in Access 95, data maintenance is easy, relatively painless, and doesn't cost anything. In fact, keeping your data updated is one of the program's main goals.

This chapter covers basic data upkeep: adding new records, deleting old ones, and fixing the ones that are broken. If you're looking for *table* maintenance hints (like adding new columns, renaming fields, and so on), check out Chapter 9, "Table Remodeling Tips for the Do-It-Yourselfer."

Dragging Your Table into the Digital Workshop

Records tend to cluster together around tables, so you need to open a table before worrying about records. Tables prefer company as well. They hang out inside databases. Databases don't care a whit about anything other than themselves, so you might find them lounging in a folder, sulking on a diskette, or holding forth on a network drive.

That fancy buildup simply means that the first step on the road to record maintenance is *opening a database*. Even though there are several different ways to do it, they all ultimately work the same way.

If you just opened Access 95, the program displays a massive dialog box (see Figure 6-1) that offers the opportunity to create a new database, reopen one you worked on recently, or wander off into another dialog box to open whatever database strikes your fancy right now.

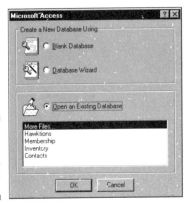

Figure 6-1:
Is this too
handy or
what?

✔ To use one of the databases listed at the bottom of the dialog box, double-click on its name. Access 95 automatically opens the database.

✔ If the database you want isn't on the list, double-click the More Files option to bring up the Open dialog box. This gives you access to all of the table files in the current file folder.

✔ What? The database you want isn't there *either?* In that case, check out the sidebar for some tips about the Open dialog box's fortuitous file-finding features.

✔ If you're in the mood to create a new table, what are you doing in this chapter? You should be back in Chapter 4 — that's where all the create-a-table stuff is.

That's all well and good if Access 95 just came roaring to life, but what if it's already running? In that case, there's a whole different way to open up your database. Here's how it works:

1. **Select File⇨Open Database from the main menu or click the Open Database button on the toolbar.**

   The Open dialog box pops onto the screen (see Figure 6-2).

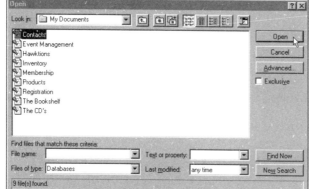

Figure 6-2:
There's the
database
I was
looking for.

2. **Scroll through the list until you find the database you're looking for.**

   If the database you want isn't on this list, it's probably in another folder, on another disk drive, or out on your network. To search for it, click the Down arrow in the Look in box (along the top of the Open dialog box) to see a list of your local and network disk drives. Click the drive you want to search. Access 95 displays a list of all databases and file folders in the current directory of that drive.

3. **When you find the database, open it by double-clicking on its name.**

   The database file opens with a flourish, as seen in Figure 6-3. This is how a normal, well-mannered database file acts in polite company. The rest of this chapter assumes that your database is behaving this way.

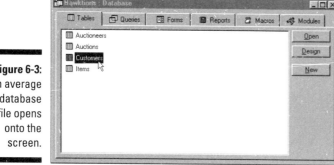

Figure 6-3:
An average
database
file opens
onto the
screen.

It's also possible that an introductory screen of some kind (known as a *switchboard*) appears instead of the tabbed dialog box. This means that your database either contains some custom programming or was created by the Database Wizard. You probably have some special forms that help you interact with the information in your database. Unfortunately, I can't tell you much more than that, because the possibilities are endless. The best suggestion I can offer is to look for instructions from your favorite local nerd.

4. **If it's not already selected, click the Tables tab.**

   This lists the tables in your database.

5. **Double-click on the table you want to edit.**

   The screen fills with your data, displayed eloquently in Datasheet view.

Adding a Little Something to the Mix

Few things are more frustrating than thinking you crammed everything you need into the car and then suddenly discovering there's *one* more thing to add (and invariably, it's something big). In the real world this is a repacking nightmare, but in the digital world of Access 95, it's effortless.

Adding another record to a table takes only a couple steps. The instructions assume that you already opened the database file and selected the table you're working on. (If you haven't, then follow the instructions in the first section of this chapter.) Here's how to add a new record to your table:

1. **Select Insert⇨Record from the main menu or click the New Record button on the toolbar.**

   Access 95 responds by opening a blank record in your table and moving the toothpick cursor there (see Figure 6-4). It's normal for an AutoNumber field to just sit there and not do anything at this point. It won't start working until the next step.

2. **Begin typing your information.**

   If the first field is an AutoNumber, press Tab and begin typing in the second field. As soon as you start typing, the AutoNumber field generates and displays a number.

Don't panic if the AutoNumber field seems to skip a number when it creates an entry for your new record (see Figure 6-5). The field remembers the last number it assigned and automatically inserts the next sequential number. Since it "skipped" a number, that means you probably entered (or at least *started* to enter) a record and then deleted it.

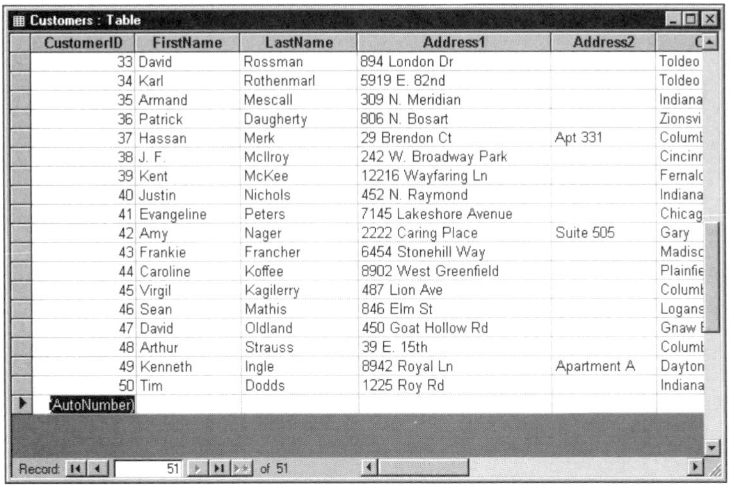

Figure 6-4:
A new
record is
born.

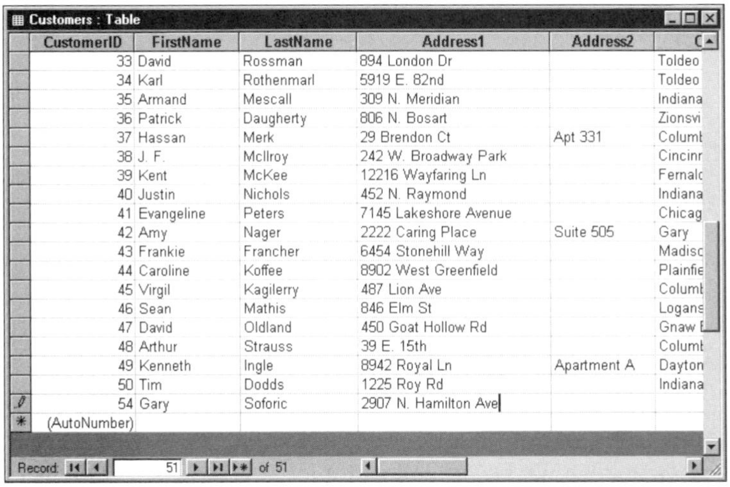

CustomerID	FirstName	LastName	Address1	Address2	C
33	David	Rossman	894 London Dr		Toldeo
34	Karl	Rothenmarl	5919 E. 82nd		Toldeo
35	Armand	Mescall	309 N. Meridian		Indiana
36	Patrick	Daugherty	806 N. Bosart		Zionsvi
37	Hassan	Merk	29 Brendon Ct	Apt 331	Columb
38	J. F.	McIlroy	242 W. Broadway Park		Cincinr
39	Kent	McKee	12216 Wayfaring Ln		Fernalc
40	Justin	Nichols	452 N. Raymond		Indiana
41	Evangeline	Peters	7145 Lakeshore Avenue		Chicag
42	Amy	Nager	2222 Caring Place	Suite 505	Gary
43	Frankie	Francher	6454 Stonehill Way		Madisc
44	Caroline	Koffee	8902 West Greenfield		Plainfie
45	Virgil	Kagilerry	487 Lion Ave		Columb
46	Sean	Mathis	846 Elm St		Logans
47	David	Oldland	450 Goat Hollow Rd		Gnaw L
48	Arthur	Strauss	39 E. 15th		Columb
49	Kenneth	Ingle	8942 Royal Ln	Apartment A	Dayton
50	Tim	Dodds	1225 Roy Rd		Indiana
(AutoNumber)					

Record: 51 of 51

Figure 6-5:
The record
takes shape,
despite
its odd
numbering.

CustomerID	FirstName	LastName	Address1	Address2	C
33	David	Rossman	894 London Dr		Toldeo
34	Karl	Rothenmarl	5919 E. 82nd		Toldeo
35	Armand	Mescall	309 N. Meridian		Indiana
36	Patrick	Daugherty	806 N. Bosart		Zionsvi
37	Hassan	Merk	29 Brendon Ct	Apt 331	Columb
38	J. F.	McIlroy	242 W. Broadway Park		Cincinr
39	Kent	McKee	12216 Wayfaring Ln		Fernalc
40	Justin	Nichols	452 N. Raymond		Indiana
41	Evangeline	Peters	7145 Lakeshore Avenue		Chicag
42	Amy	Nager	2222 Caring Place	Suite 505	Gary
43	Frankie	Francher	6454 Stonehill Way		Madisc
44	Caroline	Koffee	8902 West Greenfield		Plainfie
45	Virgil	Kagilerry	487 Lion Ave		Columb
46	Sean	Mathis	846 Elm St		Logans
47	David	Oldland	450 Goat Hollow Rd		Gnaw L
48	Arthur	Strauss	39 E. 15th		Columb
49	Kenneth	Ingle	8942 Royal Ln	Apartment A	Dayton
50	Tim	Dodds	1225 Roy Rd		Indiana
54	Gary	Soforic	2907 N. Hamilton Ave		
(AutoNumber)					

Record: 51 of 51

3. **When you're done, either press Tab to add another record or, if you just wanted to add one, simply go on about your business.**

Access 95 automatically saves the new record while you're typing it in.

If you change your mind and want to kill the new addition, select Edit⇨Undo Saved Record or press Ctrl+Z, and then click Yes when Access 95 asks about deleting the record. If the Undo Saved Record menu choice isn't available, click in the record you just added, and then select Edit⇨Delete Record. As before, click Yes when asked if you're sure about the deletion.

Bo Peep needed the Find File option

All Bo Peep needed to do was keep an eye on some animals and make sure they stayed in roughly the same geographic spot. Compared with riding herd over databases that could be on your local hard drive or somewhere in the company network, she had it easy!

The friendly folks who created Access 95 know that databases tend to run off and get lost from time to time. That's why they included the Find File options at the bottom of the Open dialog box. Although there are several options, the File name search is the most useful.

If you know at least part of the database's file name, type it into the File name box. Access 95 lists all databases in the current folder that con-

tain that text in the filename. If you click the Commands and Settings button (the one with a check mark and a menu on it in the upper right side of the dialog box) and select Search Subfolders from the menu that pops up, Access 95 looks in the current folder *and* all folders underneath it.

The real power of these two settings comes when you tell Access 95 to Look in a disk drive. Click the Down arrow in the Look in box and select a local or network disk drive from the pull-down menu. Almost immediately, your computer starts churning through the folders in the disk drive, looking here, there, and everywhere for files that match your specifications.

Changing What's Already There

Even though your stuff is safely tucked away inside a table, you can easily reach in and make changes. In fact, it's *so* easy to edit your data that I'm not sure whether this is a good feature or a bad one.

Whenever you're browsing through a table, *please* be careful! Access 95 doesn't warn you before saving changes to a record — even if the "changes" are accidental. (If I were one of those preachy authors, I'd probably make a big, guilt-laden point about how this "feature" of Access 95 makes doing regular backups all the more important. Luckily, I'm not that kind of guy, so I won't even bring the subject up.)

To change something inside a record, scroll through the table until you find the record that needs some adjusting. Click in the field you want to change. This pops the blinking toothpick cursor into the field.

What you do next depends on what kind of change you want to make to the field:

✔ To replace the *entire* field, press F2 to highlight the data, then type the new information. The new entry replaces the old one cleanly.

✔ To fix just a portion of the field, use the right and left arrow keys to position the toothpick cursor. Press Backspace to remove characters to the left of the cursor; press Delete to remove them to the right. Insert new characters by simply typing.

✔ If you're in a time/date field and want to insert the current date, press Ctrl+; (semicolon). To insert the current time, press Ctrl+: (colon).

When you're done with the record, press Enter to save your changes. If you change your mind and want to restore the original data, press Esc or Ctrl+Z to cancel your edits. If you're on a rotary-dial phone, please wait for operator assistance (hmm — perhaps I've been making too many phone calls lately).

Don't press Enter until you're *positively sure* about the changes you typed. Once you save them, the old data is gone — there's no going back.

Kicking Out Unwanted Records

There's no sense mourning over unneeded records. When it's time to bid them adieu, do it quickly and painlessly. Here's how:

1. **With the table open, click in the record you want to delete.**

   Be sure you clicked the correct record before going on to the next step! It's a *lot* less painful to discover the mistake now than it is in just a moment.

2. **Select Edit⊅Delete Record from the menu.**

   Access 95 does a truly cool screen-effect and visually swallows the old record.

3. **When Access 95 displays the dialog box in Figure 6-6, pause and reflect once more about deleting the record.**

   If you're sure, click Yes and banish the record to oblivion.

   If you're the slightest bit unsure, click No and do some more thinking before exercising the Delete Record command on anything else in your table.

   Instead of the dialog box labeled Are you sure, Access 95 might display the box in Figure 6-7. This message means you *can't* delete that record, no matter how much you might want to. In this case, you're working with a table that's related to another one. Access 95 won't let you remove the record because there are records in another table that are linked to the one you want to kill. Sorry — there's no way out of this one. If you *still* want to delete the record, ask a data hit man (or your local computer jockey) to do the dirty work for you, because there's more to this problem than meets the eye.

Figure 6-6:
Access 95
asks the
fateful
question:
Are you
sure?

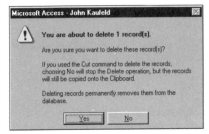

Figure 6-7:
Oops — this
record is
going
nowhere.

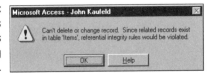

Recovering from a Baaaad Edit

I have only two suggestions for picking up the pieces from a bad edit. Unfortunately, neither is a super-cool placebo that magically restores your lost data. I wish I had better news to close the chapter with, but I'm fresh out of headlines.

First, double-check any change you make before saving it. If it's an important change, *triple-check* it. When you're sure it's right, press Enter and commit it to the table. If you're not sure about the data, *don't* save the changes. Instead, get your questions answered first and then feel free to edit the record.

Second, keep a good backup so you can quickly recover missing data and get on with your work. There's no substitute for good backups. If you make good backups, the chance of losing data is greatly reduced, your boss will promote you, your significant other will unswervingly devote his or her life to you, and you might even win the lottery. (Truth be told, backups do only *one* of those things, but it's the thought that counts.)

Chapter 7

Making Your Table Think with Formats, Masks, and Validations

In This Chapter

▶ Finding where the settings live

▶ Better formatting for prettier data

▶ Keeping bad data out with input masks

▶ Performing detailed testing through validations

Scientists have incredibly detailed, long-winded explanations of what it means to "think," but my definition is much simpler. If you see dragons in the clouds, marvel at a child's playtime adventures, or wonder what makes flowers grow, you're thinking.

Whether you use my definition or one from the experts, one thing is for sure: Access 95 tables *don't* think. If you have nightmarish visions of reading this chapter and then accidentally unleashing The Table That Ate Microsoft's Competitors, have no fear, because it's not going to happen. After all, if that *could* happen, don't you think Microsoft would've done it by now?

This chapter explains how to enlist your table's help to spot and prevent bad data from getting into your table. It covers three different tools: *formats, masks,* and *validation rules.* They may sound kinda technical, but you can work them (trust me).

Each tool has its own section, so if you're looking for specific information, feel free to jump ahead. (And pay no attention to those computers discussing philosophy in the corner.)

Finding the Place to Make a Change

There's nothing like starting with the first thing you need to know. In this case, it's nice to find out precisely *where* to make all of these cool changes. Luckily, all three options are in the same place: the General tab of the Table design window.

Use the following steps to put your table into Design view, then flip to the appropriate section of the chapter for the details on applying a format, input mask, or validation to a field in your table.

1. **With the database file open, click on the table you want to work on and then click <u>D</u>esign (see Figure 7-1).**

Figure 7-1:
It's time
for some
serious
design
work.

The table flips into Design view, showing its nerdish underbelly to the world.

 By the way, if you're already looking at the table in Datasheet view, click the Design button on the toolbar to get into Design view.

2. **Click the name of the field you want to work on.**

The General tab in the Field Properties section (the bottom half of the window) displays the details of the current field, as seen in Figure 7-2. You're ready to do your stuff!

3. **Click the appropriate box and type in your changes.**

There's a box for Format, Input Mask, and Validation Rule. (Yes, there's also one for Validation Text, but you have to look in the validations section to find out about it, because I'm not telling here.)

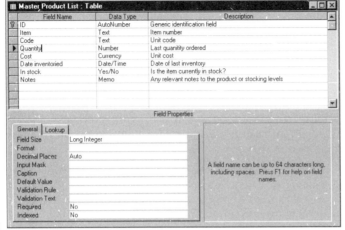

Figure 7-2:
Ready for
some work
on the
Quantity
field.

4. **If you want to work on other fields, go back to Step 2 and repeat the process.**

   You can add one, two, or all three pieces of intelligence to a field at once. Access 95 automatically saves your changes when you click another field.

5. **When you're through, close the table to save your changes.**

   There you have it!

To Format, Perchance to Better See

Formats change the way your data appears on-screen. They change the way you see the data, not how it's stored in the table. Although formats don't directly catch errors, they *do* make your information look simply marvelous (and that's gotta be worth something these days).

Each field type has its own set of formats. The following sections are organized by field type in order to make your life a little easier. Pay close attention to the kind of field you're working with, because it's both pointless and frustrating to force the wrong format into a field (and goodness knows there are *enough* pointless and frustrating things about your computer without actively courting another one).

Text and memo fields

There are four possibilities here. Unfortunately, there aren't any ready-made examples built into the Format text box like there are for the other field types. I guess that just means text and memo fields are tough and don't need the help.

Here are your four text and memo formatting options:

- ✔ The *greater than symbol* (>) makes all of the text in that field appear in uppercase, regardless of how it was entered. Although Access 95 stores the data *just as it was typed,* it displays in uppercase only. To use this, put a single greater than symbol in the Format text box.

- ✔ The *less than symbol* (<) does just the opposite of the greater than. It shows all of that field's text in lowercase. If you entered the data in mixed case, it's still stored that way. As with the greater than symbol, only the display is changed to protect the innocent. Use this by putting a single less than symbol in the Format text box.

- ✔ The *at sign* (@) forces Access 95 to display either a character or a space in the field. If the field is smaller than the format, Access 95 adds extra spaces until it fills up the format. For example, if a field uses @@@@@ as its format, but the field's data is only three characters long (like `Tim` or `now`), Access 95 displays three spaces and *then* the data. If it's displaying four characters, the format pads the beginning of the entry with two spaces. See how it works? (Kinda silly, isn't it?)

- ✔ The *ampersand* (&) is the default format. It means "display a character if there's one to display, otherwise don't do anything." Why did they create a special format for this when it's what Access 95 does by default? I don't know...for now, it remains a mystery to me.

- ✔ By the way, you include one at sign or ampersand *for each character* in the field, unlike the greater than and less than symbols, which require only one symbol for the whole field.

This is a certified Nerd Trick, but it's so useful I *had* to take the chance and tell you about it. If you sometimes need to skip a text field during data entry and want to clearly mark the fact that the field is blank, type `@;"Unknown"[Red]` into the field's Format text box. This peculiar notation will display the word *Unknown* in red print if there's no value in the field. You *must* type the command *exactly* like the example (quotation marks, square brackets, and all), or it won't work. Feel free to substitute your own word for *Unknown,* though — the command doesn't care what you put between the quotation marks.

Number and currency fields

The friendly folks at Microsoft did all the hard work for you on these two field types. They built the six most common formats into a pull-down menu right in the Format text box. To set a number or currency field format, click in the Format text box and then click the Down arrow that appears at the right side of the box. Figure 7-3 shows the pull-down menu, laden with your choices.

Figure 7-3:
Choose the
format of
your dreams
right from
the menu.

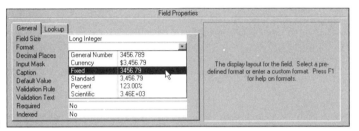

Each format's given name is on the left side of the menu. The other side shows a sample of how the format works. Here's a quick rundown of the most common choices:

- *General Number* is the default. Access 95 merely displays whatever you put into the field without making any editorial changes to it.

- The *Currency* format makes a standard number field look just like a currency field. It shows the data with two decimal places, substituting zeros if there aren't any decimals to begin with. It also adds the appropriate currency sign and punctuation, according to the Regional Settings in the Windows 95 Control Panel.

- *Fixed* locks the field's data into a specific number of decimal places. By default, it rounds to two decimal places. To specify a different number of decimal places, use the Decimal Places setting right below the Format setting.

- *Standard* does the same thing as Fixed, but adds a thousands separator as well. Adjust the number of decimals by changing the Decimal Places setting.

- The *Percent* format is especially for the percentages of life. It turns a simple decimal percentage like .97 into the much prettier 97%. Remember to enter the data as a decimal (.97 instead of 97); otherwise Access 95 displays some truly awesome percentages! If your percentages display only as 0.00% or 1.00%, see the next paragraph for a solution.

If your entries automatically round to the nearest whole number and always display zeros in the decimal places, change the Field Size setting (right above Format) from Long Integer to Single. This tells Access 95 to remember the decimal part of the number. By default, Access 95 rounds the number to an integer as you enter it. (Stupid computers.)

Date/time fields

Like the Number and Currency format options, date/time fields have a ready-to-use set of formats available in a pull-down menu. Click in the Format text box and then click the down arrow that appears on the box's right side, and the menu in Figure 7-4 dutifully pops down to serve you.

Figure 7-4:
A format for every date, and a date for every format.

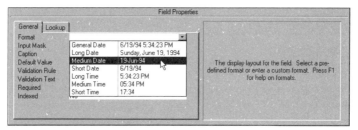

The choices are pretty self-explanatory, but I do have a couple of tips for you:

✔ When using one of the larger formats like General Date or Long Date, make sure that the datasheet column is wide enough to display the whole thing. Otherwise, the cool-looking date doesn't make sense because a major portion of it is missing.

✔ If the database is used by more than one person, it's better to choose a format that provides *more* information than one that provides less. My favorite is the Medium Date format, because it spells out the month and day. Otherwise, dates like 3/7/95 may cause confusion, because Americans and Europeans interpret that format differently.

Yes/No fields

There's only so much you can say about a field with two options. Your preset formatting choices are somewhat limited, as Figure 7-5 shows. By default, Yes/No fields are set to the Yes/No formatting (programmers are *so* clever sometimes). Feel free to experiment with the other options, particularly if they make more sense in your table than Yes and No.

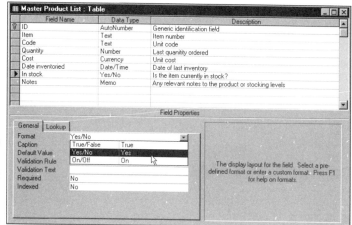

Figure 7-5:
The format
cupboard is
pretty bare.

To display your *own* choices instead of a boring Yes and No, you have to type a customized format. This works a lot like the custom text format earlier in this chapter. A good example format is ;"In stock"[Green];"REORDER"[Red]. If an item is in stock, the text *In stock* appears in green. Otherwise, *REORDER* screams a warning in bright red. Substitute your own words for mine if you like, since Access 95 displays whatever you put between the quotes without making any editorial decisions about the content.

What Is that Masked Data?

Although they have a funny name, *input masks* are filters that allow you to enter only certain data into a field. When they're paired with validations (covered in the next section), the fields in your table are *very* well protected against bad information.

An input mask is just a series of characters that tell Access 95 what kind of data to expect in this field. If you want a field to contain all numbers and no letters, an input mask can do the job. It can also do the reverse (all letters and no numbers) and almost any combination in between. Input masks are stored in the Input Mask area of the field's General tab, along with everything else in this chapter.

Each field in an Access 95 table (except a memo field) can have its own input mask. Before creating the mask, you have to know *exactly* what the field's data looks like. It won't do any good to create a mask that allows only letters into a field if your goal is to store street addresses. Know your data intimately *before* messing around with input masks.

Input masks work best with *short, highly consistent* data. Numbers and number/letter combinations that all look alike are excellent candidates. Part numbers, stock-keeping units, postal codes, phone numbers, and Social Security numbers beg for input masks to ensure the right data gets into the field.

There are two ways to create an input mask. You can either type it in manually or ask the Input Mask Wizard for some help. As luck would have it, the Input Mask Wizard isn't terribly bright — he only knows about text and date fields. And even then, he offers just a few options to make your life easier. To accomplish anything more means cracking your knuckles and doing it by hand.

Using the Input Mask Wizard

The Input Mask Wizard will gleefully help if you're making a mask for a phone number, Social Security number, United States zip code, or simple date and time field. Beyond those fields, he's clueless.

To ask the wizard's help, go through these steps:

1. **With the database file open, click on the table you want to work on and then click** <u>**D**</u>**esign.**

    The table flips into Design view.

2. **Click the name of the field you want to work on.**

    The General tab in the Field Properties section (the bottom half of the window) displays the details of the current field.

3. **Click on the Input Mask box.**

    The cursor moves to the Input Mask box, and the Build button (the one with three periods on it) appears right next to it.

4. **Click the Build button at the right side of the Input Mask text box.**

    The wizard appears, making a glorious entrance just like Figure 7-6.

    You can use the wizard only with text and date fields. Don't tempt the wizard's wrath by rousing it to work with another kind of field.

5. **Scroll through the list of available input masks to find what you want. Click on your choice and then click** <u>**N**</u>**ext.**

    The dialog box displays the sordid code behind the mask, plus some other information (see Figure 7-7).

    If you chose the Password option, there's nothing else for you to do, so click <u>F</u>inish.

6. **If you want to play with the input mask and see if it *really* does what you want, click in the Try It area at the bottom of the dialog box. When you're done, click** <u>**F**</u>**inish to use the mask with your field.**

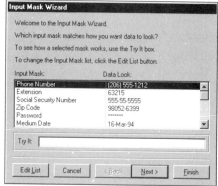

Figure 7-6:
The Input
Mask
Wizard
doesn't do
much, but it
tries hard.

Figure 7-7:
Here's what
the wizard
says you
need.

The chosen mask appears in the Input Mask area on the table design screen. By the way, click Cancel to call off the sordid mask affair and make the wizard go away.

If you click Next instead of Finish, the Wizard offers you an arcane choice about storing characters along with your data. It wants to know if you want the dashes, slashes, and parentheses that the input mask displays to be stored in your table along with the data you typed. The default is no, which I recommend sticking with. Click Finish to complete the process.

Making a mask by hand

Few things are more gratifying than making something yourself. Building an input mask with your bare hands, raw nerve, and these instructions *may* give you that same feeling of accomplishment. (If it does, please seek professional help soon — you're in danger of becoming a technoid.)

✔ What input masks *do* isn't terribly complicated, but a finished mask often *looks* that way. Don't let it worry you, though — once you get the hang of it, building powerful input masks is easy.

✔ My friends told me the same thing about water skiing, but it took only one lesson to discern that they were just trying to make my drowning look like an innocent water sports accident. You have my word that making input masks isn't anything like that.

With that confidence-building introduction behind you, it's time to roll up your sleeves and plunge your hands in the alphabetic goop of input masks. Designing and using an input mask takes just a few steps:

1. On a piece of paper, write an example of the data that the mask is supposed to let through.

Although I mentioned it earlier in the chapter, knowing your data really *is* the first step in the input mask process.

If the information you're storing has subtle variations (like part numbers that end in either a letter/number or letter/letter combination), include examples of the various possibilities so your input mask accepts them all.

2. Write a simple description of the data, including which parts are required and which are optional.

If your sample is a part number that looks like `728816ABC7`, write *six numbers, three letters,* and then *one number;* all parts are required. Remember to allow for the variations, if you have any. There's a big difference between *one number* and *one letter* or *number.*

Required information must be entered into the field (such as a phone number). *Optional* parts are just that — optional (like an area code or extension number). Access 95 uses different codes for required and optional data; that's why you need to note the difference.

3. Using the codes in Table 7-1, create an input mask for your data.

Since you know what kind of data you're storing (numbers, letters, or either one), how many of them you need, and whether each one is required or optional, it's easy to work through the table and create the mask.

To include a dash, slash, or parenthesis in your mask, put a backslash (\) in front of it. To include more than one character, put quote marks around them. For instance, the mask for a phone number with area code might be !\(999") "000\-000. This includes parentheses around the area code plus a space between the area code and phone number. (See the upcoming sidebar "The exclamation point: to know it is to love it" to find out why I included an exclamation point in that example.)

Here's a pop quiz, just to see if you're paying attention. In the example, is the area code optional or required? What about the phone number itself? Why? Write a long, detailed answer on a very small piece of paper, then rip it to shreds and throw it like confetti into the air. Wasn't that fun?

4. **If your field includes letters and you want them to always be uppercase, add a greater than symbol (>) to the beginning of your mask.**

   To make the letters lowercase, use a less than symbol (<) instead.

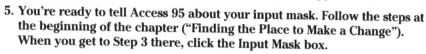

5. **You're ready to tell Access 95 about your input mask. Follow the steps at the beginning of the chapter ("Finding the Place to Make a Change"). When you get to Step 3 there, click the Input Mask box.**

   The blinking toothpick cursor hops into the box, ready for action.

6. **Carefully type your finished mask into the Input Mask area of Field Properties (see Figure 7-8).**

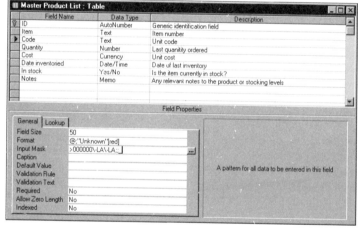

Figure 7-8:
Putting a
mask on the
Code field.

Don't worry if the mask looks like a text version of the Frankenstein monster. This is about technology; beauty is optional.

7. **At the end of the mask, add ;;_ (two semi-colons and an underscore character).**

   This tells Access 95 to display an underscore where you want each letter to appear. This step isn't required, but I think input masks make more sense with this option. Your mileage may vary.

8. Click the Table view button on the toolbar to check out your handiwork.

Try typing something into the now-masked field. The input mask should prevent you from entering something incorrectly. If it doesn't work, take the table back into Design view (click the Design View button on the left side of the toolbar) and make some repairs.

If you're adding a mask to an existing table, the mask won't ferret out incorrect data that's *already* in the table. You have to click on each entry in that field (yes, that means clicking on this field in *every* record of the table) in order to check it. If there's something wrong, Access 95 will tell you, but not until you click.

Table 7-1	Codes for the Input Mask	
Kind of Characters	*Required Code*	*Optional Code*
Digits (0 to 9) only	0 (zero)	9
Digits and +/- signs	*none*	# (U.S. pound sign)
Letters (A to Z) only	L	? (question mark)
Letters or digits only	A	a (must be lowercase)
Any character or space	& (ampersand)	C

TECHNICAL STUFF

The exclamation point: to know it is to love it

It took me a while to really get to know the exclamation point. After all, my input masks seemed very happy without it. Even the explanation in the Access 95 on-line help file didn't change my mind. (I suppose if the help file's explanation made *sense*, it might have had a better chance.)

While playing with the phone number example, I *finally* realized what the exclamation point does and why it's so useful. It tells Access 95 to fill up the field from the *right* instead of the *left*. Although this may sound like the unintelligible ramblings of an over-caffeinated nerd, this really is an important thought. Let me show you why.

In the phone number example, the area code is optional, but the number itself is required. If I leave the exclamation point *out* of the input mask, Access 95 lets me skip the area code and

type a phone number into the phone number spaces. Everything looks fine until I hit Enter. Then my seven-digit phone number displays as (555) 121-2. Eww — not exactly what I had in mind. That's because it filled the mask from the *left*, starting with the optional numbers in the area code (the numbers I didn't enter).

By adding the exclamation point to the input mask, Access 95 takes my data and fills the mask *from the right*. This time, it appears on-screen as (   )555-1212, which is what I wanted all along.

By the way, the exclamation point can go anywhere in the input mask, but you should get into the habit of putting it either at the beginning or the end. I suggest making it the first character in the mask, simply because you won't overlook it in that position.

Validations: The Digital Breathalyzer Test

Your third (and, arguably, most powerful) tool in the War against Bad Data is the *validation*. With a validation, Access 95 actually tests the incoming data to make sure it's what you want in the table. If it isn't, the validation displays an error message (you get to choose what it says!) and makes you try the entry again.

Like the other options in this chapter, validations are stored in the General tab of the Field Properties area. There are two spaces relating to validations: Validation Rule and Validation Text. The rule is the actual validation itself. The text is the error message you want Access 95 to display when some data wanders in that violates the validation rule.

Validations work best with number, currency, and date fields. It's possible to create a validation for a text field, but the validations usually get *very* complicated, *very* fast. In the name of protecting your sanity and hairline, Table 7-2 contains some ready-to-use validations that cover the most common needs. They're organized by field type, so it's easy to find the validation rule that suits your purpose.

I included different kinds of examples to show off the power of the logical operators that validations use. Feel free to mix and match with the operators. Play around and see what you can come up with!

- ✔ When using *And,* remember that both sides of the validation rule must be true before the rule is met.

- ✔ With *Or,* only one side of the rule needs to be true for the whole rule to be true.

- ✔ Be careful when combining >= and <= examples. It's very easy to come up with one that won't *ever* be true (like <= 0 And >= 100).

Table 7-2	Validations for a Lot of Occasions	
Field Type	*Validation Rule*	*Definition*
Number	> 0	Must be greater than zero
Number	<> 0	Cannot be zero
Number	> 0 And < 100	Must be between 0 and 100 (noninclusive)
Number	>= 0 And <= 100	Must be between 0 and 100 (inclusive)
Number	<= 0 Or >= 100	Must be less than 0 or greater than 100

Table 7-2 *(continued)*

Field Type	Validation Rule	Definition
Date	>= Date ()	Must be today's date or later
Date	>= Date () Or Is Null	Must be today's date or later, or blank
Date	< Date ()	Must be earlier than today's date
Date	>= #1/1/90# And <= Date ()	Must be between January 1, 1990, and today (inclusive)

The 5th Wave   By Rich Tennant

THE GREAT THING ABOUT OBJECT-ORIENTED PROGRAMMING IS, IT'S MADE SOFTWARE DEVELOPMENT AS EASY AS PUTTING ONE FOOT IN FRONT OF THE OTHER.

Chapter 8

Making Your Datasheets Dance

In This Chapter

▶ Adjusting column width, row height, and more
▶ Seeing the datasheet in a whole new font
▶ Changing the background

*I*t's pretty boring when your new datasheet looks just like every *other* datasheet. Where's the creativity in that? Where's the individuality? Where's the life, liberty, and pursuit of ultimate coolness?

Granted, Access 95 *is* a database program, and databases aren't generally known for being the life of the party. But that still doesn't mean you're trapped into a monotonous world of look-alike datasheets. This chapter explores the tools at your disposal to turn even the most dreary datasheet into a slick-looking exposition of your data.

This entire chapter focuses on datasheet tricks — things to do when you're working with information in a datasheet. These tricks work with datasheets from both tables and dynasets, so use them to spruce up every datasheet in sight. If you haven't heard about dynasets yet, don't worry. They're covered in Part III.

Seeing More (or Less) of Your Data

First on the datasheet tune-up list is fiddling with the look of your datasheet. There's plenty to fiddle with, too. At first blush, your datasheet looks pretty mundane, much like Figure 8-1. To perk it up a bit, you can change the column width, row height, and column order, and you can lock a column in place while the others scroll around it. Heck, you can even make columns temporarily disappear.

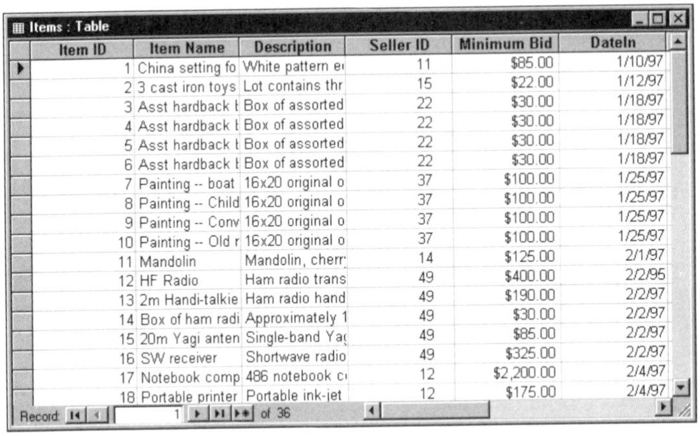

	Item ID	Item Name	Description	Seller ID	Minimum Bid	DateIn
▶	1	China setting fo	White pattern e	11	$85.00	1/10/97
	2	3 cast iron toys	Lot contains thr	15	$22.00	1/12/97
	3	Asst hardback	Box of assorted	22	$30.00	1/18/97
	4	Asst hardback	Box of assorted	22	$30.00	1/18/97
	5	Asst hardback	Box of assorted	22	$30.00	1/18/97
	6	Asst hardback	Box of assorted	22	$30.00	1/18/97
	7	Painting -- boat	16x20 original o	37	$100.00	1/25/97
	8	Painting -- Child	16x20 original o	37	$100.00	1/25/97
	9	Painting -- Conv	16x20 original o	37	$100.00	1/25/97
	10	Painting -- Old r	16x20 original o	37	$100.00	1/25/97
	11	Mandolin	Mandolin, cherr	14	$125.00	2/1/97
	12	HF Radio	Ham radio trans	49	$400.00	2/2/95
	13	2m Handi-talkie	Ham radio hand	49	$190.00	2/2/97
	14	Box of ham radi	Approximately 1	49	$30.00	2/2/97
	15	20m Yagi anten	Single-band Ya	49	$85.00	2/2/97
	16	SW receiver	Shortwave radio	49	$325.00	2/2/97
	17	Notebook comp	486 notebook c	12	$2,200.00	2/4/97
	18	Portable printer	Portable ink-jet	12	$175.00	2/4/97

Record: |◄| ◄ | 1 | ► | ►| | ►* | of 36

Figure 8-1:
Both the
ItemName
and
Description
columns are
brutally
clipped.

Each following section explores one of these techniques. You can fix one thing (like changing the column width) or a number of things — it's your choice. Each adjustment is independent of the others. Plus, these changes don't affect your actual data. They make the data appear differently on-screen, but they don't change the underlying data at all.

Most of the commands work from the mouse itself, but some send you back to the menu bar. If a command is in both places, it works the same either way.

Changing the column width

Even though Access 95 is pretty smart, it still has some trouble figuring out how wide to make a column. In fact, it usually just gives up and sets all the column widths identically, leaving some far too wide and others way too small. Pretty wimpy solution for a powerful program, if you ask me.

Setting a new column width is a quick operation. Here's what to do:

1. **With your table in Datasheet view, put the mouse pointer on the vertical bar to the right of the field name (see Figure 8-2).**

   The mouse pointer changes into a bar with arrows sticking out of each side.

2. **Click and hold the left mouse button while moving the mouse appropriately.**

   To make the column wider, move the mouse to the right. To make it smaller, move the mouse left.

3. **When the width is just right, let up on the mouse button.**

   The column is locked into its new size, as Figure 8-3 shows.

Item ID	Item Name	Description	Seller ID	Minimum Bid	DateIn
1	China setting fo	White pattern e	11	$85.00	1/10/97
2	3 cast iron toys	Lot contains thr	15	$22.00	1/12/97
3	Asst hardback l	Box of assorted	22	$30.00	1/18/97
4	Asst hardback l	Box of assorted	22	$30.00	1/18/97
5	Asst hardback l	Box of assorted	22	$30.00	1/18/97
6	Asst hardback l	Box of assorted	22	$30.00	1/18/97
7	Painting -- boat	16x20 original o	37	$100.00	1/25/97
8	Painting -- Child	16x20 original o	37	$100.00	1/25/97
9	Painting -- Conv	16x20 original o	37	$100.00	1/25/97
10	Painting -- Old r	16x20 original o	37	$100.00	1/25/97
11	Mandolin	Mandolin, cherr	14	$125.00	2/1/97
12	HF Radio	Ham radio trans	49	$400.00	2/2/95
13	2m Handi-talkie	Ham radio hand	49	$190.00	2/2/97
14	Box of ham radi	Approximately 1	49	$30.00	2/2/97
15	20m Yagi anten	Single-band Ya(	49	$85.00	2/2/97
16	SW receiver	Shortwave radio	49	$325.00	2/2/97
17	Notebook comp	486 notebook c	12	$2,200.00	2/4/97
18	Portable printer	Portable ink-jet	12	$175.00	2/4/97

Record: 1 of 36

Figure 8-2:
Ready to
widen the
column.

Tell Access 95 to save the changes to your table, or all of your hard work
will be lost forever. The program automatically asks about saving changes
when you close the table.

Changing the row height

Access 95 does better in the row height department, leaving enough room to
separate the rows while displaying plenty of information on-screen, but there's
still room for improvement. If you have large fields in your table, changing the
row height lets you see more data in each field while *still* displaying the same
number of fields on-screen.

Like changing column width, adjusting the row height takes only a couple of
mouse clicks:

Item ID	Item Name	Description	Seller ID	Minimum Bid
1	China setting for 8	White pattern e	11	$85.00
2	3 cast iron toys	Lot contains thr	15	$22.00
3	Asst hardback books (1 of 4)	Box of assorted	22	$30.00
4	Asst hardback books (2 of 4)	Box of assorted	22	$30.00
5	Asst hardback books (3 of 4)	Box of assorted	22	$30.00
6	Asst hardback books (4 of 4)	Box of assorted	22	$30.00
7	Painting -- boat on lake	16x20 original o	37	$100.00
8	Painting -- Children	16x20 original o	37	$100.00
9	Painting -- Convertible	16x20 original o	37	$100.00
10	Painting -- Old man	16x20 original o	37	$100.00
11	Mandolin	Mandolin, cherr	14	$125.00
12	HF Radio	Ham radio trans	49	$400.00
13	2m Handi-talkie	Ham radio hand	49	$190.00
14	Box of ham radio magazines	Approximately 1	49	$30.00
15	20m Yagi antenna	Single-band Ya(	49	$85.00
16	SW receiver	Shortwave radio	49	$325.00
17	Notebook computer	486 notebook c	12	$2,200.00
18	Portable printer	Portable ink-jet	12	$175.00

Record: 1 of 36

Figure 8-3:
That looks a
whole lot
better.

1. **While viewing your table in a datasheet, put the mouse pointer in the far left side of the window on the line between any two rows in your spreadsheet (see Figure 8-4).**

   The mouse pointer changes into a horizontal bar with arrows sticking out vertically.

2. **Click and hold the left mouse button; then move the mouse to change the row height.**

   Move the mouse down to make the row higher. Move it up to squash the row and put the squeeze on your data.

3. **When the row height is where you want it, release the mouse button.**

   Access 95 redisplays the table with its new row height (see Figure 8-5).

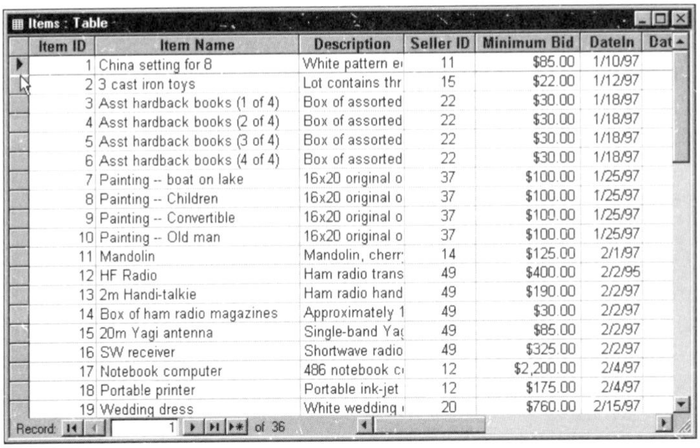

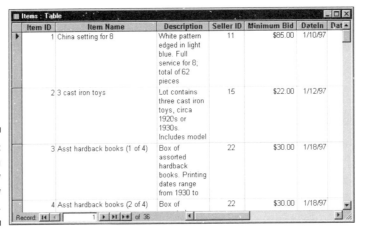

Figure 8-4: One wider row, coming right up (or is that down?).

Figure 8-5: The data automatically fills the new field space.

Reorganizing the columns

When you laid out the table, you put a lot of thought into which field came after which other field. Most of the time, your data looks just the way you want it on-screen, but occasionally it helps to stir things up a bit.

To move a field to a different place on the datasheet, use these steps:

1. **Click on the field name of the column you want to move; then click and hold the left mouse button.**

   The whole column darkens, with a smaller box at the bottom of the column, and the mouse pointer changes to an arrow (see Figure 8-6).

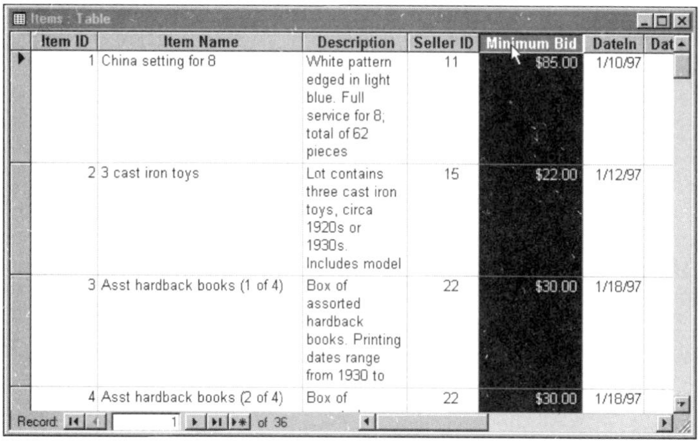

Figure 8-6:
You're ready
to move that
column.

2. **Drag the column to its new destination.**

   As you move the mouse, a dark bar moves between the columns, showing you where the column will land when you release the mouse button.

3. **When the column is in place, let up on the mouse button.**

   The column, data and all, moves to the new spot (see Figure 8-7).

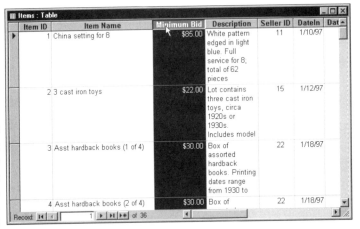

Hiding a column

This is one of those features that seem totally unimportant until the moment you need them, and then they're worth their weight in gold. If you want to temporarily not display a particular column, just hide the little fellow. The data is still in the table, but it doesn't appear on-screen. Too cool, eh?

To hide a column, follow these steps:

1. **With your table in datasheet view, right-click on the name of the column to hide.**

   The whole column goes dark and a pop-up menu appears.

2. **Select Hide Columns from the menu (see Figure 8-8).**

   {Poof!} The column vanishes.

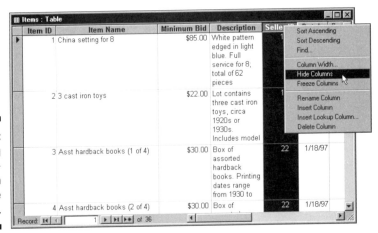

To hide more than one column at once, click and drag across the names of the columns you want to squirrel away, then select Format➪Hide Columns from the main menu.

When you're ready to bring back the temporarily indisposed column, use these steps:

1. **Select Format➪Unhide Columns from the main menu.**

   This displays a small dialog box listing all of the fields in the current table. The fields with a check mark in the box next to them are already displayed.

2. **Click in the check box next to each field you want to see on-screen again, then click Close (see Figure 8-9).**

   Depending on the number of fields in the list, you may have to scroll around to find all of the fields.

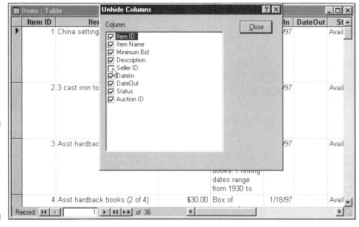

Figure 8-9:
Aha — I
found its
hiding
place!

Freezing a column

If you have a lot of fields in a table, they don't all fit in the window. As you scroll from one side of the table to the other, fields are constantly appearing on one side and disappearing from the other. What if you want to keep looking at a column way over on one side of the table *while* looking at fields on the other?

The secret is to freeze the column in place. This locks a column into the left side of the window so it just sits there while you scroll merrily back and forth through the table. Of course, there's an *unfreeze* step to go along with it — you don't want your tables catching cold, do you?

Here are the steps to freezing a column:

1. **Right-click on the column you want to freeze.**

   The column turns dark, and the ever-anticipated pop-up menu appears.

2. **Select Freeze Columns from the menu.**

   The column is now locked in place. You can now scroll back and forth through your table with impunity (and you don't have any restrictions, either).

To unfreeze the column when you're done, select Format⇨Unfreeze All Columns from the main menu.

Fonting Around with Your Table

Being your basic, business-oriented program, Access 95 displays your table in a basic, business-oriented font. You're not stuck with that font choice forever, though (and it's a good thing, too, because it's boring). You have control over the font, style, and even the *color* your data appears in. It's up to you, so why not live on the edge and try a new look on your table?

These settings apply to the *entire table,* not just a particular row or column.

To change the font, style, or color of your table, follow these steps:

Making design changes in Datasheet view — danger, Will Robinson!

So far, everything in this chapter changes the look of the datasheet without doing anything to the table underneath it. Moving or hiding columns, changing column widths, adjusting row heights — all of these are innocuous settings that simply make your digital world a prettier place.

The story changes with the *Insert Column, Insert Lookup Column, Rename Column,* and *Delete Column* options on the right-click pop-up window. These choices actually *change* the structure of your table, so go slow and treat them carefully!

Rename Column changes the field name. Insert Column adds a new column on the datasheet, which translates into a new field in the table. Insert Lookup Column starts the Lookup Wizard and helps you insert a column for data pulled in from another table. Delete Column is pretty self-explanatory (remember that Access 95 undoes only the *last* thing you did, so don't delete anything until you're sure it's the right thing to kill).

You're altering the table's structure with these options. Have a look through Chapter 9 for more about these options and how to use them safely. (It's *that* important.)

1. **With the table in Datasheet view, select Format⇨Font from the main menu.**

   The font dialog box elbows its way onto the screen.

2. **Click on your choice from the Font list on the left side of the screen (see Figure 8-10).**

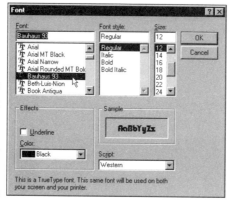

Figure 8-10: It's a cool font, but will it look good on the table?

Access 95 previews the font in the Sample box on the right side of the dialog box.

It's best to pick a TrueType font instead of the other options. TrueType fonts have the little double-T symbol next to them in the list.

3. **Click on the preferred style in the Font style list.**

   Some fonts may not have all of the common style options (normal, bold, italic, and bold italic). It depends on how the fonts were loaded onto your system. For more about fonts and font files, check out *Windows 95 For Dummies* (IDG Books Worldwide).

4. **To select a different size, click on a number in the Size list.**

   As with style, not every font is available in all sizes. If you chose a TrueType font back in Step 2, this isn't a problem because TrueType fonts are scaleable (Windows simply makes them whatever size it needs).

5. **If you want a new color, click in the arrow next to the Color box and pick your favorite from the drop-down menu.**

   You're almost done — now's a good time to look at the Sample box and see if your choices look good together. If they don't, click Cancel and start over with Step 1.

6. **Click OK to apply your font selections.**

   The datasheet now displays your table in its new digs (see Figure 8-11).

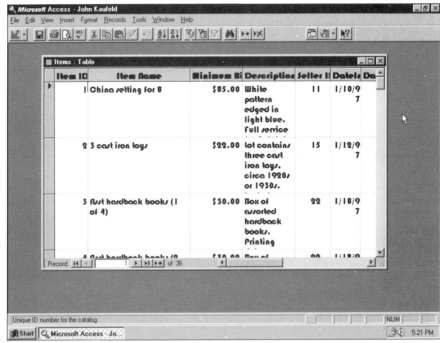

Figure 8-11:
Ewww . . .
back to the
font drawing
board.

Giving Your Data the 3-D Look

This final change is purely cosmetic, but even tables like to feel good about how they look. Access 95 gives you a couple of cool looking, three-dimensional options for your datasheet. If there's a solution to the problem of boring-looking datasheets, this must be it (because it serves no other purpose).

To turn your datasheet into a cool work of art, follow these steps:

1. **Select Format⇨Cells from the menu bar.**

   The Cells Effects dialog box pops onto the screen.

2. **For a cool, 3-D look, click either the Raised or Sunken radio buttons in the Cell Effect area (see Figure 8-12).**

   The Sample box previews your selection. (I think Raised both looks cool and is easy to work with, but that's personal preference.)

   If you don't want the gridlines (the lines separating the rows and columns) cluttering up your datasheet, leave the Cell Effect set to Flat and click the Gridlines Shown check boxes so they're blank.

Cells Effects
Gridlines Shown
Horizontal
Vertical
Gridline color:
Gray
Background color:
Silver
OK
Cancel
Cell Effect
Flat
Raised
Sunken
Sample:

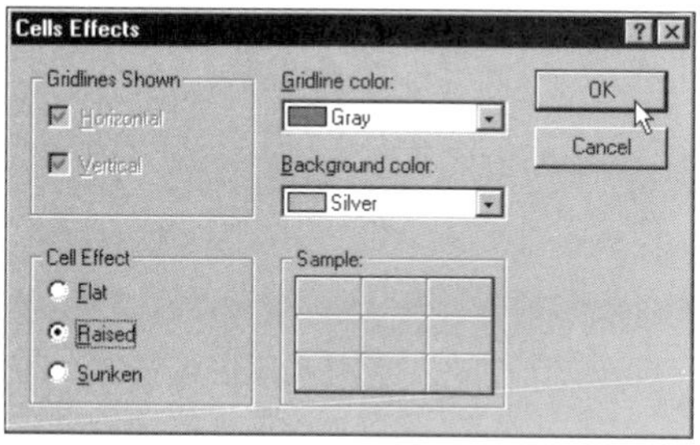

Figure 8-12: The choice is made — let's see how I did.

3. **Click OK when you're done.**

   The datasheet changes according to your selections, just like Figure 8-13.

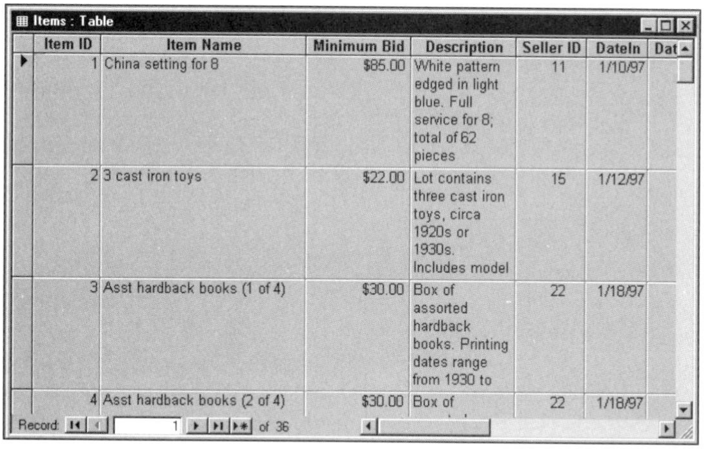

Items : Table
Item ID
Item Name
Minimum Bid
Description
Seller ID
DateIn
Dat
1 China setting for 8 $85.00 White pattern edged in light blue. Full service for 8; total of 62 pieces 11 1/10/97
2 3 cast iron toys $22.00 Lot contains three cast iron toys, circa 1920s or 1930s. Includes model 15 1/12/97
3 Asst hardback books (1 of 4) $30.00 Box of assorted hardback books. Printing dates range from 1930 to 22 1/18/97
4 Asst hardback books (2 of 4) $30.00 Box of 22 1/18/97
Record: 1 of 36

Figure 8-13: That works for me!

WARNING!

Unless you're really good with color combinations, leave the color settings alone. Since I regularly attempt to wear stripes and plaid together, I let Access 95 handle this on its own.

Chapter 9

Table Remodeling Tips for the Do-It-Yourselfer

*R*emodeling is a part of life — at least it is if you're a home owner. A touch of paint here, a new wall there, and pretty soon your entire house is a mess, because the jobs never *quite* get finished. For instance, I think my house has given up hope that I'll finish updating the electrical outlets. I've been working on the job for three years now, and I still have eight outlets to go. I do about one outlet per quarter, usually spurred to action because I need to plug something in and it won't work in the old outlet.

My databases, on the other hand, are completely organized and up to date. When I start changing a table, I finish the job right then and there. My wife says the difference has to do with physical labor and my aversion to it, but the real reason is the tools that Access 95 provides to get the job done.

Whether you're adding a new field, removing an old one, or making some subtle changes to your table, this chapter guides you through the process. Be sure to read the chapter's first section before attempting any serious surgery on your tables. Some serious pitfalls await you out there, and I want you to miss them cleanly.

Even though you can do some of the stuff in this chapter (specifically, add and delete columns) through Datasheet view, I don't generally recommend doing it that way. It's too easy to make a mistake and damage your table. Instead, make your changes through Design view, where you're in full control of the process. That's how the steps in this chapter do it.

This Chapter Could Be Hazardous to Your Table's Design

There's nothing like starting on a pleasant note, but *this* isn't the time for it.

To properly set this chapter's mood, I wanted to open with pictures of things that naturally say "don't touch — things like snapping alligators, roaring lions, and the *please audit me* box on your income tax form. My editor suggested that I use a warning icon instead. In the name of compromise (and because it's so hard to find good editors these days), I agreed.

Tread lightly in this chapter. You're tinkering with the infrastructure of your entire database system. A mistake (particularly of the *delete* kind) could cause massive hair loss, intense frustration, and large-scale data corruption. Put simply, it would be bad.

Putting a New Field Next to the Piano

No matter how well you plan, sometimes you just forget to include a field in your table design. Or, after using the table for a while, you discover some unforeseen data that needs a home. Regardless of the circumstances, Access 95 doesn't make a big deal out of adding a new field.

Dropping a new field into your table takes just a moment. Before starting, make sure you know the following things:

- ✔ What data the field will hold
- ✔ The field type (text, number, yes/no, and so on)
- ✔ The size, if applicable
- ✔ What you're planning to call the field
- ✔ Where the field fits in the table design

Is it a column or a field?

The answer to this lyrical question — is it a column or a field — is *yes*. In Access 95 lingo, *columns* and *fields* are really the same thing. When you insert a column into a table in Datasheet view, you're actually adding a new field to every record. If you build a field in Design view, you're creating a new column for the datasheet. Either way you say (or do) it, you get the same result.

With that information in hand, you're ready to make a new field. To add the field in Design view, follow these steps:

1. **With the database file open, click the table you want to work on and then click <u>D</u>esign.**

   This summons forth the table's structure in Design view.

2. **Highlight the row *below* where you want to insert your new field by clicking on the row button (it makes more sense in Figure 9-1).**

   This highlights the entire row. Pretty cool, eh?

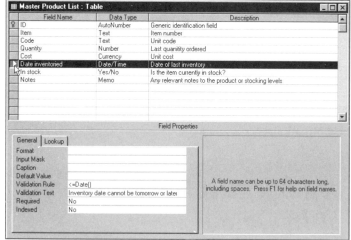

Figure 9-1:
Click the
button on
the left to
highlight an
entire row.

3. **Select <u>I</u>nsert⇨<u>R</u>ow from the menu.**

   A blank row appears *before* the row you clicked in Step 1.

4. **Click in the Field Name column of the new row and then type the name of your new field.**

   The field name flows smoothly into the text area.

5. **Press Tab to move into the Data Type area. Click the Down arrow and pick the data type from the pull-down list (see Figure 9-2).**

   If you're uncertain which data type is for you, refer back to "Frolicking through the Fields" in Chapter 4.

6. **Press Tab to hop into the Description area. Type a short description of the data in this field.**

   Although this is optional, I *highly* recommend doing it.

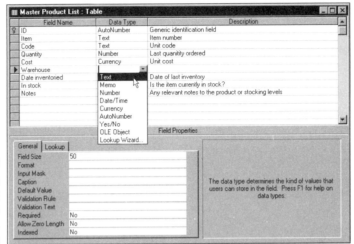

Figure 9-2:
Pick a data
type from
the list.

7. **Save your changes by selecting File⇨Save from the menu or clicking the Save button on the toolbar.**

Congratulations — you did it!

Saying Good-bye to a Field (and All of Its Data)

Times change, and so do your data storage needs. When one of your fields is past its prime, send it to that Great Table in the Sky by deleting it from your design. Getting rid of the field *also* throws out all of the data *in* the field. You probably know that already, but it's important enough that I want to make sure.

✔ Killing a field *erases all data* in the field. Proceed with caution!

✔ If the data in this table is important to you, make a backup copy before deleting any fields.

✔ If this data *isn't* important, why bother with it at all? Why not do something fun instead?

Here's how to delete a field from your table:

1. **Open the database file, click on the table you're planning to change, and then click Design.**

The design window pops onto the screen.

2. Click the gray button on the left side of the row you want to delete.

This highlights the doomed field so that all the other fields know what's about to happen and who the victim is.

3. Select Edit⇨Delete Row from the menu.

The Dialog of Doom appears, asking if you really want to do the deed (see Figure 9-3).

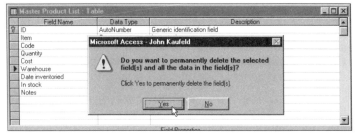

Figure 9-3:
Don't click that button unless you're positively sure!

4. Click Yes to delete the field; click No if you're having second thoughts.

If you delete the field and immediately wish you hadn't, press Ctrl+Z or select Edit⇨Undo Delete from the menu (see Figure 9-4). Your field instantly comes back from beyond.

5. Make the deletion permanent by selecting File⇨Save or clicking the Save button on the toolbar.

Figure 9-4:
Change your mind? Click here to restore the field.

The key word in this step is *permanent,* as in *never to be seen nor heard from again.* There's no undoing this step — when it's done, it's done.

A Field by Any Other Name Still Holds the Same Stuff

Access 95 really doesn't care how you name the fields in a table. Granted, it has some technical rules for what a legal field name looks like, but editorially speaking, it doesn't care. Field names are really a human thing (silly humans, we're always running around naming stuff).

There are two ways to change a field name. You can either use Design view (which is the *official* way), or you can do some right-clicking in Datasheet view (the fun, visual, and intuitive way). This section explains both. Even though I warned you earlier about the evils of changing the table structure in Datasheet view, I don't have a preference for this step — go with whichever one makes the most sense to you.

Here's how to change a field name in Design view:

1. **Open the database file, click on the table of the day, and then click <u>D</u>esign.**

   The table appears, laid out in Design view. (Granted, every first step in the chapter opens with this, but you have to start somewhere.)

2. **Click on the field you plan to rename and then press F2 to highlight it (see Figure 9-5).**

   You're ready to replace the field name.

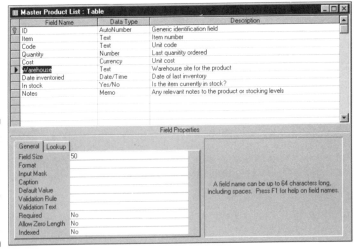

Figure 9-5:
The field name is highlighted and ready for the change.

3. Type the field's new name.

The new name overwrites the old one, just like Figure 9-6.

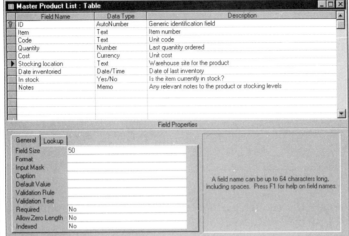

Figure 9-6:
The new name gracefully takes its place in the table.

4. To save the change, select File⇨Save or click the Save button on the toolbar.

The process is complete!

As I said before, you can also rename a field in Datasheet view. It's about the same number of steps, but some people think it's easier. In the name of diversity, here's how to change a field name in Datasheet view:

1. Open the database file and double-click the table name.

Surprise — it's a different first step! After surviving the shock of a new set of instructions, you'll notice the table is on-screen in Datasheet view.

2. Right-click on the name of the field you want to change.

The column highlights, and a pop-up menu appears.

3. Select Rename Column from the menu (see Figure 9-7).

The name of the column is highlighted, braced for the change.

4. Type the new name. Press Enter when you're done.

Even though you made the change in Datasheet view, Access 95 actually changed the table's design.

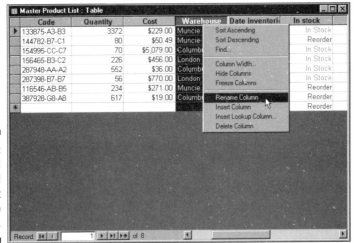

Figure 9-7:
Ask and
you shall
receive, but
right-click to
rename.

 5. **To make the change permanent, click Save on the toolbar or select File⇨Save.**

You're Done!

Reorganizing Things for a New Look

Seeing the *same* data in the *same* order gets old after a while. Even the most sedentary person longs for a little change of scenery every now and then. Whether the need is cosmetic or to make the data easier to work with, Access 95 lets you shuffle a table's fields with ease.

✔ You can move any field in the table, including the key field. Some database programs make you put the key field first in the table, but not Access 95. In this program, the key field can be *anywhere* in the table — it's entirely up to you.

✔ Even though you can move fields around in Datasheet view, those changes *do not* affect the table's design. Only changes made in Design view alter the table's structure. Datasheet changes are strictly cosmetic.

To reorganize a table's fields, follow these steps:

1. **Open the database file, find the table you're going to adjust, and click Design.**

The table jumps into action, appearing in a design window.

2. Click the gray button to the left of the row you want to move.

The row highlights, so you know which one is ready to go.

3. Press and hold the left mouse button on the same button and then slide the mouse up or down to move the row to a new location.

A dark bar appears in the place where the row will land (see Figure 9-8).

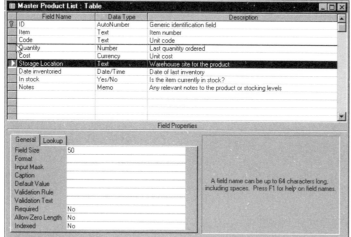

Figure 9-8:
The Storage
Location
field heads
north.

4. To position the field, release the mouse button when the dark bar is in the correct place.

When you let up on the mouse button, the field information moves to that position.

5. Save your work by clicking the Save button on the Toolbar or selecting File⇨Save.

Houston — the field has landed.

Part III
Finding the Ultimate Answer to Everything (Well, Not Really)

"Oh, Scarecrow! Without the database in your laptop, how will we ever find anything in Oz?"

In this part . . .

Electronically collecting the data together in one place is nice, but if you're just stacking it on the hard disk instead of piling it around your office, what did you gain (apart from a less cluttered office)?

At the risk of sounding like a marketing brochure, the ability to interact with your data is one of the truly cool features of Access 95. Since this *is* a computer product, we can't just say you're *interacting with* or *questioning* the data. No — that would be too easy. In database lingo, you're *querying* the tables.

Even though it sounds a lot cooler to *query* something than to *ask a quick question,* the basic concept is the same. Part III digs into the whole query thing, starting out with simple questions and leading you into progressively more complex prognostications. This is juicy stuff, so work up a good appetite before digging in.

Chapter 10

Quick Searches: Find, Filter, and Sort

· ·

In This Chapter

▶ Using the Find command

▶ Sorting your database

▶ Filter by selection

▶ Filter by form

· ·

*T*he real superpowers of Access are revealed when you create queries to answer your questions, covered in Chapter 11. But before you move that far along the Access Yellow Brick Road, you should know how to use some almost-super-powered techniques that organize your data and get quick answers to some simple questions. These are the commands Find, Sort, and Filter.

Locating Records: "Toto, Find My Ruby Slippers"

Oh no! Dorothy has lost her Ruby Slippers among all the other data, and she desperately needs them to escape the Wicked Witch of the West and get back home. How will she find them in time?

Although you don't have to deal with the Wicked Witch of the West in all her green glory, you probably have a boss (or a spouse or a friend) who can be a good substitute for her at times, and you may need to locate a specific record on demand.

Fortunately, Access 95 has a quick-and-dirty way to allow you to find one specific piece of data within the tables and forms of your project: the <u>F</u>ind command. When you're looking at an Access table or form, the <u>F</u>ind command is available under the <u>E</u>dit menu or as a button on the Toolbar. Whichever way you do it, starting the <u>F</u>ind command brings up the dialog box conveniently shown in Figure 10-1.

Figure 10-1:
The Find
dialog box
helps you
locate one
specific item
out of all
your data.

Enter what you are looking for here.

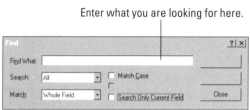

The Find dialog box is a tool nearly as miraculous as the Ruby Slippers themselves. You get to play with three text boxes and three check boxes, and (believe it or not) that's all you need to locate information stored in any record in your database. The Fi<u>n</u>d What text box is where you type in what you are using to locate the record. Dorothy would naturally type **Ruby Slippers** in here.

Finding first, finding next: Oh Toto, have we found them?

Once you fill in the Fi<u>n</u>d What text in the Find dialog box, click on the Find Fir<u>s</u>t button to start your search. Access moves you to the location of the first record in the database that matches your request and highlights the match. That's nice, isn't it?

But what if the record that Access finds isn't the one you're looking for? The Find request matches the record, but it's not the right one. Do you have to go through the hassle of a new search? No! You can send the Munchkins back out to find the next record that matches your request by clicking on the <u>F</u>ind Next button. This locates the next entry that matches your request.

If you are currently in the middle of your records and you click on Find Fir<u>s</u>t, the Munchkins go to the beginning of the database and find the first record that matches your request. If you click on <u>F</u>ind Next, the Munchkins proudly present you with the next record that fills the bill *after the current record* (the one that's highlighted on screen). Of course, nothing in computers is really ever that simple, so how the Find command behaves can change depending upon which direction you tell Access to start looking (see "Continuing the Search: Where in Oz could they be?" below).

To end your search, click Close. The Find dialog box disappears and the Munchkins can take a nap.

Continuing the Search: Where in Oz could they be?

Sometimes just providing the information in the Find What box isn't enough. Either you find too many records, or the ones that you match aren't really the ones that you want. One thing you can do to reduce the number of times you find the wrong record is to provide more details. This also makes your searches even faster.

It would really speed up Dorothy's search for her lost footwear if she knew the general direction in which she had last seen them. There's no reason to look to the South if she had been in the East the last time she remembered wearing them. To speed up the search, you can use the Search list box, shown in Figure 10-2.

Figure 10-2:
The Search list box gives a direction.

When you click on Search, a drop-down list appears with the options of Up, Down, and All. Use *Up* if you know that the record you need is listed earlier than your present location in the database. Use *Down* if you know that the record is lower down in the file. *All* searches both up and down for you, which assures that you find the record.

You can play with the Search command all you want, but if you click on the Find First button, Access *always* goes to the beginning of the data to find the *first* record that matches your search criteria.

In addition to telling Access 95 the direction you wish to search, you may want to narrow down the location where Access 95 looks for matches. If you know that you're looking for a record of someone in the city of Columbus, you don't want to look at records for people named Columbus.

The Search Only Current Field check box solves the problem for you. If you know you are looking for Columbus, Indiana, click on the City field of the table or form *before* you open the Find dialog box. Then, click on the Search Only Current Field box to place an X inside the box. The Title bar of the Find dialog box then shows that Access 95 will only look in the field that you've told it to. The Munchkins then look only through addresses to find the word Columbus (as shown in Figure 10-3) — or whatever it is that you are looking for.

Finding a Match: Whose slippers are they, really?

All this *Find* stuff is great if you know exactly what you're looking for, but what if the data is hiding under a slightly different name? Access 95 won't find "The Ruby Slippers of the Wicked Witch of the East" (or even "The Well Worn but very Comfy Slippers of Aunty Em") if you just tell it to look for "slippers." Luckily, the Match list box solves the problem. Match list helps you find something that's in Any Part of Field, Whole Field, or Start of Field (yes, I too think a nerd wrote those options).

If you select Whole Field, your entry in Find What must match an entire field in a record. If you select Start of Field, then Access 95 looks to match your Find What request with the beginning of every field. If you use Any Part of Field, Access 95 shows you a record that contains your Find What request *somewhere* within it.

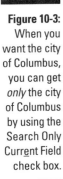

Figure 10-3: When you want the city of Columbus, you can get *only* the city of Columbus by using the Search Only Current Field check box.

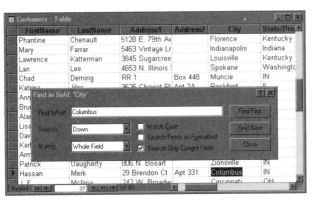

For example, suppose you think that Mr. Rothenmarl lives on 82nd Street, but you can't remember the actual address. You can't even remember whether his name is actually Rothenmarl and not Rothencarl or whether 82nd is a street or an avenue. In fact, the only thing you're sure of is that it's 82nd something. Don't panic. You can use the Any Part of Field option of Match to locate his record by matching any record that contains 82nd (as shown in Figure 10-4). Keep in mind, you may see some other records first, but eventually you'll find the right one.

Figure 10-4:
If you want
them to, the
Munchkins
can locate
any part of
any field by
using the
Match list
box.

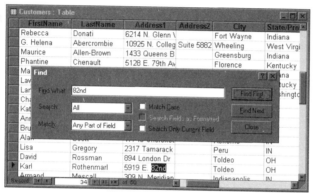

Casing for clues: "Ruby Slippers," or "RUBY slippers"

The options on the Find dialog box give you even greater control over what Access considers to be a match. The Match Case check box tells Access whether or not to worry about capitalization. If you leave this box blank, Access 95 finds the records regardless of whether they're in ALL CAPITALS, MixEd cASe, or all lower case letters. With this box checked, a record must *exactly* match the case of what you typed in the Find What box before Access 95 considers it a match.

For example, if the Match Case check box is checked and you type *Mcnally* in the Find What box, Access won't find the record for *Ms. Kay McNally* because the lowercase *n* won't match with the uppercase *N*. If Match Case is turned off, then a search for *Mcnally* would turn up *McNally, MCNally,* and *mcnally.*

Sorting Out Life on the Planet

It seems like very few databases are already organized into nice, convenient alphabetical lists. So what do you do when your boss wants the world neatly sorted and on her desk within the hour?

The solution, of course, is the <u>S</u>ort command and it's *really* easy to use! The Sort command is on the <u>R</u>ecords menu, plus there are two buttons on the Toolbar (Sort Ascending and Sort Descending) that do the job as well.

 Sort Ascending sorts your records alphabetically from top to bottom, so records that begin with A are at the beginning, and records that begin with Z are at the end.

 Sort Descending is just the opposite, records that begin with Z are at the top, A is at the bottom of the list.

The Sort command handles dates and number with equal ease. Sort Ascending organizes numbers from smallest to largest and dates from oldest to most recent. Sort Descending puts the largest numbers and most recent dates at the start of the list.

To use the <u>S</u>ort command, click on the field that you wish to sort by, then click on either the Sort Ascending or the Sort Descending button. Your records will change their order to organize the fields you have selected in alphabetical and numeric order. Figure 10-5 shows the auction customer list, sorted by Last Name.

Sometimes, the Sort function has limited usefulness. If you want to sort by a field that has numbers mixed in with spaces and letters (such as street addresses), Access 95 sorts the numbers by position rather than value. This can give you a result where "10608 W. Verm" actually comes before "119 Spring Mill." (The 0 in the second position comes before the 1 in the second position.) Oh well, you can only expect *so much* from a mere program.

Figure 10-5:
If you want
to organize
your data by
a certain
category,
click on that
category
before
you sort.

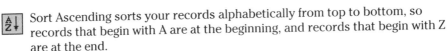

CustomerID	FirstName	LastName	Address1	Address2	City
21	G. Helena	Abercrombie	10925 N. Colleg	Suite 5882	Wheeling
22	Maurice	Allen-Brown	1433 Queens B		Greensburg
12	Theodore	Backmeyer	114 N. 3rd Ave	#3A	Richmond
11	Melanie	Cae	4487 Rose Pkw		Carmel
23	Phantine	Chenault	5128 E. 79th A\		Florence
6	Jean	Coffie	5269 N. Rural S		Indianapolis
8	Gerald	Curtis	3775 State St		Connersville
36	Patrick	Daugherty	806 N. Bosart		Zionsville
27	Chad	Deming	RR 1	Box 448	Muncie
50	Tim	Dodds	1225 Roy Road		Indianapolis
20	Rebecca	Donati	6214 N. Glenn \		Fort Wayne
24	Mary	Farrar	5463 Vintage Lr		Indianapolis
43	Frankie	Francher	6454 Stonehill \		Madison
19	Neil	Garret	205 Glasgow Lr		Fort Wayne
32	Lisa	Gregory	2317 Tamarack		Peru
2	Karen	Harvill	7601 E. Newber		Indianapolis

Record: |◄| ◄| 7 |►| ►I| ►*| of 50

Filtering Finds Records with Something in Common

Sometimes you need to see a group of records that share a common value — they're from a particular city, have a certain job title, or read the same genre of books. Access 95 has a special tool for this purpose — the Filter command.

Filters take the criteria that you want to look for and pull out all records that match the criteria. This creates a sort of mini-table that has only those records that match what you want. You can find the Filter commands on the Records menu or on the toolbar.

 There are three kinds of Filter commands: Filter by Form, Filter by Selection, and Advanced Filter/Sort. They each do the same basic thing, but in different ways and with different bells and whistles attached. Filters work in tables, forms, and queries. Although you *can* apply a filter to a report, that's really a different kind of beast. Each section below shows you how filters work in tables, but the same concepts apply when you're working with queries and forms.

Filter by Selection

 The Filter by Selection command is the easiest of the three filter commands to use. It assumes that you already found one record that matches your criteria. It's much like Dorothy grabbing a Munchkin out of the crowd and shouting: "OK, everybody who's like him, line up over there."

To use Filter by Selection, click in the field that has the information you want to match. For example, suppose that you're looking at the items for sale at the auction and decide that you only need to look at those items that have a minimum bid of $30.00 (no more, no less). So, you find one item that meets that criteria and move to the MinimumBid field. Then you click on the Filter by Selection button (if you'd rather, you can choose the Records⇨Filter⇨Filter by Selection command). Your result is a table of five items (see Figure 10-6), each with a minimum bid of exactly $30.00. Too cool, eh?)

Figure 10-6:
Filter by Selection finds the records that match highlighted criteria.

Item Name	Description	S	Minimum Bid
Box of ham radio magazines	Approximately 100 amateur radio		$30.00
Asst hardback books (1 of 4)	Box of assorted hardback books.		$30.00
Asst hardback books (2 of 4)	Box of assorted hardback books.		$30.00
Asst hardback books (3 of 4)	Box of assorted hardback books.		$30.00
Asst hardback books (4 of 4)	Box of assorted hardback books.		$30.00
			$0.00

Record: 1 of 5 (Filtered)

The Apply Filter button clicks in by itself and turns into the Remove Filter button when you click on the Filter by Selection button. When you are done with the filter, you can click on the Remove Filter button on the toolbar to return your table or form to its regular arrangement.

✔ To find the items with a minimum bid of $30 or more is too much work for a Filter. Instead, you need to use a real live, full-fledged query like the ones discussed in the Chapter 11.

✔ What if you're looking at that list and decide that you want the books but not the magazines? You can Filter by Selection again! Only this time, you want all the books listed. If you highlight any full field in the Item Name column, you only get those items that exactly match that field. The secret is to highlight *only part of the field*. In this case, highlight only the word "books" in one field and use Filter by Selection again. When you do, you get rid of those pesky ham radio magazines, as seen in Figure 10-7.

At this stage of the game, you may want to save a list of everything that matches your filter. Unfortunately, you can't. If you want a permanently saved record of your filtered search, you need to create a query (see Chapter 11).

Figure 10-7:
You can
Filter by
Selection
more than
once to
tighten up
the results
of the filter.

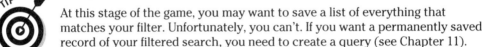

Filter by Form

You can tighten a search by using additional filters to weed out undesirable matches, but that's limited because you can only narrow your current search or start a new one. What if you need to create a group of records that are based on more than one criterion or on criteria using more than one field?

Filter by Form is a useful tool for sifting through records using more than one criteria. Say, for example, you need a list of all the customers at your auction who came from Illinois or from Indiana. Well, you can do two different Filter by Selection searches and write down the results of each to get your list. The Scarecrow, however, showed Dorothy an easier way using Filter by Form just once to get all the information in one table.

To use Filter by Form you can either select Records⇨Filter⇨Filter by Form from the Access menu or you can click on the Filter by Form button on the Toolbar. Of course, you have to have the database that you want filtered open at the time. When you open Filter by Form, you see an empty replica of your table like the delightful one for the auction customers shown in Figure 10-8.

The first thing that you want to be aware of is that the Access 95 toolbar changes when you command Filter by Form to appear. The most significant change is the arrival of the three buttons, Close, Clear Grid, and Apply Filter. These are discussed in the appropriate sections below.

Figure 10-8:
The Filter by Form table lets you give detailed instructions on what to look for in your data.

Notice in Figure 10-8 that there is an arrow button in the FirstName field of the table. That's because that was the field that was active when the Filter by Form command was selected. That's nice if you want to filter by first name, but you're going to look at states of residence. If you move your cursor to the State/Province column and click once, the little arrow will obligingly jump to that column. You can then click on the arrow to open a list box showing all of the entries for that field in your open database, as displayed in Figure 10-9.

In the lower-right corner of the table there is a tab labeled Look For. When that tab is highlighted, you can click on an entry to designate that as your primary search. So you click on the abbreviation IL in the drop-down list of the State/Province list box, and IL moves into the State/Province column.

Figure 10-9:
The little arrow opens a list box showing all the entries for that field.

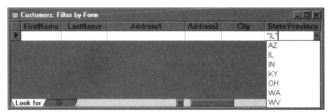

But wait! What about the records that have the state entered as "Illinois"? Don't worry — that's what Filter by Form is all about. Look back at the lower-left corner of the table, you see the little tab labeled Or next to the Look For tab? Click on Or and then open your list box again. You can click on any other entry and the Munchkins will search for it as well as for "Illinois."

Repeat this process as many times as you need and in any field you need. Every time you click on the Or tab, another Or tab comes into existence to let you add another criterion to your search. Figure 10-10 shows how the Filter by Form table looks with an extra Or tab in place.

Figure 10-10:
You can
use as
many "Or"
statements
as you need
to define all
the criteria.

When you have entered all the criteria you want for the filter, click on the Apply Filter button and Access 95 does the rest. Figure 10-11 shows the results.

Sometimes, you may want to create a group of records based upon the information in more than one field. For example, Dorothy may want to list everyone who is both a member of the Lollipop Guild and who wears a blue hat. Since her database has fields for both the Guild and the Hat Color of each individual, she can easily do that with Filter by Form. All she needs is to type the matching information into each of the fields (the word **blue** in the Hat Color field and the **Lollipop** in the Guild field). Now, when she selects Apply Filter, all of the records for people who are in the Lollipop Guild and wear a blue hat are listed.

Figure 10-11:
The
Munchkins
have found
all the
records that
you asked
for using
Filter by
Form.

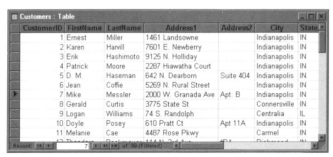

Although you can get very fancy and combine And searches and Or searches to your heart's content, it gets pretty tough to keep track of your creation in no time at all. Before creating *The Filter That Identified Incredibly Detailed Sub-Sets of Manhattan,* remind yourself that Queries work better than Filters when you're asking complicated questions. Flip ahead to Chapter 11 for the low-down on Queries.

What to do when good criteria go bad

What do you do if you enter criteria by mistake? Or if you decide that you really don't want to include Ohio in your filter right after you click on OH? Well, it's inconvenient, but not really a problem. Undoing this is what the Clear Grid button is for.

When you click on the Clear Grid button, the Munchkins get out their pails of soapy water and their brushes and they scrub away all the criteria you put into the Filter by Form table. Then you get to start over. What fun!

If you want to get rid of just a single Or tab, you can select that tab and then use the Edit➪Delete Tab command.

When you are done working with the Filter by Form command, click on the Close button and your database returns to normal. If you're a toolbar fan, you can also click the Remove Filter button to get things in shape again.

Chapter 11

Make a Simple Query, Get 10,000 Answers

*Q*ueries are the true heroes of Access 95. You use queries to make sense of all the data that you've slavishly typed in for lo these many hours or days; with queries, you start getting a return on all your labor.

So what is a query? Simply put, a query is a question about the data in your tables. Queries can make lists from one or more tables, count records, and even do calculations based on what they find lurking in your database. Queries are the power behind the Access 95 throne.

Since queries are such powerful and flexible tools, there's a lot of information to cover about them. To get you started, this chapter explains how to do queries on a single table. Chapter 12 gets into the details of working with linked tables in a single query.

On Your Way with Advanced Filter/Sort

The Advanced Filter/Sort command is essentially the simplest type of query. It will work with only one table or form in your database at a time, so you can't use an Advanced Filter/Sort with a bunch of linked tables. In addition, you can only ask certain types of questions with Advanced Filter/Sort (there's more about that later in the chapter).

You open the Advanced Filter/Sort from an open table or form by selecting Records⇨Filter⇨Advanced Filter/Sort. This brings up the Design view of the Advanced Filter/Sort shown in Figure 11-1.

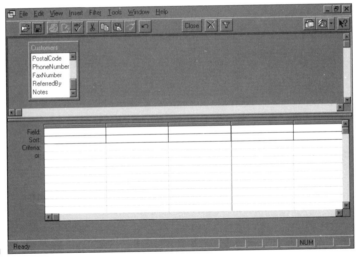

Figure 11-1:
Advanced
Filter/Sort is
a cross
between a
powerful
filter and a
simple
query.

Notice in Figure 11-1 that the window is split. In the lower half of the screen is a blank grid; in the upper half is a small box labeled Customers. This box, which I call the *Field List box*, lists all the fields in the currently open table or form that you can work with.

Although I only mention filtering tables and forms, you can also filter a query. Why you'd *want* to filter a query is a little beyond me, so just let the nerds worry about this feature — it definitely falls under the heading *Features for People with Too Much Time on Their Hands*.

You can work with the Field List in two ways:

✔ You can double-click on a field's entry in the Field List and watch the little guy magically appear in the table below.

✔ Or you can click on the field you wish to insert and drag the field down to the table yourself.

Once you include that field in your table, the Munchkins look at that field's information when trying to answer your question. When you move a field onto the query table, the table changes to include that field, as shown in Figure 11-2.

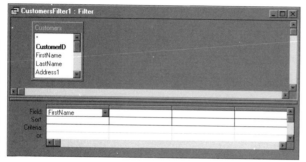

Figure 11-2:
Double-click on a field in the Field List to include it in the filter.

Notice that, when you move the field down to the table, a downward-pointing arrow appears in the table next to the field name. This indicates that you can open a list box in that field. If you click on this box, you see a drop-down list that allows you to select a different field name from your table or form. You can then move on and select other fields for the other columns of the query.

If you do want to include all the fields in your query, you can do this quickly in two ways:

✔ If you double-click on the heading for the Field List, you highlight all the fields and can then drag the whole list down to the table. This places a separate field in each column of the table. Doing this allows you to use your entire database, but to establish separate criteria for each field and to arrange the fields in the order you want for just that query (but more on that later).

✔ The second way is to locate the asterisk (*) at the top of the list in each Field List. If you drag or double-click on this *, all fields for that table are inserted into a single column of the query. This allows the query to search all fields for your data, but you can only establish a single set of criteria for all fields, and the fields print in the their default order.

Sorting things out

After inserting all the fields you need for your query, you determine which field you want the data sorted by and click on the Sort row for that column. The arrow that indicates a list box appears, and you choose between ascending and descending sorts. Figure 11-3 shows a query table for a mailing list, with the data to be sorted by zip code.

Figure 11-3:
You can
tell the
Munchkins
to sort by
whatever
field most
suits your
needs.

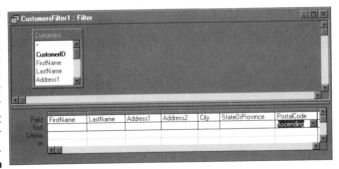

Figure 11-3: You can tell the Munchkins to sort by whatever field most suits your needs.

You can instruct Access 95 to sort by more than one field, but it always *starts* with the field that's furthest to the left in the table. When it finds records with the same information in that field, it starts sorting by the other fields you specified, working from left to right through the list.

Adding selection criteria

The third row of the query table is labeled Criteria. In this row, you tell Access what you want it to look for.

Say, for example, that you only need a mailing list for customers in Indiana. In the State column, you type in **"IN."** Press Enter when you are done. Access 95 automatically puts quotation marks around your entry.

You can also use the Expression Builder by right-clicking on the field name and selecting Build. I'm not going to talk about the Expression Builder right now. I'm saving that for a later chapter, say Chapter 15.

What if you also want to include Illinois in your mailing list? Unlike the simple-minded Filter by Selection tool from the last chapter, Advanced Filter/Sort lets you include more than one criteria in the same filter. Simply move to the Or row of the same column and type in **"IL"**; Access includes the Land of Lincoln in its search.

There are limits to this flexibility, though. You can only include a maximum of nine criteria in the same column. (Okay, so it's not *that* much of a limitation.) Figure 11-4 shows what the table looks like now that all the information needed for the search has been entered.

Figure 11-4:
You're
almost
ready to
create a
mailing
list of
customers
in Illinois
and Indiana.

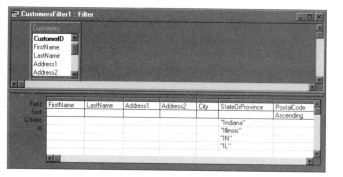

Access does one thing when you are entering criteria that can be very confusing. You may have noticed that, when you went to type **IL** on the Or line of the table, the word IN disappeared! No, you didn't destroy the Hoosier state. What happened was that Access scrolled the table down to make room for the new criteria. Go ahead and click on the up arrow of the scroll bar to see Indiana again in all its flat and muggy glory. (I'm allowed to say things like that about the state — I live there.)

When you use more than one column or row within the grid, you are actually combining criteria. Criteria are combined by arranging them so that Access either tries to match both rules (AND) or either of the rules (OR). Working with the many rows and columns of the query grid is the topic of Chapter 13, "Lions AND Bears? Lions OR Bears?"

Operators and other flying monkeys

Operators are supposed to be designed to help you tell Access exactly how you want the data to be matched to the criteria. In theory, this is a wonderful idea. But unless you have a degree in Boolean Logic (you don't, do you?), operators can be as scary and intimidating as the Wicked Witch's flying monkeys. But do not despair! I am here to help, and with a little good ole' plain English, you can figure out how to use an operator like a pro. (By the way, Access also uses the term *comparison operators* for these things, and that's where you find information about them in the Help file.)

Boolean operators are symbols that are used to make equations that can be answered with either a Yes or a No. You might begin to suspect that Boolean was actually the first name of the Wizard, but that's not the case. George Boole was actually a famous 19th-century mathematician, although the distinction between mathematicians and wizards is a blurry one.

An *operator* defines the relationship of the data to the criteria you established. Just typing in the state name is fine if a state name is all you need. But what if you want a list of all the items for auction that are valued below $100.00? You can use eight operators with the Criteria row for all queries. Table 11-1 lists these operators, how they should be typed in, and what they really mean.

Table 11-1		Comparison Operators
Symbol	*Name*	*What Does It Mean?*
Is	Is	This is what you get when you just type something into a Criteria row. The information you enter must match the information in the field exactly.
Like	Like	You can put the word Like before text in a field to ask Access to search through the contents of that field to see if it can find the text anywhere within the field. If it can, then that counts as a match. The criteria Like "The" matches "The Wizard," "Home on the Range," and "Many Meanings of The."
<	Less Than	This operator is used with numeric fields. If you need to have a list of all values that are *Less Than* your criteria, use this. Example: <30 in the MinimumBid field finds all bids from $0 to $29.99.
>	Greater Than	Another numeric operator, this lists all values in the field that are *Greater Than* the criteria. Example: >30 in the MinimumBid field finds all bids that are more than $30 (starting with $30.01).
>=	Greater Than Equal to	Like Greater Than, except that it also includes all entries that exactly match the criteria. Example: >=30 finds all values from 30 to infinity.
<=	Less Than or Equal to	If you add the = sign to Less Than, your query includes all records that have values below the number or which have that number. Example: <=30 includes not only those records with values less than 30 but also those with a value of 30.
<>	Not Equal (a.k.a. Less Than or Greater Than)	This operator finds all entries that do not match the criteria. If you want a list of all records except ones with a value of 30, enter this as <>30.
=	Equals	This operator finds only those records that exactly match the criteria. Example: =30 will only find values of 30.

Applying the filter

When you have completed filling out the criteria for the Advanced Filter/Sort, you are ready to take that bold step and ask your Munchkins to apply the filter to your data. Scary isn't it? To apply the filter, you can either select Filter⇨Apply Filter/Sort from the menu or simply click on the Apply Filter button on the Toolbar. You should see results similar to those shown in Figure 11-5.

Figure 11-5:
Ta dah!
You've just
completed
your first
query!

	FirstName	LastName	Address1	Address2	City	State/	Postal Code
▶	Alan	Scott	17748 Cherokee Lane		Kokomo	IN	44203-
	Theodore	Backmeyer	114 N. 3rd Ave	#3A	Richmond	IN	44551-
	Sean	Mathis	846 Elm Street		Logansport	IN	44557-
	Gerald	Curtis	3775 State St		Connersville	IN	45273-3989
	Tim	Dodds	1225 Roy Road		Indianapolis	IN	46226-
	Kay	McNally	10608 W. Vermont	Suite 481	Indianapolis	IN	46228-
	Jean	Coffie	5269 N. Rural Street		Indianapolis	IN	46228-
	Armand	Mescall	309 N. Meridian		Indianapolis	IN	46228-
	Dagmar	Rosen-Sheid	119 Spring Mill Lane		Greenwood	IN	46272-
	Charles	Pak	1112 N. Bradbury Lane		Greenwood	IN	46272-
	Chad	Deming	RR 1	Box 448	Muncie	IN	46287-
	Doyle	Posey	610 Pratt Ct	Apt 11A	Indianapolis	IN	46287-
	Mike	Messler	2000 W. Granada Ave	Apt. B	Indianapolis	IN	46287-
	Justin	Nichols	452 N. Raymond		Indianapolis	IN	46287-
	D. M.	Haseman	642 N. Dearborn	Suite 404	Indianapolis	IN	46287-1357
	Patrick	Moore	2287 Hiawatha Court		Indianapolis	IN	46338-4988

Record: 1 of 30 (Filtered)

Some of you may wonder how I could fit all of the columns on Figure 11-5. Although you may know that column widths are adjustable, you may not know that you can automatically adjust a column to fit the widest field in the table. To do this, move your cursor to the top right edge of the column. Keep moving the cursor around until it changes to a downward-pointing arrow with a crossbar. When you see this, double-click on the right border of the column you want to adjust, and the whole column changes size automatically.

Sweeping up the debris: clearing and deleting

There are a couple of nifty tools associated with all queries that you can also find in the Advanced Filter/Sort. On the bottom of the Edit menu, you see two commands: Delete Column and Clear Grid.

- ✔ You use the Delete Column command to remove a field from your query. Simply click in the column that you want to remove, select Edit⇨Delete Column, and that field goes away.

- ✔ The Clear Grid command is more comprehensive. In fact, it's sort of like a swarm of killer bees. When you select Edit⇨Clear Grid, *all* of your fields in the query table are removed, and you can create your query again from scratch without having to start a new one.

What if you decide you want to change the order of your fields in a query? Well, you *could* start over, but I don't like hearing that kind of language from my readers. You can rearrange the columns of your queries and tables quickly, easily, and without all that nasty language:

1. **Simply click on the column header to select the whole column, point to the column head again, and drag with the mouse.**

   You see a little box below your cursor, which tells you that your mouse is carrying something heavy.

2. **When your cursor is where you want the column to be repositioned, release the mouse and that column pops into place.**

This also works in Design view and Datasheet view.

Save me, Toto!

Once you've created your query, you may want to save it for later. If you click on the Save button on the toolbar, you see the dialog box shown in Figure 11-6, which allows you to save your Advanced Filter/Sort as a query and to open it again from the Query tab.

Figure 11-6:
You can
save your
Advanced
Filter/Sort as
a query.

All you need to do is give your query a name so that you will recognize it later. Rather than a friendly name like Bob or Rita, I suggest you use a descriptive name that provides some information about what the query does — something like "Indiana and Illinois Customers" might be good.

Finding Elusive Answers with a Well-Placed Query

To work with Queries and the Query Wizard go to the main database window (the one with the tabs for Table, Query, Form, and so on) and click on the Query tab. Under the Query tab you see a window that most likely at this time is empty (unless you saved an Advanced Filter/Sort). On the right side are three buttons: Open, Design, and New. To work with a new query, go ahead and click on New.

At this point, you see the New Query dialog box shown in Figure 11-7, which gives you a choice of how you want to set up your query.

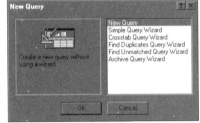

Figure 11-7:
The New
Query dialog
box.

If you select the New Query option and click on OK, you see the Show Table dialog box in Figure 11-8.

Figure 11-8:
From the
Show Table
dialog box
you can
select what
tables or
forms you
need to
look
through.

You can select a table and/or a query from the Show Table dialog box and click on the <u>A</u>dd button to include your selection in your search. You can select more than one table for your query, but that's a topic for Chapter 14.

After you select the Items table for the query and click on the <u>A</u>dd button, you can then Close the Show Table dialog box and go directly to the Design view for your query. Figure 11-9 shows this view. Looks familiar, doesn't it?

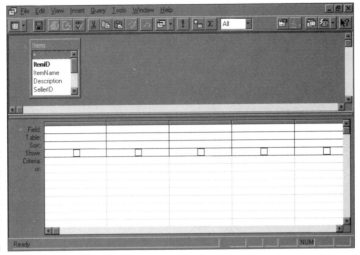

Figure 11-9: Hey — you're back in Design view!

Notice the amazing similarity between this screen and the one shown in Figure 11-1? Except for the some additions to the menu and Toolbar, this window is the same as the Advanced Filter/Sort window I talked about earlier.

The Select Query functions like the Advanced Filter/Sort; you can move fields from your source table onto the query table, establish sort order, and define what criteria you want to use the same way as you do for the Advanced Filter/Sort. There are some differences, however, and they can be important.

One advantage of working with a query over using the Advanced Filter/Sort is that you can limit your table to only the information that is relevant to your question. For example, if you are looking at developing a mailing list from your Customer list, you probably don't need or want a table cluttered up with phone and fax numbers.

Using Top Values: Who IS the top lion in the forest?

In Figure 11-9, there is a list box along the toolbar that I've labeled Top Values. This is a very useful tool that is only available in true queries. The Top Values function lets you only show either the top or the bottom values in the field you designate.

Say, for example, that you want to know what the five least expensive items on sale at the auction are. You click on the MinimumBid field in your query table and designate an ascending sort (so that the lowest priced items are at the start of the list). Next, click on the Top Values list box. You can then type the number **5** or select it from the drop-down list. When you tell Access 95 to run your query, it presents you with a list of items with the five lowest minimum bids in the auction. Figure 11-10 shows the results of using the Top Values command.

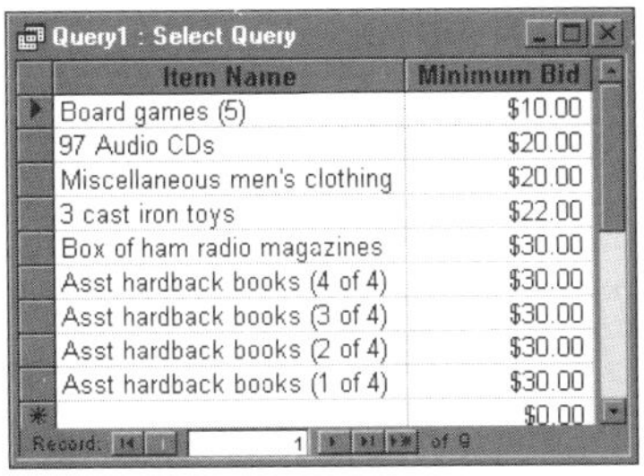

Figure 11-10: These nine items are the ones with the lowest prices in the auction.

Item Name	Minimum Bid
Board games (5)	$10.00
97 Audio CDs	$20.00
Miscellaneous men's clothing	$20.00
3 cast iron toys	$22.00
Box of ham radio magazines	$30.00
Asst hardback books (4 of 4)	$30.00
Asst hardback books (3 of 4)	$30.00
Asst hardback books (2 of 4)	$30.00
Asst hardback books (1 of 4)	$30.00
	$0.00

Record: 1 of 9

Note that you get more than five items. The list has the five lowest minimum bids and each item with one of those bids. Because some items have the same bid, the list of items has more than four entries.

If you would rather have a list of items that have the four highest prices at the auction, change the sort order for the field to descending.

Run, Toto, run!

How are you supposed to tell Access 95 to start working?

There are two answers to that: the Run button on the toolbar will crack the whips on the little guys, or you can use the menu and select Query⇨Run to do the same thing.

Alternately, you can use the Design View button on the toolbar. This button allows you to switch between Query Design view (where you set up your query), SQL view (which is used for working with databases on other computers — stay far away from this), and Datasheet view (which shows you the results of your query). You can find these same commands on the <u>V</u>iew menu.

If you click on the arrow to the right of the Design View button, you see a command list showing all the different views available. Or you can just click on the button, and your screen will switch to the Datasheet view (if you are currently in the Design view) or the Design view (if you are in the Datasheet view). Notice how even Access 95 tries to avoid the SQL view. The advantage of this button is that it easily allows you to switch between views, make changes to your design, and see how that changes the results.

 With a standard query, it doesn't matter whether you use the Run button or the Datasheet button. With an Action query like those discussed in Chapter 16, the difference can be quite important. For now, use the Datasheet button to look at the results of your query. Leave the Run button alone until you have a chance to wander through Chapter 16.

 Sometimes you need Access 95 to use certain fields in a query but display others in the in the Datasheet view. There is a really easy way to do this. In the Design view of every query is a row labeled Show. Each column in this row has a box with a check mark inside. By default, Access 95 wants to show *all* of the columns in the Datasheet. To remove a column from Datasheet view, click in the check box for that field. If you change your mind and want to put a column back into the Datasheet view, just click in the column's Show check box one more time. When you open the Datasheet view, Access 95 only displays the fields you told it to.

Toto, Can the Wizard Help?

Once you know how to work with the New Query function, you can understand how the Simple Query Wizard operates and use it to your best advantage. Like all the other Wizards in the land of Access, the Simple Query Wizard takes care of the behind-the-scenes work for you, but you have to enter the sorting and criteria information on your own. (Such is life in the 90's — maybe they'll include that feature in Access 2000!)

The next time you click on the <u>N</u>ew command from the Query tab, choose the Simple Query Wizard instead of New Query. When you do, the Wizard appears in a flash of flame and thunder. You can see this wizardly manifestation in Figure 11-11.

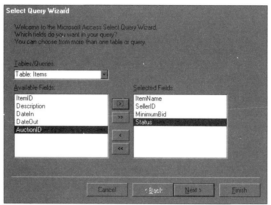

The wizard asks you to provide three bits of information:

- The first, Tables/Queries, allows you to select which tables you want to use in this query. Click on the arrow to see the drop-down list and choose from the available choices. Don't worry, the wizard is wise and includes all of the queries and tables in the current database.

- After you've selected what table to use, the Available Fields box shows what fields are in use in that table. You can move these fields over to the Selected Fields box by highlighting the fields that you want to use and clicking on the > button. Or, if you know that you want to use all of the fields in the database, click on the >> button to see everything transfer over.

- If you decide that you don't want a field that you've already transferred, highlight that field in the Selected Fields box and click on the < button. If you want to remove all of the selected fields, click on the << button.

When you're done telling the wizard what fields you want to use, go ahead and click on the Next> button to see another face of the wizard, as revealed in Figure 11-12.

In the Select Query Wizard screen, you can type in a label for your query at the top. You can also determine if you need to add sorting and criteria information to the query. If you do, click on the button marked Modify the query's design to be sent to the Design view when you click Finish. If you are satisfied with what you can get at this point, select the Open the query to view information button to see the Datasheet view.

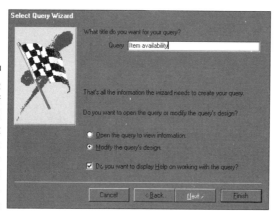

Figure 11-12:
This side of
the wizard
lets you put
a label on
your query
and ask
for help.

The last check box on this screen is labeled Do you want to display Help while working with the query? This check box automatically opens a Help file explaining how you can customize your query. After you make your selections, you are ready to click on the Finish button to see your handiwork.

That's it! That is all you need to know to work with single table queries. I'm sure that if Dorothy gets this information, she won't lose track of the Yellow Brick Road again.

Looking Ahead

There is a lot more to queries than I've covered here. Chapter 12 covers the great joy of creating a query using multiple tables (both with and without the Simple Query Wizard). Chapter 13 shows you how to combine criteria in a query, and Chapter 14 focuses on how to use crosstabs and create totals. Chapter 15 gives you tips on how to make mathematical computations and invoke Boolean logic on your behalf. Finally, Chapter 16 tells you how to make big changes in your queries using a few simple commands.

Chapter 12

Searching a Slew of Tables

. . . .

. . . .

You can go beyond creating simple queries using only one table for your data. In this chapter, you'll see how to work with multiple tables in the same query, and I lightly cover some of the different — more complex — types of queries that you can create. Ready? Get set. Go!

Queries Using Multiple Tables

You may need to look at information from a variety of tables to get full use from your data. (In fact, if you're in the corporate world, it's almost a forgone conclusion.) Fortunately, Access is specifically called a *relational database* because it allows you to establish *relationships* between the different tables you work with. This means that queries can look at two or more tables and recognize information that goes together.

In most cases, a multiple table query works the same as a single table query. You merely need to let Access 95 know that you are drawing on information from different sources, and let the software do the rest. The primary difference between a multiple table query and a single table query is that, with queries that use more than one table Access creates a link between the tables so that the relationship between them can be explored. This link, called a *join* in Access, is represented in your Query Design view by the line that is drawn between two or more field lists, shown in Figure 12-1.

Figure 12-1:
In a multiple
table query,
the tables
are linked
to share
their data.

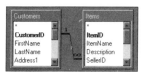

It is always best to link the tables when you first design them (check out Chapters 4 and 5 for more about that). If you didn't link the tables then, but you want to merge their information in a single query, you can still do it. If two or more tables have a field with the same name and the same type of data, Access invokes its *Auto-Join* feature and automatically link these fields together. If the fields have even *slightly* different names, you have to link them on your own. There is more to be said about Join and Auto-Join (lots more, in fact), so see "Joining Your Tables in Holy Matrimony," later in this chapter.

Your first step toward a good query is to determine what problem you are trying to solve. With the problem well in hand, you can build a query that answers your need.

Imagine that you are running an auction house. (Granted, it's not as much fun as going to Oz, but Oz never had to worry about cash flow or inventory track-ing.) You need a list of the people who have contributed items, what those items are, and how much the items are selling for. The database has one table listing Customer information and another with the items that are for sale. You *could* print both lists and spend an afternoon flipping between the pages, but that kinda defeats the purpose of using Access 95.

Instead, why not have Access 95 match the customers with their items? Given the example above, you need the Seller Name, Item Name, and Minimum Bid fields. The fields for Seller Name are in the Customer table, while Item Name and Minimum Bid are comfortably located in the Items table. Not a problem.

Calling on the Wizard

The Query Wizard wouldn't be much of a wizard if all it could do is create single table queries; you can use it for multiple table queries as well. Figure 12-2 shows you the first screen of the Select Query Wizard. (To get to this point, you just start a new query and double-click on the Select Query Wizard option in the New Query dialog box.)

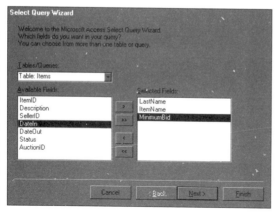

Figure 12-2:
You can use
the Select
Query
Wizard to
create
queries
using more
than one
table.

If you need to create a multitable query, just open the Simple Query Wizard as described in Chapter 11, select one of the tables you need data from, and transfer what fields you need into the Selected Fields list box. Then, select the next table you want to use and repeat the process. All you have to do is tell the wizard what you need and it'll do the rest. Isn't that nice?

Selecting the type of summary

After you indicate what fields you want to use and click on the Next button, you should see a screen similar to the one shown in Figure 12-3. This screen does not appear if you are using only one table for your query.

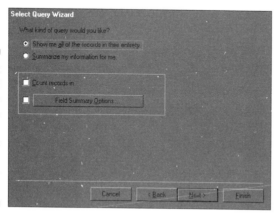

Figure 12-3:
The wizard
needs more
information
from you
when it's
creating a
multitable
query.

This dialog box lets you tell the wizard how you want the information presented. You have two basic options here. The first option — Show me all of the records in their entirety — creates the type of datasheet that has all records listed, as shown in Figure 12-4.

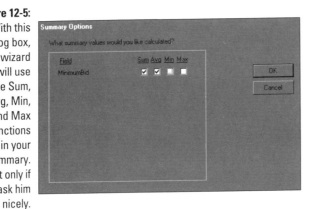

Figure 12-4:
The wizard
has created
a query with
all the
records
listed.

The second option — Summarize my information for me — tells Access that you aren't interested in each record, but just in the summary information. When you select the Summarize option, the check box labeled `Count records in` is checked. This is the default summary; simply put, it counts the number of entries that are included in the Datasheet. (This is described more completely in Chapter 14.) If you need something different for your summary, click on the Field Summary Options button to see the dialog box shown in Figure 12-5.

Figure 12-5:
With this
dialog box,
the wizard
will use
the Sum,
Avg, Min,
and Max
functions
in your
summary.
But only if
you ask him
nicely.

NOTE

There is a lot of statistical fire and smoke involved in understanding the Sum, Avg, Min, and Max functions, but they are actually quite easy to use. It just seems to be a part of the nature of wizards to want to try and impress people with their awesome knowledge and power. If you really want to see the man behind the curtain, check out "Do you know other tricks, Toto?" in Chapter 14 to get a full explanation of these functions.

The Summary Options dialog box lets you determine what other summary information you want your query to provide. Notice in Figure 12-5 that both Sum and Avg are checked. You can also check the Min and Max functions if you want, and the wizard will include those. You can even use these functions in conjunction with the Count function discussed in the previous paragraph. In fact, you can mix and match functions just like you can the clothes in your summer wardrobe.

After you select which functions you want to use, click on OK, and then on Next. You are prompted to name your query and choose a format to display your query. When you finish with these chores, click on the Finish button.

Setting the criteria

If you are using the Field Summary Options, you are not yet done (I'm so sorry). As soon as you click on Finish, you see a series of dialog boxes such as the one shown in Figure 12-6 that ask you to type in parameter values for each field.

Figure 12-6:
The wizard insists that you define your parameters for a summarized query.

A parameter is simply a value that will be listed on the Criteria row of your query. If you'd rather fill in the these values later, just leave the dialog box blank. Access will ask you for a parameter for each field, but you need only provide as many or as few as you like.

After you jump through all the wizard's hoops, you finally get to see a table summarizing the information you've requested. Figure 12-7 shows you the Datasheet view of your summarized query.

The wizard inserts the necessary expressions into the Total row of the design grid for you. Using the wizard in this manner means that you don't have to remember the tedious little details of where to put the AVG expression, or which field needs a SUM, or if Dorothy remembered to curtsy to the Good Witch of the North.

LastName	First Of ItemNa	Sum Of Minim	Avg Of Minimu	Count Of Items
Abercrombie	Treadle sewing	225	75	3
Allen-Brown	Asst hardback k	120	30	4
Backmeyer	Notebook comp	2375	1187.5	2
Cae	China setting fo	85	85	1
Coffie	100 skeins woo	100	50	2
Donati	Wedding dress	1350	337.5	4
Haseman	Board games (5	45	22.5	2
Hashimoto	Quilt rack	120	120	1
Ingle	HF Radio	1030	206	5
Merk	Painting -- boat	400	100	4
Peters	Animation cell	2245	3.333333333333	3
Rosen-Sheid	3 cast iron toys	22	22	1
Vaubel	Mandolin	125	125	1
Williams	Home theater s	750	250	3

Record: 4 of 14

Figure 12-7:
The
Datasheet
view of the
multitable
summarized
query.

How many wizards are there, Toto?

Is there a collective noun for a group of wizards? If there isn't, there needs to be because Access is loaded down with a whole plethora of wizardly assistants. Chapter 11 discusses the Select Query Wizard because it's the simplest and most useful wizard for your general needs.

There are four other Query wizards that you can call on at need, but only one of the group is discussed elsewhere in this book. You can find out everything you need about the Crosstab Query Wizard in Chapter 14, "Using the Total row/CrossTab Queries."

The remaining three wizards (Find Duplicates Query Wizard, Find Unmatched Query Wizard, and Archive Query Wizard) were exiled to the Land of the Nerds because they're just too weird for normal folks to need.

Adding tables to the grid

In Chapter 11, when I created a New Query, I had to select which table to use from the same Show Table dialog box seen in Figure 12-8.

When you want to work with multiple tables and you are creating a new query, simply click on the first table that you need and press the Add button, then click on the next table, click Add again, and so on, until you have all the tables that you need. You can click on Close to move to the next step. Figure 12-9 shows the Design view of a query with two tables selected.

Few things are more frustrating than going through all the work of designing an item and then realizing that you forgot something, so you have to start over again. What do you do if you've set up a wonderful query that you think will give you the answers that you need, only to realize that you forgot to include a field from another table?

Figure 12-8:
The Show Table dialog box brings Munchkins from different tables together to work on your queries.

Figure 12-9:
You can set up a query using more than one table.

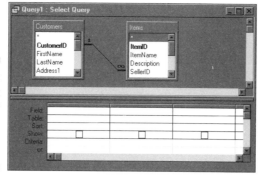

 Use the Show Table button to add the missing table to your query — that's what!

 Why do you use something called *Show Table* to add another table to your query? Beats me. I honestly have no idea why this feature isn't called *Add Table* instead. I guess the programmers didn't like that name because it's too close to what the feature actually does — you know how those programmers get sometimes.

To use this feature, go to the Design view of your query and click on the Show Table button. You see the Show Table dialog box, where you can choose which table or tables you want to add. Highlight those tables you want to include, click on <u>A</u>dd, and watch them magically appear in your query screen.

You can, if you like, add each table individually as described above. But another way to do this is slightly quicker. In the Show Table dialog box, click on the first table you need to add, hold down the Ctrl key and click on the next table you want, and repeat. As long as you hold down the Ctrl key after the first selection, you can choose multiple tables from your database. After you select all the tables you need, simply click on the Add button and the tables are all transferred to your query.

Please don't get caught in the trap of thinking that you can only use one or two tables. For ease of explanation, I only use two in the discussion, but just so you remember it, here's Figure 12-10, that has three tables included.

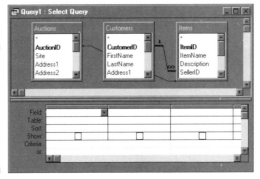

Figure 12-10: You can use three, four, or even more tables in a single query.

From one to two, from two to three, just keep on until you have as many tables as you need. Access lets you use all of the tables from the current database in your query.

Which Table Am I Using?

Okay, so you've slogged your way through the process of creating a multitable query. Don't break out the champagne yet. There are still some things that you may want to know before imbibing the bubbly.

Figure 12-11 shows you the Design view of my multitable query. Notice that in this view there is an extra row in the grid called Table. Access uses this row to remind you where that particular field came from.

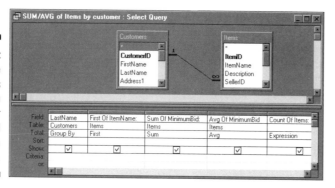

Figure 12-11:
The Table
row helps
you
remember
which field
goes with
which table.

You can let Access show you this row if you really need it. But if this one little bit of extraneous information is about ready to put you over the edge, you can make the whole row disappear into the bushes. Simply click on the <u>V</u>iew menu and click on the Table <u>N</u>ame command to remove the check next to it. The Table row then obediently slinks away to quietly whimper in the corner.

If, however, you find that you really do need to know where each field in your query is coming from, you can easily call the row back by putting the check back next to the Table <u>N</u>ame command.

Joining Your Tables in Holy Matrimony

When you are working with multiple tables in a single query, the top half of the query screen shows the field lists of each table contributing information to the query. Notice in Figure 12-12 that the two field lists are attached to each other by lines with symbols on each end.

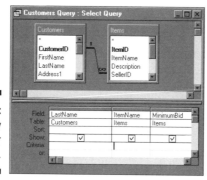

Figure 12-12:
The query
under
construction.

Notice that the line connecting the Items field list and the Customers field list is a little darker than the others and also has an infinity symbol (∞) next to the Items list and a 1 next to the customers list. This means that Access recognizes that one customer may have contributed more than one item to the auctions, but each item could have been contributed by only one person. This is a called a one-to-many relationship (there's more about this back in Chapter 5).

You may also notice that there is a lighter line between the Auctions field list and the Items field list. This represents that while there is a link between the two tables (the AuctionID field) Access does not care how the records are related.

These connections are part of the Join feature of Access and are important to understanding how the relational aspect of the database works, especially when you are asking questions through queries. Chapter 5 discusses how to create the link when you set up your database, but sometimes you may need to create a link between two or more tables long after they have been designed.

To create a link after tables have been designed, do you need to create new tables and reinput the data? No! Access is smarter than that, and several features let you merge the information between tables when you are working with queries.

One little feature of working with multiple tables can help you keep the relationship straight. You can rearrange the field lists to get a clearer understanding of the relationships between the tables by clicking on the table name and dragging the list to a new location on the screen.

When you move the tables, the connecting lines between the tables move as well. Don't worry if the lines seem to lead to the very top or bottom of one of the table windows. This happens because the connecting lines try to go directly to the fields that establish the relationship. If the field has scrolled off the top or bottom of the list, the line just attaches itself to the top of bottom of the list area, trying to get as close as possible to the field.

Using Auto-Join

If you put two or more tables that do not have a Join connection between them into the same query, Access attempts to automatically join the tables together by comparing all the fields in each table. If two fields have the same name and the same type of data, then Access links them together with Auto-Join.

So, if you set up your Auction database without linking tables and then realize that you need a query that lists the ItemName field (in the Items table) with the Auction the items are to be sold at, you can just add an AuctionID field in the

Items table and designate it as a number field. Then fill in that AuctionID field in the Item database based on the ID number automatically designated by Access for the particular auction, and you're all set.

When you put the two tables together in a query, Access recognizes that they both have numerical fields labeled `AuctionID` and links the two together.

Creating a joined connection

If your tables do not have fields that Access can recognize and Auto-Join, you can still manually Join two tables together in a query. Your first step is to make sure that your tables actually *do* have fields that share the same information. The two fields don't need exactly the same name, but they *must* contain the same type of information.

If your tables don't have any fields in common, you're sunk — there's no way to link two tables that are completely different.

Once you're sure that your tables are ready, go ahead and set up the design grid for the query. Figure 12-13 shows what a three-table query looks like when one table is not joined to the other two.

Figure 12-13:
Your query
can include
tables that
are not
joined.
Notice that
the Auctions
table is not
connected
to the
Customers
or the Items
tables.

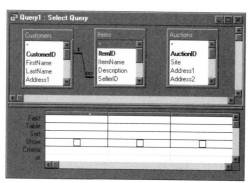

Your next step is to locate the fields in the two tables that you will use to establish your connection. In this case, you scroll down on the Items table until you find the AuctionID field. Then you click on the field in one of the tables (it really doesn't matter which) and drag it to the same field in the other table. It's really that simple. When you release the mouse button, Access creates the link, as shown in Figure 12-14.

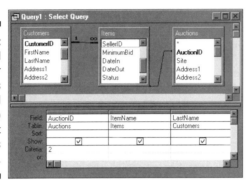

Figure 12-14:
Access will
join your
tables
together, all
you have to
do is tell it
what fields
to connect.

At this point, all that's left for you to do to finalize your link is to right-click on the connection between the two tables, select Join Properties, and choose the option that best fits your data.

Changing the Join

Whether Access creates the link for you (with Auto-Join) or you design it into your original database, a time may come when you want to change the way in which two tables are linked. You can do that anytime you see the line representing the connection. To make changes, start by right-clicking on the connection to see the pop-up menu shown in Figure 12-15.

Figure 12-15:
You get this
pop-up
menu if you
right-click
on the
connection
between
two tables.

If you select the Delete option, you remove the link between the two tables. On the other hand, if you select the Join Properties command, you see the dialog box shown in Figure 12-16.

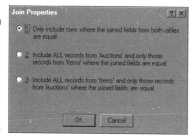

Figure 12-16:
This dialog
box tells
how two
tables are
related.

The Join Properties dialog box gives you three options that relate to the kinds of connections discussed in Chapter 5. If you select the Only include rows where the joined fields from both tables are equal option Access only reports information from either of the two tables if there is a direct one-to-one relationship between the information (in other words, if one entry in Auctions relates only to one entry in Items).

If you select one of the other two options, Access will Join the two tables assuming that one table has many records that are connected to one record in the other table. In the case of the Auctions example, you want to select option #3, Include ALL records from 'Items' and only those records from 'Auctions' where the joined fields are equal because each auction will have many items for sale, but the items are not for sale at more than one auction. That's a *one-to-many* relationship (but you probably figured that out already).

Adding Records to Tables

Another way that you can work with more than one table within Access is to use a query to select records from one database and add them to a new table, to an existing table within the current database, or to another database. You do this by changing the query type. If you change your Select query into a Make Table query (by selecting Make Table from the Query menu), Access displays the dialog box shown in Figure 12-17.

Figure 12-17:
The Make
Table query
dialog box.

In the Make Table dialog box, you can create a table name where the information is to be stored and determine whether or not this table is to be added to the current database or to another database. When you run the query, all the fields that are displayed as a result of the query are added to the new table, and those records that match the criteria that you are using are inserted into that new table. In general, this technique is useful only if you are breaking your main database into smaller chunks or are in the process of redesigning it. If you simply want to create a report based on a subset of your database, base the report on the results of the query rather than on its own table.

You can also change the query type to an Append To query by selecting Append from the Query menu. When you do, Access displays the Append dialog box rather than the Make Table dialog box. The only difference between the two dialog boxes is the name and the fact that, in the Append To dialog box, it says Append To around the controls rather than Make New Table. When you run an Append query, the table to which you are adding the information needs to already exist, the fields that result from your query should match, and the field names should match. The new information is simply added to the end of the existing database.

Appending to an existing table is one of the most complex things you may ever try within Access, so be warned that everything has to match perfectly. Access won't let you create duplicate primary keys, nor empty primary key fields, so you must make sure that the records that you add will fit into the existing table. If you're a little fuzzy on the whole *key* thing, refer back to Chapter 5 for help.

Chapter 13

Lions AND Bears? Lions OR Bears? Oh, my!

· ·

In This Chapter

▶ The difference between AND and OR

▶ Using the AND function

▶ Using the OR function

▶ Using AND and OR in the same query

· ·

*I*t seems to be a fact of life that the longer you work with a database, the more complex the questions that you want to ask of it. It's not enough for Dorothy to know which Munchkins are in the Lollipop Guild and which are in the Lullaby League. No, now she has to look at questions that combine these things. For example, she may be interested in seeing everybody who's in either group, or getting information about only those little folks who wear green and have met Glinda the Good Witch.

Comparing AND to OR

One of the things that makes it so difficult to write queries using ANDs and ORs is the fact that we speak English, and our databases don't. For example, when Dorothy says that the forest is filled with lions and tigers and bears, she is not talking about some creature that is a lion and a tiger and a bear. She is talking about a group of creatures, each of which falls into one of the three categories. She really means that she's afraid of running into a creature that is a lion or a tiger or a bear.

To put her problem into database terminology, she has three *expressions* which describe things she doesn't want to meet on a dark, tree-lined forest path. To assemble the three individual expressions into a single Access 95 query, you need an OR criteria (there's more in a little while about *why* that's the criteria of choice for her problem — for now, just nod acceptingly and go on).

So, in the peculiar language of the database world, Dorothy is afraid of meeting lions OR meeting tigers OR meeting bears. She's apparently not afraid of meeting Moose or meeting Elks, which just goes to show that she's never been in the same hotel as one of their big conclaves.

Here are some easy rules that make remembering this stuff really easy:

- An AND criteria always makes your list more restrictive, giving you fewer answers.
- An OR criteria always makes your list encompass more items, giving you more answers.

For example, if you start looking for an individual with blue eyes and red hair and over six feet tall and female, you have a very small group of possible candidates. (Nobody involved with this book meets all of those criteria.) If, on the other hand, you look for someone who has blue eyes or red hair or is over six feet tall or is female, you find out that quite a few people meet one, two, three, or maybe all four of these criteria. The group is much, much bigger. In fact, almost everyone who worked on the book — including my Spitz puppy — would be in this group.

Finding Things Between Kansas AND Oz

One of the most common ways to combine expressions is to try to restrict the list to entries that are between two values. For example, you may want to know all of the records that were entered after January 1, 1997, and before January 1, 1998. To ask this type of question, you need to use an AND criteria.

You simply put your two conditions together on the same line, separated with an AND. Figure 13-1 shows the query screen restricting DateIn in the Items table of the Auction database to sometime during the year 1997. Pay particular attention to the formula used to write this criteria.

The way in which Access 95 looks at this is to check the records and ask the first question, "Was the record entered after January 1, 1997?" If it wasn't entered then, Access 95 ignores the record and goes on to the next one. If it was entered after January 1, 1997, Access 95 goes ahead and asks the second question, "Was the record entered before January 1, 1998?" If yes, Access 95 includes the record in the results. If not, the record gets thrown out and Access 95 moves on to the next one. Notice that the comparison uses greater than or equal for the first date (January 1, 1997). That's because you want to include records written on the first day of the year as well.

Figure 13-1:
The AND
function
finds all
dates
between
January 1,
1997, and
January 1,
1998.

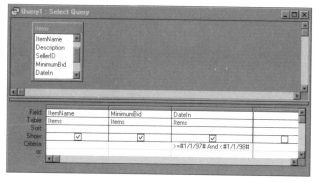

You can create this type of "between" instruction for any type of data. You can list numeric values that fall between two other numbers or work with names that fall within a range of letters.

Use the AND criteria when you want to ask a more specific question or reduce the number of matches that you find.

Multiple ANDs: AND Then What Happened?

You are not restricted to using an AND operator within the same column. You can instead combine a number of criteria in different columns, restricting a group by using additional rules. In that case, each rule that you are combining must fall within the same row. Access 95 checks each record to make sure it matches each of the expressions before allowing it to appear in the result table. Figure 13-2 shows an example of a query which uses three fields, with a rule in each, joined together on a single row (combining the rules with an AND statement).

The first part of the rule restricts the list to those items that are for sale at the auction at The Ranch. That gives a total of 21 records. The second part of the rule looks at those 21 records and finds the items that were submitted for sale by the Donati family. That brings the list down to only two records. The final part of the criteria asks for only those items with a minimum bid of less than $25. That gives a list of only one item — a bunch of men's clothing.

When you have a very large database and are trying to restrict your results down to a very few records, you will find that combining AND expressions is the most useful way to go.

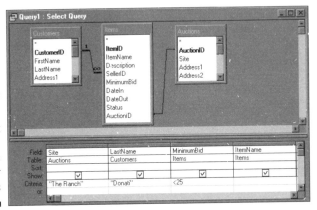

Figure 13-2:
Finding that
one record
that meets
all of your
requirements

Access 95 now enables you to create a Datasheet view of a table using a query and then further restrict that table using the filter and sort techniques discussed in Chapter 10.

Are You a Good Witch OR a Bad Witch?

Often, you may want to find a group of records that fall into a variety of possibilities, as I explained in the Advanced Filter/Sort for a mailing list in Chapter 11, where records were searched for people in Illinois OR Indiana. To use an OR in your criteria, you simply use a new line for each comparison.

To work with OR, simply list each criteria on its own line. The instructions can be listed in the same field as the same criteria. So, for example, with Dorothy database, you could look in the Animals field for Lions on one row, Bears on another, or Tigers on a third row, as shown in Figure 13-3.

Figure 13-3:
The OR
command
lets you find
all the scary
beasties in
the forest.

Alternatively, you could list the criteria in different columns. For example, Figure 13-4 shows the Items table of the Auction database with a request for items that were entered by the Donati family OR which have a MinimumBid of $30 or less.

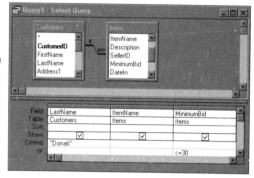

Figure 13-4:
You can create OR criteria from different fields.

Notice that each of the criteria is on a separate line. If the criteria were listed on the same line, you would be doing an AND operation, and only those records that matched both rules would appear.

Figure 13-5 shows the results of the query with labels indicating why each record is included. Notice that you have some records that match each of the rules and a few records that actually match both. Had you set this up as an AND query, you would have had only the records that matched both.

LastName	Item Name	Minimum Bid
Ingle	Box of ham radio magazines	$30.00
Donati	Wedding dress	$760.00
Donati	Engagement ring	$550.00
Donati	97 Audio CDs	$20.00
Donati	Miscellaneous men's clothing	$20.00
Haseman	Board games (5)	$10.00
Rosen-Sheid	3 cast iron toys	$22.00
Allen-Brown	Asst hardback books	$30.00
Allen-Brown	Asst hardback books	$30.00
Allen-Brown	Asst hardback books	$30.00
Allen-Brown	Asst hardback books	$30.00

This record is $30.

These records match only the 'Donati' criteria.

These records match both criteria.

These records are $30 or less.

Figure 13-5:
Breaking down the results of the query.

AND and OR? AND or OR?

Sometimes, using the AND and OR operators by themselves isn't enough. You need to ask a question about several different groups. Part of the question involves restricting the groups (with an AND), and other parts require including records based on a different criteria (with an OR).

Be careful with these queries. They get *really* fancy *really* fast. If a query grows to the point that you're losing track of which AND the last OR affected, then you're in over your head. Either start over or seek help from a qualified database nerd.

The most important thing to remember is that each OR line (each line within the criteria) is evaluated separately. If you want to combine several different criteria, you need to make sure that each OR line represents one aspect of what you are doing.

For example, in the Auctions database, it may be useful to know those items that will sell for less than $30 or more than $100 at auction site one. Well, finding the items in those price ranges requires the use of an OR condition. (If we were trying to find those items with a MinimumBid between $30 and $100, we would use an AND criteria here). That means that the entries go on separate lines.

However, that's not sufficient. We only want the items that are for sale at site one (The Ranch). For this query to work, we need to repeat that information on each line. In order to set this up, we need to ask for those items that are less than $30 AND at site one, OR those that are over $100 AND at site one. Notice that the OR separates two complete thoughts — the two price points — and neatly splits which criteria are put on separate lines. Figure 13-6 shows how to combine some ANDs with an OR.

Figure 13-6:
Any criteria on the same line are AND functions and restrict the search. Criteria on different lines are OR functions and expand the search.

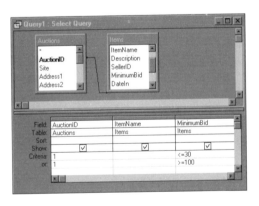

When reviewing your criteria, look at each line separately to make sure that line represents a group you want included in the final answer. Then check to see that the individual lines will work together to distill the answer you're seeking.

The AND criteria all go on the same line and are evaluated together. OR criteria go on separate lines, and each line is evaluated separately. If you have criteria that you want to use in each of the ORs, they must be repeated on each of the separate lines.

As with other types of queries, you don't have to use the same fields on each OR row. In fact, each row can be entirely separate. For example, Figure 13-7 shows a criterion which is asking for those items sold by the Donati family at site one OR items that are being sold for less than $100 at site two. Notice that both rows use the site location, but that the items that are combined with them are separate.

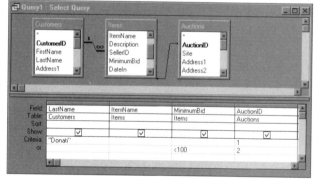

Figure 13-7:
Your OR rows can be represented in different fields.

The two groups that you get are those items sold by the Donati family at site one along with any records that match the second row — items sold for over $100 at site two.

To add an additional OR row, simply fill in another row. As soon as you press enter, you can use the scroll bars on the right side of the screen to see additional query rows. The additional rows, even though they are not labeled, all function as separate OR rows.

Counting the Lions, Tigers, and Bears

Once Dorothy found out how to determine what animals are in the forest, she decided it would be a good idea to know how many animals there are. The Tin Man pointed her in the right direction with the Total row of the Select Query screen, the topic of Chapter 14. Using this feature of Access 95, you can perform calculations with the contents of any field in your database and organize your information by any combination of other fields.

The 5th Wave By Rich Tennant

"I SUPPOSE THIS ALL HAS SOMETHING TO DO WITH THE NEW MATH."

Chapter 14
Teaching Queries to Count

. . . .

In This Chapter

▶ Using the Totals row

▶ Grouping entries together

▶ Understanding the Count and Sum functions

▶ Asking Crosstab queries

▶ Applying more functions

. . . .

*G*etting quick answers to simple questions about the stuff in your database is nice, but there's more to life than finding out precisely how many Munchkins bought pastel-colored back scratchers between January and May of the previous year. What if you needed to know the total amount of money they spent on back scratchers? Or the number of orders they placed?

In what's rapidly becoming a recurring theme of the book, it's Access 95 to the rescue. Well, technically speaking, it's actually Access 95 *query calculations* to the rescue.

Queries can do simple math, count matching entries, and do several other tricks while they're at it, provided you know how to ask for their help. This chapter explains the inner workings of these helpful functions. Read on and put those queries to work!

Totaling Everything in Sight

In addition to just answering questions, the standard query screen can also be used to perform simple calculations using the information that it finds. For example, if you tell the system to only find Munchkins who belong to the Lollipop Guild, you can then have it count the Munchkin members while it's there.

The first step in creating a total is to make the Total row appear. In order to do that, simply select View⇨Totals, or click on the Totals button. Figure 14-1 shows the Select Query screen with the Total row added.

Figure 14-1:
The Total row is added between the Table row and the Sort row.

 Your screen may have an additional line called Table, which lists the name of the table for each item. I discuss use of the View⇨Table Names command in Chapter 12.

The symbol shown on the face of the Totals button is called the *sigma*. This is a Greek letter meaning "to add everything up" and is used as a mathematical symbol for Sum. Fortunately, the *sigma* starts with an *s,* and so does the word *sum,* so it's easy to remember. After all, a total is just a sum.

Grouping the Suspects

To use the Total row, you start by adding to the grid the fields that you want to use in the query. You do this the same way you do for a Select query as discussed in Chapter 11. (Simply drag the field name from the list at the top to one of the columns in the grid.) As you add the fields to the grid, the Total row fills in with the Group By entry. This indicates that Access is trying to use that field to organize your information.

You use the Group By field to have Access organize the information that you are displaying into groups based on that particular field. This can be useful for getting a list of all of the different entries that appear in a single field. For example, Figure 14-2 shows a query with the Group By instruction in the DateIn category (from the Items database).

Figure 14-2:
The Group
By
instruction
lists each
entry in the
field only
once.

By doing Group By with the DateIn field, it is possible to generate a list of all of the dates in which new items were added to the auction. When you use this query, you get the results shown in Figure 14-3.

Figure 14-3:
Group By
lets you
group
records
together by
one set of
criteria.

Each date is listed only once, even though on some of them several items may have been brought to the auction (which means several records with that date exist in the database). Without the Group By instruction, the list would have repeated the date each time it appeared in the database.

Dorothy can use this same feature to get a list of all of the guilds within Munchkin Land simply by dragging over the Guild Name field and putting the Group By instruction on the Total row.

The Group By entry needs to stay in each field that will be used to organize your data. In other words, if you are going to use a criteria for your field, it needs to have Group By on the Total rows.

If you have more than one field showing with the Group By instruction, it lists each unique combination of the two fields. Figure 14-4 lists the results of having the DateIn and Item Name fields listed from the Items table of the Auction database.

Item Name	DateIn
HF Radio	2/2/95
China setting for 8	1/10/97
3 cast iron toys	1/12/97
Asst hardback books	1/18/97
Painting -- boat on lake	1/25/97
Painting -- Children	1/25/97
Painting -- Convertible	1/25/97
Painting -- Old man	1/25/97
Mandolin	2/1/97
20m Yagi antenna	2/2/97
2m Handi-talkie	2/2/97
Box of ham radio magazines	2/2/97
SW receiver	2/2/97
Notebook computer	2/4/97

Record: 4 of 31

Here each date shows every different type of item that was added on that date. Notice now that for dates such as February 2, several different items are listed as having come into the auction. On the other hand, when the same type of item was brought in (such as the four boxes of books that came in on January 18), the item type is only listed once.

Counting the Good Count

Although getting a list of the different entries within a field can be useful, the Total line can also be used to give you information about the contents of a field. If you want to work with the contents of the field, you must use an instruction other than Group By. One of the easiest types of instructions to work with is Count, which tells you how many records are in the group. (You create a group from the entries in the field, using the Group By entry.)

To find out how many records are in each group, you simply need to use the Count function on one of your other fields (columns). This means that your query uses two fields — the one you are using to create the groups (Group By) and the one you are counting (Count).

The most difficult thing is deciding which field to use for counting. If you want to make sure to count each record that matches, you must be certain that the field you use has an entry for each and every record. For example, Figure 14-5 shows the Query that Dorothy would use to count the number of members in each of the guilds.

Figure 14-5: Access calculates the number of members in each guild.

Select the Count function by clicking on the cell in the Total row for the field that you want counted. When you click, a down-arrow button appears. Click on the down arrow to see a drop-down list of functions, one of which is Count.

In the Guild field's Total row, Dorothy used the Group By instruction. For her other field in this query, she used LastName. To do the arithmetic, she included a Count instruction in the LastName field's Total row. Count told Access to group the records by the entry in the Guild field and, within each group, to increase the count by one for each of those records with a last name. Because all Munchkins have names, this means Access will count the number of Munchkins in each guild. Figure 14-6 shows the results of Dorothy's search.

Figure 14-6: The Great Guild Membership Count is complete.

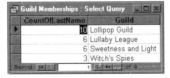

Select 'em, Then Count 'em

With Dorothy's problem solved, it's time to check back at the auction and see how Access is helping there. The managers of the auction are considering whether to require a minimum bid of $50 for all items. Before they change the minimum bid, however, the managers want to find out how many items will be affected. To do this, they need to create a query that selects the items affected and then counts them. The only problem is that a different field must be counted than the one being used for the criteria. Figure 14-7 shows a query that can do this.

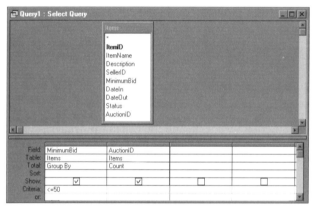

Figure 14-7:
The results of this query will list the number of records for each minimum bid amount less than $50.

When you're working with the Total row, remember that *each field* you include must have an instruction on the Total row, even if it's only Group By. (It's just one of those Access 95 things.)

You can use a criteria in any field — even one you're not including in the final results. To do this, put a Where instruction on the field's Total row. When you put the Where instruction in a field, Access uses any criteria you create in the field, but does not display the field in the results of the query.

You can also use a Where instruction in a field that you want to have treated as one group. If the managers used a Where instruction rather than a Group By instruction, the results would have a single row — the total count of records in the database with minimum bids of less than $50.

If you want to use a criteria in one of the fields that you are summarizing, add the field to the grid a second time and use the Where instruction. For some reason, Access can only use a criteria with the Total row when you mark it with the Where instruction.

Counting with Crosstab

Some types of information naturally lend themselves to being grouped by two categories. For example, polls often use gender to break down their results. You can do the same thing in Access with a crosstab (or *cross tabulation*) query.

Figure 14-8 is an example of what a crosstab looks like. It shows a breakdown of the auction information organized by the state of the customer and the location where their items were sold. Each row represents a different state, and each column represents one of the sites. Each box within the table contains the number of customers from that state who sold items at that site. Four states and two sites make eight values in the table.

Figure 14-8:
The Datasheet view of a Crosstab query.

State/Province	Exposition Hall	The Ranch
IL	3	3
IN	7	15
OH	3	2
WV	2	1

Record: |◄| ◄ | 1 | ► | ►I | ►* | of 4

A Crosstab query grid includes both the totals and the Crosstab row (as shown in Figure 14-9). Crosstab queries always have three fields. *Row Heading* is used for the row categories. *Column Heading* tells Access 95 where to find the column category. The third field explains where the values for the crosstab come from.

Figure 14-9:
In a Crosstab query, one field becomes the Row Heading, one the Column Heading, and one the value.

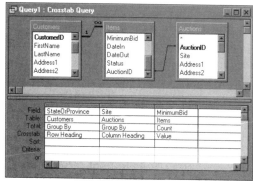

Field:	StateOrProvince	Site	MinimumBid	
Table:	Customers	Auctions	Items	
Total:	Group By	Group By	Count	
Crosstab:	Row Heading	Column Heading	Value	
Sort:				
Criteria:				
or:				

Both of the fields used as headings have a Group By instruction on the Total row. The field used for value has the function (usually Count, Sum, or Avg) that is to be used for calculating the values for the table.

You can also use a criterion (or several criteria) to limit which records are included in the summary. As with other queries in this chapter, you do so by adding a criteria to one of the fields already being used. You can do this by adding an additional field to the query using the Where instruction.

Of course, you don't have to do all this by hand. The Crosstab Query Wizard can guide you through each of the steps for a basic Crosstab query. Take advantage of it; otherwise, the wizard begins to feel lonely.

Does It All Add Up?

You can use other functions on the Total row instead of Count. One of the most useful is the Sum function, which simply gives you a total. For example, you may just use the MinimumBid field from the Items table of the Auction database with the Sum function and no other field. By doing that, you get the total amount of all minimum bids, as shown in Figure 14-10.

Figure 14-10:
Total all the values in a field by using the Sum function.

To create a query that sums a total, add the MinimumBid field to your query grid and use the Sum instruction on the Total row. The rest of the grid is left blank. The records are put into one large group and then values in the MinimumBid field are added together to create the sum.

As with the Count function, you can combine the Sum function with other instructions on the Total row (or even with criteria). For example, you may want to find out what the total is for each Seller ID. To do that, you simply add the Seller ID to your query with a Group By instruction, as shown in Figure 14-11.

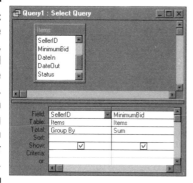

Figure 14-11:
If using the
Total row,
each field
must have
an entry.
Here, I'm
calculating
the minimum
bids total for
each seller.

When you run that query, you see the results shown in Figure 14-12. Each Seller ID is listed individually with the total for that seller.

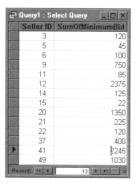

Figure 14-12:
If you add
Seller ID
with Group
By, you get
the total
value of the
minimum
bids for
each seller.

If you wish to have the seller's name rather than the ID, all you need to do is organize this with a multiple table query that links to the Customer table by the ID number. To complete the process (for this example), you would use the LastName field for your Group By rather than your Seller ID, as shown in Figure 14-13. When you run the query, the information is organized by Last Name with the total minimum bid for each individual instead of simply listing the seller number.

Here's a tidbit from the Since You're Already Here School of Access 95: You can also activate the Sort function and have the list organized in descending order (largest to smallest) by any field in your query. To do that, put the *Descending* instruction on the Sort line under the field you want to sort with. Figure 14-14 shows the Auction query set up with a descending sort on the MinimumBid field.

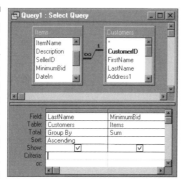

Figure 14-13: Using the Customer table, you can organize your query by seller name rather than ID number.

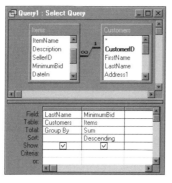

Figure 14-14: Having Access 95 sort the minimum bids in descending order is easy.

Figure 14-15: The results are in — and in order from largest to smallest.

LastName	SumOfMinimumBid
Backmeyer	2375
Peters	2245
Donati	1350
Ingle	1030
Williams	750
Merk	400
Abercrombie	225
Vaubel	125
Hashimoto	120
Allen-Brown	120
Coffie	100
Cae	85
Haseman	45
Rosen-Sheid	22

Record: 8 of 14

The query's results are in Figure 14-15.

There's more about the Sort line in Chapter 11. If you're curious about sorting in general, flip back to Chapter 10.

There's More to Life than Sum and Count

Don't get the idea that the world of queries begins and ends with Sum and Count. Access 95 includes many other functions to organize, evaluate, and generally figure out what your data is saying. Some of more popular and useful functions are listed in Table 14-1.

Table 14-1	Access Functions and What They Do
Function	*Purpose*
Group By	Use this column to organize the query results.
Sum	Add up all the values from this field in the query results.
Avg	Calculate the average of the values in this field.
Min	Tells you the lowest value the query finds.
Max	Gives you the highest value the query finds.
Count	Tells you the number of records that match the query criteria.
First	Returns the first record that Access 95 stumbles across that meets the query criteria.
Last	Same as First, except this is the last matching record Access 95 finds.
Expression	Tells Access you want a calculated field (check out Chapter 15 for more information).
Where	Use this field as part of the query criteria.

Each entry in the table includes the name of the function and a brief description of what it does. Each function can be selected from the drop-down list on the Total line.

Chapter 15

Automated Editing for Big Changes

· ·

In This Chapter

▶ Developing an expression

▶ Performing more complex calculations

▶ Using fixed values in a calculation

▶ Calculating text fields

▶ Using the Expression Builder

· ·

*W*hen you first learn to create your database, one of the rules is to put in only fields that you need and not to bother with things that can be calculated based on information already in the database. Well, this chapter shows you how to do those calculations. The secret to this wizardly magic is the *calculated field*.

A calculated field takes information from another field in the database and perform some arithmetic on it to come up with new information. In fact, a calculated field can take data from *more* than one field and combine it to create an entirely new field if that's what you want.

Although the examples in this section deal with calculated fields within queries, you use the same techniques to add them within a report. There's more information about adding calculated fields to reports in Chapter 20.

A Simple Calculation

When you want to create a calculated field within a query, first make sure that all of the tables containing fields that you want to use in the calculation are included at the top of the query screen. As an example, say that you want to calculate an expected price for items in an auction. Doing this requires only that the Items table be added to the query and — so that you know which items are which — that the ItemName field be added to the query grid (see Figure 15-1).

Figure 15-1:
To calculate the expected price for an item, you just need the ItemName and MinimumBid fields.

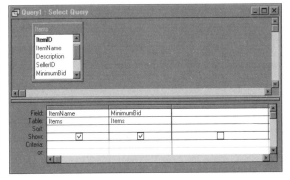

To start building your calculated field, simply click in the field name box of the column where you want the results to appear. Instead of selecting an existing field, you simply type the calculation that you want Access 95 to perform.

Say that you've done your research and know that, in most auctions, an item sells for 47 percent more than the minimum bid price. So to calculate the expected price, you simply need to add 47 percent to the MinimumBid. One formula to do this is

```
[MinimumBid] + ([MinimumBid] * .47
```

In this case, the expected price will go into the field next to the ItemName. Start typing the formula in the first field that you will be using; in this case, MinimumBid. In order for Access 95 to recognize what you are typing as a field, you need to enclose **MinimumBid** in square brackets, as shown in the preceding sample formula and in Figure 15-2.

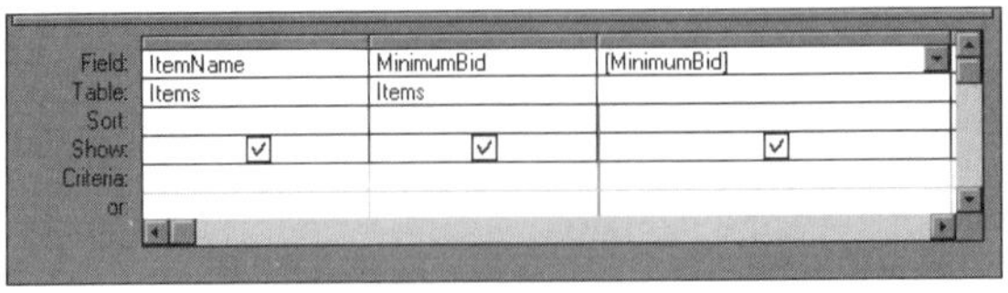

Figure 15-2:
Using square brackets tells Access that you are discussing a field.

You can now type the rest of the formula in the field; however, you may not be able to see all of your formula at one time. You have two choices: either keep typing and trust that what you are typing is actually going into the field, or enlarge the field so that it is wide enough to display the entire formula. Figure 15-3 shows the entire formula for calculating the expected price displayed in the field.

Figure 15-3:
The formula for the expected price of your sale items.

Field:	ItemName	MinimumBid	[MinimumBid]+([MinimumBid]*.47)
Table:	Items	Items	
Sort:			
Show:	☑	☑	☐
Criteria:			
or:			

Because Access 95 isn't smart enough to recognize the percent sign, you need to convert any percentages to decimals; in this case, 47% is written as **.47**. In order to convert a percent to a decimal, just divide it by 100.

You have to type each field name into your formula; you can't just drag the field name down from the table list. This is because dragging down the field name adds it as a field itself.

When you run this query, it produces a table showing the item name and an expected price for each entry (see Figure 15-4). If you like, you can take a calculator and check that Access 95 did its job correctly. You should find that if you take the value in the MinimumBid field and multiply it by 1.47, you get the result shown in the new calculated field.

Figure 15-4:
It actually works!

Item Name	Minimum Bid	Expr1
China setting for 8	$85.00	124.95
3 cast iron toys	$22.00	32.34
Asst hardback books	$30.00	44.1
Asst hardback books	$30.00	44.1
Asst hardback books	$30.00	44.1
Asst hardback books	$30.00	44.1
Painting -- boat on lake	$100.00	147
Painting -- Children	$100.00	147
Painting -- Convertible	$100.00	147
Painting -- Old man	$100.00	147
Mandolin	$125.00	183.75
HF Radio	$400.00	588
2m Handi-talkie	$190.00	279.3
Box of ham radio magazines	$30.00	44.1

Record: 13 of 36

Notice that the column for the expected price is labeled a little strangely with the column heading Expr1 (which stands for *Expression 1*). If you want to change the expression heading, that's easy to do. If you look at the grid after creating an expression, you find that Access 95 inserted the field name and a colon in front of your equation. To give the field a different name, simply highlight the field name and replace it. Figure 15-5 shows the calculated field after it's been given the field name Expected Price.

Figure 15-5:
The words
before the
expression
create the
label for the
field name.

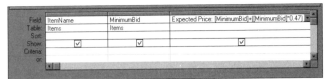

In addition to changing the field name, you may want to change its format. To change the format of the field, simply right-click on the field and, from the pop-up menu that appears, select Properties. In the Field Properties dialog box (shown in Figure 15-6), click in the Format line and then click on the button that appears on the right end of the field (the one with the downward-pointing arrow).

Figure 15-6:
Use the
Field
Properties
dialog box
to change
the
formatting
of your
fields.

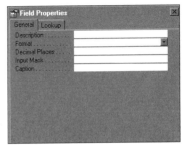

In the drop-down list that appears, select the type of format that you want to use for the field. For this example, select Currency. Figure 15-7 shows the resulting table after you change the name of the field to Expected Price and use the Currency format for all of the values.

Figure 15-7:
Using the
Format
section of
the Field
Properties
dialog box,
you can set
any field
to fit a
particular
format.

Item Name	Minimum Bid	Expected Price
China setting for 8	$85.00	$124.95
3 cast iron toys	$22.00	$32.34
Asst hardback books	$30.00	$44.10
Asst hardback books	$30.00	$44.10
Asst hardback books	$30.00	$44.10
Asst hardback books	$30.00	$44.10
Painting -- boat on lake	$100.00	$147.00
Painting -- Children	$100.00	$147.00
Painting -- Convertible	$100.00	$147.00
Painting -- Old man	$100.00	$147.00
Mandolin	$125.00	$183.75
HF Radio	$400.00	$588.00
2m Handi-talkie	$190.00	$279.30
Box of ham radio magazines	$30.00	$44.10

Once you get the hang of simple calculations, you can more confidently use
Access for more powerful operations.

Bigger, Better (and More Complicated) Calculations

You can use more than one field in your calculation to create a result. Figure
15-8 shows the Items table after a couple of options have been added. In
addition to the fields previously discussed, Actual Price, DateIn, and DateOut
fields have been added, and, for many of the records, the DateOut and
ActualPrice fields have been filled in with dates and amounts as the items sold.
For some items, the Status field has been changed from Available to Sold, and
there are entries for the two new fields. (You may notice that a couple of items
have been withdrawn.)

Figure 15-8:
I've added
the
ActualPrice
field — an
important
field — to
the Items
table.

Item Name	DateIn	Minimum	DateOut	Status	ActualPrice
China setting for 8	1/10/97	$85.00	2/1/97	Sold	$130.00
3 cast iron toys	1/12/97	$22.00	2/1/97	Sold	$35.00
Asst hardback books	1/18/97	$30.00		Available	
Asst hardback books	1/18/97	$30.00		Available	
Asst hardback books	1/18/97	$30.00	2/1/97	Sold	$30.00
Asst hardback books	1/18/97	$30.00	2/1/97	Sold	$40.00
Painting -- boat on lake	1/25/97	$100.00		Available	
Painting -- Children	1/25/97	$100.00	2/1/97	Sold	$150.00
Painting -- Convertible	1/25/97	$100.00		Available	
Painting -- Old man	1/25/97	$100.00	2/1/97	Sold	$165.00
Mandolin	2/1/97	$125.00	2/5/97	Withdrawn	
HF Radio	2/2/95	$400.00		Available	
2m Handi-talkie	2/2/97	$190.00		Available	
Box of ham radio magazines	2/2/97	$30.00		Available	
20m Yagi antenna	2/2/97	$85.00		Available	
SW receiver	2/2/97	$325.00	2/1/97	Sold	$475.00

When items in the auction have started selling, it might be convenient to know how much more than the expected bid each item earned and how long each item took to sell. You can find out by creating three calculated fields.

One field calculates the number of days it took an item to sell by subtracting the DateIn field from the DateOut field.

A second field calculates the difference between the amounts in the ActualPrice and MinimumBid fields.

A third field calculates the percentage of difference between the minimum bid and the amount above the minimum bid for which the item actually sold. This percentage can be calculated by taking the difference — in this example, Expr2 — and dividing it by the amount in the original MinimumBid field. Notice in Figure 15-9 that the Expr2 reference is treated like a field name and is enclosed in brackets.

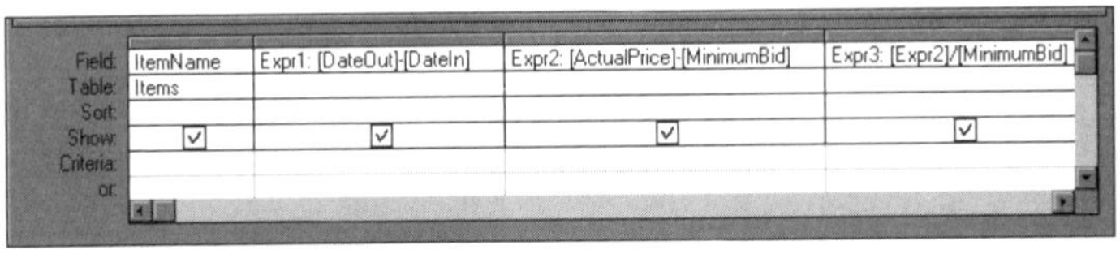

Figure 15-9:
This query
uses three
different
expressions.

Field:	ItemName	Expr1: [DateOut]-[DateIn]	Expr2: [ActualPrice]-[MinimumBid]	Expr3: [Expr2]/[MinimumBid]
Table:	Items			
Sort:				
Show:	☑	☑	☑	☑
Criteria:				
or:				

Although these formulas produce correct results, the fields would be clearer if they had names that were more descriptive and formatting that was more logical. Figure 15-10 shows the query grid after the names of the fields have been changed to DaysToSell, AmountAbove, and Increase. Note that if you change the field name for the second field (the one calculating the difference between the actual sale price and the minimum bid), you need to change the reference to that field in the third formula from Expr2 to AmountAbove.

After looking at the query for a minute, you may realize that it's not necessary to display the AmountAbove field — you can just include the information for that field directly in the formula for the Increase field. Instead of having AmountAbove above the divisor, your formula would be

```
([ActualPrice]-[MinimumBid])/[MinimumBid]
```

Whichever way you do it is up to you.

Figure 15-10:
If you change the name of a field, you need to change any reference to it in any other calculated field.

When this name changes...

then this reference has to change.

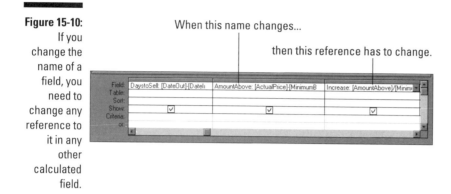

Figure 15-11 shows the results of the query using these formulas. Rather than show all of the items, the list includes only those that have been sold (and therefore have ActualPrice and DateOut fields). Setting up such criteria is discussed in Chapter 11, but to refresh your memory — just add the Status field and type **Sold** in the Criteria row.

Figure 15-11:
The results of your calculations for auction items already sold.

Item Name	DaystoSell	AmountAbove	Increase
SW receiver	13	$150.00	46.15%
Portable printer	11	$125.00	71.43%
Wedding dress	0	$440.00	57.89%
Miscellaneous men's clothing	0	$5.00	25.00%
Treadle sewing machine	21	$45.00	56.25%
Box of asst silk thread	6	$5.00	10.00%
50 asst laser disks	2	$50.00	25.00%
Board games (5)	0	$5.00	50.00%
China setting for 8	36	$45.00	52.94%
3 cast iron toys	20	$13.00	59.09%
Asst hardback books	42	$0.00	0.00%
Asst hardback books	14	$10.00	33.33%
Painting -- Children	21	$50.00	50.00%
Painting -- Old man	7	$65.00	65.00%

Record: 1 of 14

Making Access 95 ask

At times, you may want a value included in a formula that's not in your database. If you already know the value, you can simply type it into the formula as done earlier with **.47** for 47%. But if you'd rather be able to enter that value as you run the query, that's easy to do, too.

Simply create a field name to use within your formula. For example, you might choose to calculate an Expected Price field by using a percentage value that you'll enter when you run the query. To make it easy, imagine that this field is called PercentIncrease. You then create your calculated field using the formula

```
[MinimumBid]+([MinimumBid]*[PercentIncrease])
```

When you run the query, Access displays a dialog box like the one shown in Figure 15-12. This lets you enter a value for the increase that you're expecting.

Figure 15-12:
Access asks you to provide a value for your calculation.

When the dialog box appears, just enter the value of your expected increase (as a decimal value), and then Access 95 does the rest. This means that you can use the same query with different values to see how changing that value affects your results.

Working with words

Numbers aren't the only thing you can use for calculations. In fact, often it can be more useful to perform the calculation using a text field. Figure 15-13 shows one of the most common database formulas, which is used to combine the FirstName and LastName fields to provide the full name.

Figure 15-13:
You can turn a name into a calculated field.

This formula consists of the FirstName field, a plus sign, then a single space inside of quotation marks, followed by another plus sign, and then the LastName field:

```
[FirstName]+" "+[LastName]
```

When you run this query, Access 95 takes the information from the two fields and puts them together, inserting a space in between them. The results of this query are shown in Figure 15-14.

Figure 15-14: See! You can join the names back together again.

Notice that each individual's name appears as it would on a mailing list label. This makes it very easy to take information from your database and turn it into a more readable format.

Help with Expressing Yourself

There are two basic problems with creating calculated fields. First, you have to be able to figure out what the formula should say. And then you have to know how to enter the formula so that Access 95 can recognize it.

 Unfortunately, there's no help for the first problem — but there is for the second. To get help creating a calculated field the way Access 95 wants it, click on the Build button and bring out the Expression Builder.

The Expression Builder has several parts to it, as you can see in Figure 15-15. The top part is the area where you actually create the expression, and immediately below that are the operators you can use to work with the information in your expression.

The expressions are put together here.

These are your tools.

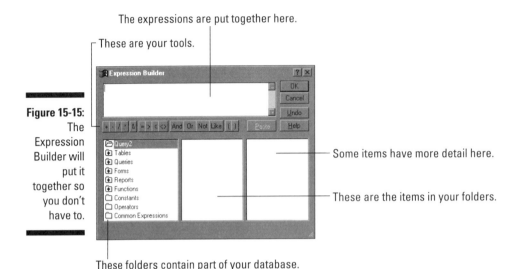

Figure 15-15:
The
Expression
Builder will
put it
together so
you don't
have to.

Some items have more detail here.

These are the items in your folders.

These folders contain part of your database.

The first group of these operators does simple mathematical operations: addition, subtraction, multiplication, and division. The next operator is similar, in that it can be used to combine two text fields (in most cases, you can also use the plus sign to do this).

The next group of operators does logical comparisons. These operators create expressions similar to those used in the Criteria field and return a response of True or False. The final two buttons in this collection allow you to enter parentheses. (You can also simply type these symbols directly from your keyboard, which is often much easier.)

The bottom of the dialog box has three windows. The left one contains folders of the various parts of your Access 95 environment, including all of the information in your tables.

To add a field from one of your tables, simply open the Tables folder and then open the folder for the table that you want to use. A second column will then appear, displaying a list of all of the fields in that table. To add a field to the expression, simply double-click on it. Figure 15-16 shows the Expression Builder with the Items folder open and the MinimumBid item already added to the expression.

Notice that when you use the Expression Builder to add a field, it includes the table name in front of the field name with an exclamation mark in between the two. The format for this is

```
[Table Name]![Field Name]
```

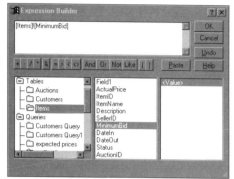

Figure 15-16:
You can find
a field in the
lower half of
the builder
and add
it to an
expression
by double-
clicking
on it.

The other folders listed in the first window often contain much more information. In some cases, this information is organized into categories within the
folder. For example, the Functions folder contains a variety of built-in functions,
as well as some that you or others may have defined in your database. These
functions can be used to perform calculations using the information in your
database.

To use one of the built-in functions, simply open the Functions folder, select a
category of functions from those in the second window, and then look through
the list in the third window until you find the one you want to use. Figure 15-17
shows the Built-In Functions folder open, with the math functions displayed in
the third window. To select a category of functions, simply click on it in the
second window. To select a function, double-click on it in the third window.

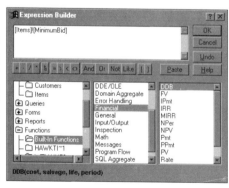

Figure 15-17:
In the lower
left, you see
a brief
synopsis of
the function
that you've
selected.

There are useful items in the other folders, as well. The Constants folder
contains constants that are defined for you for use in comparisons, including
True, False, and some that can represent empty fields. The Operators folder
contains symbols used for creating expressions.

The Arithmetic category includes the same four operators that are available as buttons. It also includes the caret (^), which is used for exponents (raising a number to a higher power); MOD, which is used to return the remainder of a division operation; and the backslash, which is used for integer division. With integer division, dividing 5 by 2 (5\2) gives you the answer 2, and 5 MOD 2 gives you the result of 1, the remainder.

Finally, the Common Expressions lets you include various common entries. These are most useful for creating a report and are discussed in Chapter 20.

One of the advantages to using the Expression Builder is that it helps to remind you what you need to do. For example, when you are creating an expression, the Expression Builder won't let you just add two fields, side by side. Figure 15-18 shows what would happen if you double-clicked on the DateOut and DateIn fields, one after the other.

Figure 15-18:
The
Expression
Builder tells
you when
you need to
add an
operator
to an
expression.

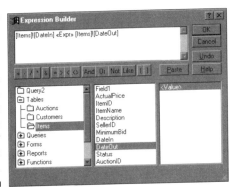

Notice the angle bracket (the two less than signs), Expr, and angle bracket (the two greater than signs)

```
<<Expr>>
```

that appear between the two fields. They remind you that you need to insert an expression between the two fields. If you click on the `<<Expr>>` entry, the entire text will highlight and then you can click on one of the operators to insert it between the two fields (for example, the minus sign).

Chapter 16

Action Queries

*I*t's pretty easy to fix an incorrect entry in an Access table. A couple of clicks, some typing, and {poof!} the problem is gone.

But what if you need to fix 26,281 records? Suddenly, we're talking about a whole *lot* of clicking and typing and clicking and typing. Maybe it's just me, but editing an entire table by hand doesn't sound like a {poof!} experience to me — it sounds more like a clean-the-elephant-herd-with-a-toothbrush kind of experience.

Fortunately, Access has a variety of large-scale housekeeping and editing tools. These tools let you make widespread changes to your database without wearing down your fingers in the process. This chapter explores the tools available within Access and gives you examples of how to use them to make quick work of the elephant herd in your life.

Quick and Easy Fixes: Replacing Your Mistakes

Before moving on to the elaborate techniques that you can use in queries, you should know about one particular editing technique: using the Replace command to change a mistake into a different value. When you open a table in the Datasheet view, you can select the Replace command from the Edit menu to display the dialog box shown in Figure 16-1.

In this dialog box, you can enter the word that is currently in your database (the wrong information) in the Find What box and enter the proper information into the Replace With box. When you have entered text in both fields, the buttons on the right side become available; you can use these buttons to move through your information, making changes as you go.

If you've misspelled "Munchkin" throughout your data and need to change all of its occurrences to the proper spelling, you can simply put the incorrect spelling in Find What, the proper spelling in Replace With, and click on the Replace All button. Your computer goes off and does your bidding, changing each and every word in the Find What box to the one in the Replace With box.

You can, however, have greater control over what's going on. Some features that control how Access locates specific records are discussed in Chapter 10 as part of the Find command. Two additional options, though, are unique to the Replace command.

One option, Match Whole Field, tells Access to only bother looking for cases where the information in the Find What box is all that is in the field. If there are any additional characters, even a single letter, and the Match Whole Field box has a check next to it, Access skips over that field.

The other option gives you both a Find Next and a Replace button to move you through the data. You use the Find Next button to move to the next information that matches what is in the Find What box without changing the current selection. You use the Replace button to change the current selection and move on to the next match.

This lets you browse through your database making changes only in certain cases. Click on Find Next to move on without changing; click on Replace to make the change and move on. (Clicking on Replace All makes each and every change without asking your permission first. It does tell you how many changes were made when it finishes.)

Different Queries for Different Jobs

Although Select queries are the most useful types of queries within Access because they answer your questions and can be used as the basis for reports, other types of queries are also useful (otherwise, Microsoft wouldn't have bothered including them). You can change the type of query that you are using by selecting from the Query menu (found in Query Design View) or by using the Query Type button on the Query Design View Toolbar. When you click the downward arrow on the right side of the Query Type button, a list of query types is displayed, as shown in Figure 16-2.

Figure 16-2: You can tell the current type of query by the image on the button and the dot next to its name.

The Crosstab query is discussed in Chapter 14; the Append query and Make Table query types are discussed in Chapter 12. To change the type of query you are using, simply select the type that you want from the list (either the Query menu or the Query Type button).

 You may notice that the last four types of queries (Make Table, Update, Append, and Delete) are marked with exclamation marks. That's to remind you that these types of data actually change the way your information is organized. When you are working with these four types of queries, you can use the Query View button to preview which records will be affected by the query. I strongly recommend that you do a preview before running any of these queries because that's the only way to make sure the changes you are making are really the ones you intend.

With a Select query, there isn't much difference between using the Run button and the Query View button, and with most other types of queries, the difference is minor. When you are using either the Delete query or the Update query, there is a BIG difference. When you use the Query View button with these two functions, you are looking at the results without really changing your database. If you use the Run button instead, your information will be changed for all time and eternity (well, unless you have a backup).

You're Outta Here: The Delete Query

One of the easiest types of editing queries to create is a Delete query. Unfortunately, the Delete query is also one of the most dangerous queries around. When you go to create a Delete query, you use the same commands and setup as you do for a Select query. In fact, consider doing a Select query first to make sure that you are matching the records you mean to match before converting the query to a Delete query.

 At the very least, click on the Query View button before you use the Run button.

1. **To begin, set up all of your criteria in a normal Select query for identifying your records.**

2. **Run the query and make sure that, in fact, the records that you want to work with are being displayed.**

3. **Return to the Design view and use the Query Type drop-down list to select a Delete query or select <u>D</u>elete from the <u>Q</u>uery menu.**

   You see the Delete Query option on the Query Type list.

When you switch to a Delete query, the name in the Title Bar changes, and the Sort line changes to the Delete line. Figure 16-3 shows a typical Delete Query screen. Notice that information for locating records is already in this query because it was converted over from the query I used to list out these records (the original Select query).

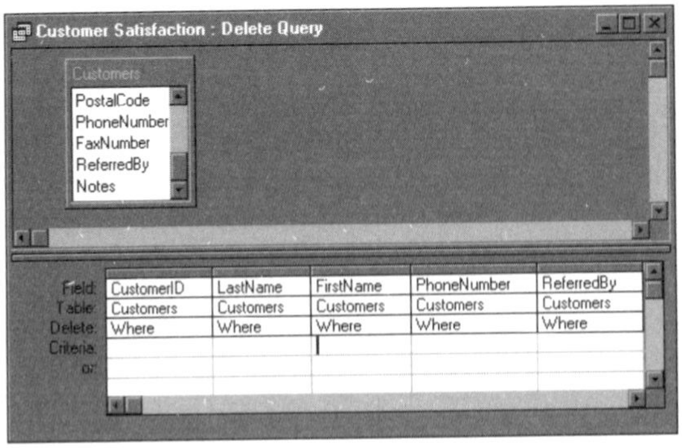

Figure 16-3:
The Delete Query window sets your Munchkins to scrubbing out the data you don't want.

Those fields that are going to be used to select the records are identified with the Where instruction on the Delete line. This simply means, "Find records *where* this criteria is true." Once you set up your criteria, if you want to delete all of the records that match your criteria, once you have converted to a Delete query you are ready to go. When you start to run the query, you see a message asking if you're sure you want to delete the records and reminding you that you won't be able to get the data back.

You cannot undo the changes made this way. Once you delete these records, they are gone — period. Gone for good, never to be seen or heard from again. Are you sure you really mean to do this?

If you realize that this is all a bad dream and you really want to keep those records in your table, carefully click No. If you're *sure* (really sure) that you want to delete the records, click on the Yes button; Access then will go out, find the records that match the criteria, and remove them from the table. That's all you need to do.

You can, in fact, create Delete queries that use more than one table to locate their information. Be very careful when doing this, however, as the number of changes that you are making can go up dramatically. Again, I suggest doing a Select query first to list out the records that you will be deleting.

You actually don't need to run a separate Select query before you begin. You can simply click on the Query View button on the left side of the standard toolbar to switch to a Dataview and see what records will be affected by your query.

If you wish, you can emphasize which records are to be deleted by dragging the asterisk symbol from the appropriate table. When you drag in the asterisk, the information on the Delete line for that field changes to the From instruction, indicating that this is the table that the record will be deleted *from*.

Things get a bit more complicated if you create a query using more than one table. When deleting from more than one table, Access can only figure out by itself when it should delete records that are linked one-to-one — in other words, each record that is linked only to a single record in the other table. When you look at the relationship grid at the top of the Query screen, one-to-one links are shown with a "1" symbol. If your relationships are one-to-many (indicated with an infinity symbol at the end of the link), you need one query to delete all of the matching records from the Menu table and a second query to delete the single record from the other end of the relationship.

Making Big Changes

There comes a time in every database's life when it needs to change. Fortunately, changes of the large variety can be made automatically using an Update query. An Update query allows you to use a query to select records and then use instructions to change the information.

As with other types of queries which modify your data, particularly the Delete query discussed previously in this chapter, it's important to make sure that your query is working only with the records you want to change. That's why I always suggest setting up your criteria and then running the Select query.

When you select the Update query, either by selecting Update from the Query menu or by selecting Update query from the Query Type list, your query grid changes to resemble the one shown in Figure 16-4.

Figure 16-4:
The Update Query Design view gives you a field to update the entries of selected criteria.

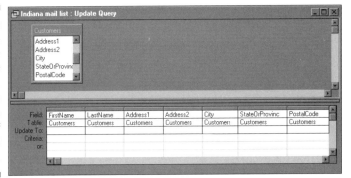

The one difference is the addition of the Update To line. You can use any criteria to select your records, just as you can in a normal query. For example, you may want to select all of the records in your auction database which belong to the Allen-Brown family.

To do that, you can set up your criteria with LastName field and the entry "Allen-Brown" on the Criteria line. You may also want to include the Item Name and its MinimumBid to make sure that you are finding those records that you want. When you run your Select query, your grid should resemble the one shown in Figure 16-5.

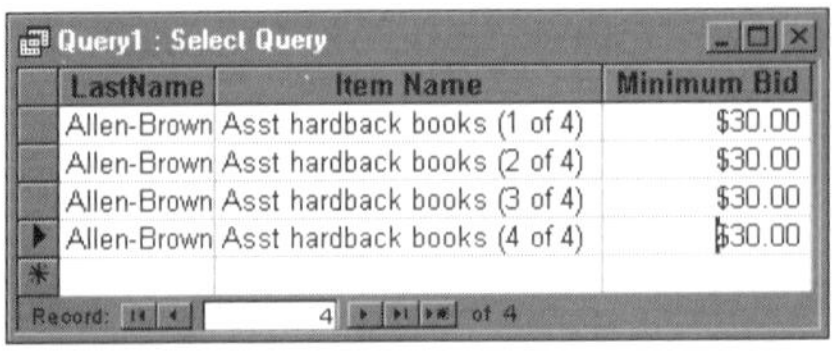

Figure 16-5:
A Select query shows the items contributed by the Allen-Brown family.

LastName	Item Name	Minimum Bid
Allen-Brown	Asst hardback books (1 of 4)	$30.00
Allen-Brown	Asst hardback books (2 of 4)	$30.00
Allen-Brown	Asst hardback books (3 of 4)	$30.00
Allen-Brown	Asst hardback books (4 of 4)	$30.00

Record: 4 of 4

When you run this query, you see that, in fact, you are getting only the records for the items submitted by the Allen-Brown family, four boxes of assorted books.

The Allen-Brown family has decided to raise the price of the books that they have in the auction. To raise the price of the books, you can simply go through and change each record by hand, but using an Update query is easier. The Allen-Brown family has decided on a price of $35.00 as the MinimumBid. So your Update query screen looks like the one shown in Figure 16-6. Notice here that the new value has been put in the Update To row for the MinimumBid field.

When you run the query, you get a warning message that you are about to update records. Click on Yes to go ahead and make your changes.

You can also make changes based upon the existing value in a field. For example, you may decide to apply a 10% discount to all minimum bids over $100. To do that, you simply need to use a calculation in the Update To field.

Figure 16-6:
The Update query allows you to change the values of all the items in a field that correspond to your criteria.

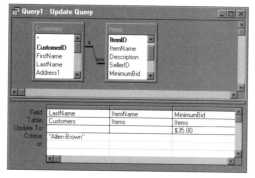

You can use the Expression Builder, discussed in Chapter 15, in order to create your calculation. In this case, the MinimumBid is equal to .9 x the MinimumBid. Taking 90% of the current cost is the same as taking away 10% (100% - 10% = 90%), and .9 is the same as 90%. Figure 16-7 shows how this Update query is set up.

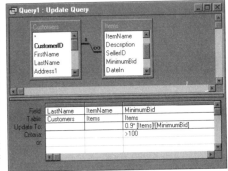

Figure 16-7:
The
expression
for
calculating
how to
update the
values of a
field can be
based on
the current
contents of
the field.

When you run this query, Access attempts to update 20 of the Auction records, discounting the MinimumBid price to 90% of its original, but only on those records that have a MinimumBid of more than $100.00.

To combine additional tables and criteria, you may want to update all the MinimumBids that will be at one of the auction sites. To do that, you can use a grid like the one shown in Figure 16-8.

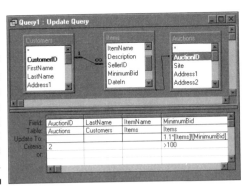

Figure 16-8:
You can
update
fields using
criteria from
more than
one table.

In Figure 16-8, the criteria being used is the Auction ID code for the auction, and the update is being done again to MinimumBids — in this case, increasing the price of the items by 10% (multiply the old price by 1.1).

Part IV
Turning Your Table into a Book

The 5th Wave   By Rich Tennant

TYPE? NAW, I JUST SORT OF HUNT AND PECK.

In this part . . .

Someone said that the computer revolution would do away with paper. Needless to say, they were wrong. (The last I heard, that person is now compiling the annual psychic predictions page for one of the national tabloids.)

So far, you put the data in and then mixed it up a little. Now it's time to pull the data out, clean it up a bit, and record it for posterity on the printed page. Access 95 has some strong reporting tools to make your multithousand page reports look truly cool. Better still, it offers some great summary tools to make those multithousand page reports a thing of the past. Stick your head in here and see what you can see!

Chapter 17

The Model-T Report: It's Clunky, but It Works

*1*f you're comfortable with designing and filling out forms, tables, and queries and moving around Access 95 like a pro, you probably feel as though you can go forth and solve the mysteries of the universe — like where those socks go when they disappear from the dryer — with your mastery of your database. Being able to answer questions and solve problems like the legendary Oracle of Delphi creates such an awesome feeling, doesn't it?

But you're not done yet. What do you do if someone (like your boss) wants you to share your new-found omniscience, preferably in detail? Do you try to lug your computer into the conference room so that you can have all the vice presidents of your company stand around and watch you pull up queries and tables? I thought that would make you shudder!

Fortunately, you don't have to figure out a way to strap your CPU to your back to bestow your knowledge upon the unenlightened, because Access 95 has yet another tool to make your life easier; this time the tool is generically referred to as a *report*. Which just so happens to be the topic of this and the next four chapters. Incredible coincidence, isn't it?

The Report on Reports

While anyone who survived high school English knows what a report is (usually to their regret), it may be helpful to redefine reports in the terms that Access 95 uses. Access 95 considers a report to be a component of your database (like a query or a form) used to organize and present your data. Specifically, reports are used to format your information so that you can present it to others in an understandable and sensible fashion. (*Very* different from any of *my* reports in high school, I can tell you).

Access is designed so that the creating and printing of reports is just another part of the whole database system. Like queries, reports can take information from the other parts of your database (specifically, tables or queries) and organize it for you based on your instructions. Access even has Report Wizards to walk you through the steps of designing a report to meet your needs.

Getting started

Access 95 has several ways to generate a report, and you begin them all in the same way: simply click on the Reports tab from your main database screen to see the screen shown in Figure 17-1.

Figure 17-1:
The Reports tab contains all of your reports and allows you to create new ones.

When you decide (or it's decided for you) that a new report is in order, simply click on the <u>N</u>ew button to the right of the screen. When you do, you open the dialog box shown in Figure 17-2. This screen is very important; you need it to determine what kind of report you want Access 95 to create for you.

Determining the type

The first thing to do is determine what type of report you are going to generate. In this chapter, I focus on the simplest report that Access 95 lets you create: the AutoReport. There's more about some of the other report options (like the Report Wizard and such) later in this Part.

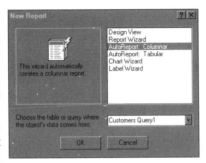

Figure 17-2:
The New
Report
dialog box
lets you
choose the
type of
report and
what table
or query it
comes from.

Notice in Figure 17-2 that there are two kinds of AutoReports: Columnar and Tabular. Both organize the same data, but they don't organize data the same way. A Tabular AutoReport places all information for each record on one row, with a separate column for each field. A Columnar AutoReport, on the other hand, organizes the data of each record vertically on the page, in two columns — one for the names of the fields (the *labels*) and one for the contents of the fields. Each record generally starts its own page. (You can adjust the report so that more than one pair of columns appears across the page.)

There isn't a profound answer to the question of when to use one or the other of the two types of AutoReports. It is more a matter of personal choice and aesthetics than anything else. The Tabular format is generally more useful if your report has lots of records with small fields, while the Columnar format is better for reports with large fields but not that many records.

One limit to using an AutoReport is that it works with only one table or query, but it is still a very useful tool to have available.

Using Columnar AutoReports

I'll start with Columnar reports (they do tend to be the default that Access 95 prefers). Go ahead and, in the list box in the New Report dialog box, click on AutoReport: Columnar. Then move down to the drop-down list at the bottom of the dialog box and click on it to choose which table or query you want to use.

Once you select the format of the report and the table or query, click OK.

That's it! Your report is now ready for you to print and wow your neighbors with. Okay, not really — though you *can* at this point choose to print your document, and it *may* even turn out well. But you may want to check on a few things first.

The query advantage

The fact that Access lets you base a report on a query is actually a wonderful thing. When you base a report upon a table, you get an entry in your report for each and every record in the table. But what if you only want a few of the records? The answer is to create a query and then to base the report upon that query (it may be better to think of this as basing the report on the query's datasheet, just as it's good to think of the report as a fancy presentation of the table's datasheet).

The advantages don't stop there. If you create a query based upon multiple tables, you get your results neatly organized into a single datasheet. If your query produces the information that you want in its datasheet, then a report based upon that query's datasheet will organize and present the information in the way you want. (For more on creating queries using more than one table, see Chapter 12, "Searching a Slew of Tables.")

There is one circumstance where a query datasheet won't give you what you need. If you want to create a report with several levels of information, you need to use the techniques discussed in the next chapter, "Wizardly Control and Multilevel Reports." Reports that are based upon a datasheet are always organized with all of the records in a single group.

Previewing your printing

After you click on the OK button, Access 95 thinks about things for a while and then gives you the Print Preview window shown in Figure 17-3. This window lets you see what the document will look like.

When you are in Print Preview, you can't do a whole lot with your report *except* print it. Well, that's not quite true. Print Preview gives you the important ability to closely check out exactly what your document looks like, and a number of tools help you do that.

 The first button on the Print Preview toolbar allows you to print your report. This is very straightforward. Simply click on the button and your printer begins spewing forth like a manic. But you may not want to print just quite yet; there's still more for you to do and know.

 The second button is called *Zoom*. This allows you to change the size of the image on your screen and works in conjunction with the Zoom Control drop-down list. These two controls are very important. If you look back at Figure 17-3, you can see that not all of the page is visible; what you can see is legible, but you can't see the whole record, let alone the page. This is 100 percent magnification and is a life-size representation of a sheet of paper with your data on it.

Click here to leave Print Preview.

Click here to
start printing.

Don't try this one yet.

These let you see
the rest of the page.

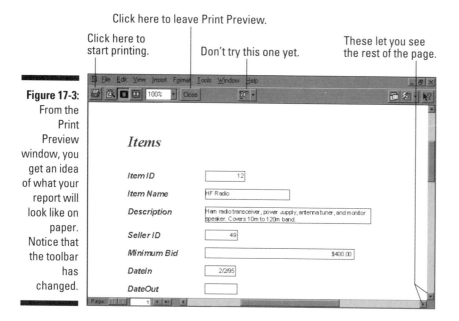

Figure 17-3:
From the
Print
Preview
window, you
get an idea
of what your
report will
look like on
paper.
Notice that
the toolbar
has
changed.

But what if you need to see what the whole page will look like? If you click on Zoom, you will see the view shown in Figure 17-4. This is called the Fit view, because Access 95 sizes the view to fit the whole page on your screen, and the Zoom Control text box will show this change. The Fit view is nice because you get an idea of the bigger picture. You can't read the text, but you can see what it looks like on the page.

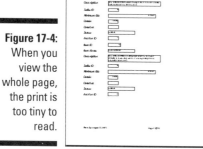

Figure 17-4:
When you
view the
whole page,
the print is
too tiny to
read.

When you want to go back to the 100 percent view, click on the Zoom button again, and Access 95 obligingly switches for you. But what if you want to see a view that fits more on the page but is still legible? Not a problem; that's what Zoom Control is for. Click on the Zoom Control arrow to see a drop-down list with a variety of percentages listed. These percentages determine the magnification of your view. Click on a size other than the one currently in use and your view will change. If you don't like any of your choices, you can use your own setting by typing a percentage into the Zoom Control and then clicking somewhere else on the screen.

Notice that when you move your cursor over the view of your report, the image of your cursor changes to look like a magnifying glass. This tells you that if you click on any area of the report, Access 95 will switch you to the previous view. Not only that, but if you are increasing the Zoom, your screen automatically shows the area that you clicked on. Click again, and your view is changed back.

The One Page and Two Pages buttons control whether you see one or two pages in the Print Preview. You can select only one of these at a time, and clicking either button will set the Zoom view to the Fit setting. The only other thing you need to know about these buttons is that, when you have two pages showing, the odd-numbered page is always on the left. (In book publishing, the odd-numbered page is always on the right — unless the production department is having a very, very bad day.)

You can also right-click anywhere on the Print Preview screen to see a pop-up menu that gives you the choice of switching the Zoom or viewing a specific number of pages. When you select the Zoom command, a submenu appears with the same choices as on the Zoom Control. If you select the Pages command, Access 95 shows you a new trick — you can see more than two pages simultaneously on the screen. When you select the Pages command, you see the submenu shown in Figure 17-5.

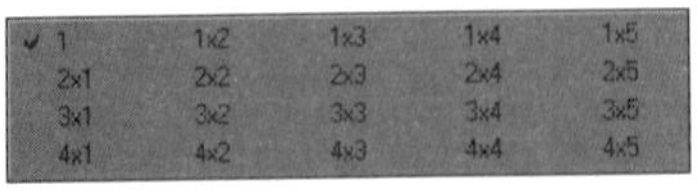

Figure 17-5:
This menu allows you to view up to 20 pages of your report at once.

Clicking on one of the options will change your view to display the arrangement you've chosen; in Figure 17-6, I've set up a 3 x 5 configuration.

Figure 17-6:
You certainly can't read it, but a multipage Print Preview can, at a glance, show you how your report will look on paper.

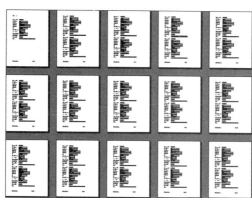

Two other commands are available when you right-click on the Print Preview screen: Save As/Export and Send. Save As/Export lets you save your Access 95 report in a format used by another program, and Send lets you take a copy of your Access 95 report and Send it as a mail message. By the way, the Zoom and Pages commands are also available on the View menu.

There is one other feature of AutoReport that I'd like you to notice when you have the Print Preview open. Go ahead and adjust the Zoom to a size you can read comfortably and then scroll to the bottom of the on-screen page. You should see something like the picture in Figure 17-7.

Figure 17-7.
You get the date and page number as a footer in AutoReports.

Friday, August 18, 1995   *Page 1 Of 18*

Notice that Access 95 automatically inserts a footer with the date the report was generated and the page number. The footer will appear at the bottom of each and every page of your report. You can find out about changing the contents of the footer by looking at Chapter 20, "Grouping Ducks and Apples (and Counting Them, Too)."

If you've finished looking at your report and don't want to print it yet (perhaps it might need a few *teensy* little changes), click on the Close button. No, you won't close out of the report, unless you've saved it already. If you *have* saved your document, it *will* close, but otherwise you are taken to the Design view for your report. Designing reports by hand is an odious little task that I personally try to avoid. You will have to learn about doing it eventually, but not quite yet. (I'm saving it for Chapters 19 and 20.) For now, let's move on to do something that will be both more meaningful and less frustrating for you at this stage in the game.

Laying out your pages

Once you've looked at the Print Preview of your report, you have a decision to make. If you are happy with how your report looks, great! Go ahead and print your document. However, a few minutes of extra work can do wonders to even the simplest reports, and I'm here to tell you how to do it.

You can click on File⇨Page Setup from any Report view in Access 95. When you do, you will see the dialog box shown in Figure 17-8.

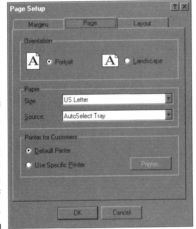

Figure 17-8:
The Page
Setup dialog
box will help
you improve
the look of
your report.

The figure shows you the Page tab of the Page Setup dialog box, but don't worry if that isn't what you see when you first open this dialog box. Just go ahead and click on the Page tab at the top, and I'll cover the rest a little later.

The most fundamental decision that you must make about your layout is which direction you want your paper to go. The default choice is Portrait, with the long side of your paper running from top to bottom of your text (the way most magazines and books appear). Your other choice is Landscape, where the long side of the paper runs horizontally from left to right so that the page is wider than it is tall.

There are more than just aesthetics to this decision. If you are using columns, Landscape allows you to use a wider column that can convey more information for each field; the columns will be much shorter, however, so there is always a trade-off. After all, that piece of paper is only so big.

Generally, with a Columnar report, Landscape limits your reports to one record per page (depending, of course, upon the nature of the fields in your records). Figure 17-9 shows you how the same report you've seen before looks if you change the orientation to Landscape.

Figure 17-9:
Landscape orientation usually creates much more white space in your report, which can make it easier to read.

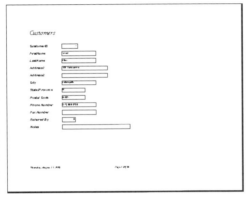

Your other choices for the Page tab are determined by your printing capabilities. The two drop-down lists in the Paper section of the tab allow you to determine the Size of the paper you will use. The Source drop-down list gives you the option of choosing to use your regular paper feed (the AutoSelect Tray choice), another automatic source, or to manually feed your paper into the printer.

The last part of the Paper tab is labeled "Printer for [report name]" and has a pair of radio buttons. You can either use the Default Printer, or the Use Specific Printer options. If you decide to go with the latter option, the Printer button then becomes available, and clicking on it gives you a dialog box that lets you choose from among your available printers. (When you look at your own Page Setup dialog box, the silly-looking [report name] will be replaced with the name of your report.)

After you've finished with the Page tab, you will probably want to click on the Layout tab. This is where the work really starts. The Layout tab of the Page Setup dialog box is shown in Figure 17-10.

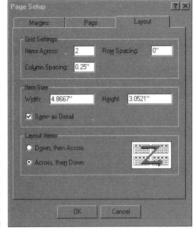

Figure 17-10:
The Layout tab of the Page Setup dialog box lets you redesign your report.

This card is divided into three sections. The Grid Settings section allows you to control how many columns your report uses and how far apart the different elements are from each other. The Items Across setting allows you to determine the number of columns that you are using on each page (remember that with a Columnar report, each column is a different record). Your default setting is one column to a page, but you can change that; just keep in mind that with more columns, your reports can show less information for each record. If you use enough columns that some of the information won't fit, you'll see a warning similar to the one shown in Figure 17-11.

Figure 17-11:
You may not be able to fit more than one column on a page.

If the number of columns you've selected will fit (or if you're willing to not see part of the information from some of your fields), you can click OK to see a view of what your document will look like with multiple columns. Figure 17-12 shows a two-page Fit to Screen view of a report where two columns — at least as they are currently formatted — can cause you to lose data.

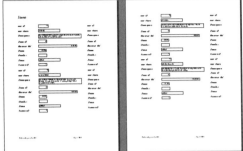

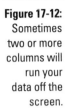
Figure 17-12:
Sometimes
two or more
columns will
run your
data off the
screen.

Back to the Grid Settings section of the Layout card in the Page Setup dialog box: Row Spacing lets you determine the size of the area between the rows, measured in inches. Simply click on this box and type in the amount of space that you want between each row. Again, this is a matter of personal preference. The Column Spacing option allows you to determine the width of the space between your columns; if you narrow this width, you can make more room, but your entries could be more difficult to read.

The bottom section of the Layout tab, called Layout Items, lets you control how your columns are organized on the page. You have two options here. Down, then Across tells Access 95 to start a new record in the same column if your last record has not filled up the page. With this, Record 13 will start below Record 12 on the page (provided there's enough room), and then Records 14 and 15 will appear in the second column. The Across, then Down option would start Record 13 across from 12, and then put Record 14 below 12, and Record 15 below 13.

The last tab of the Page Setup dialog box is called Margins. And guess what! It controls how wide the margins of your report are. Figure 17-13 shows you the Margins tab.

This tab is really straightforward; you have a text box for the Left, Right, Top, and Bottom margins. Double-clicking on each of those boxes highlights the setting and you can type in a new setting, using inches as your measurement. (The *margin* is the space on each edge of the paper where Access 95 is not allowed to print.) To the right of these boxes is a Sample, to show you how your current margin settings will work. Figure 17-14 shows you a Fit to Screen view of the report I've been working on, after I've made a few changes to the margins.

Once you make all the changes you want to the layout of the report, go ahead and click the OK button at the bottom of the dialog box. At this point, you may want to go back to Print Preview and check the report over to make sure that everything is the way you want it. If it isn't, simply go back to Page Setup and play with the options until everything works out. Then, you can click on the Print button (or select File➪Print) and let your printer do its job.

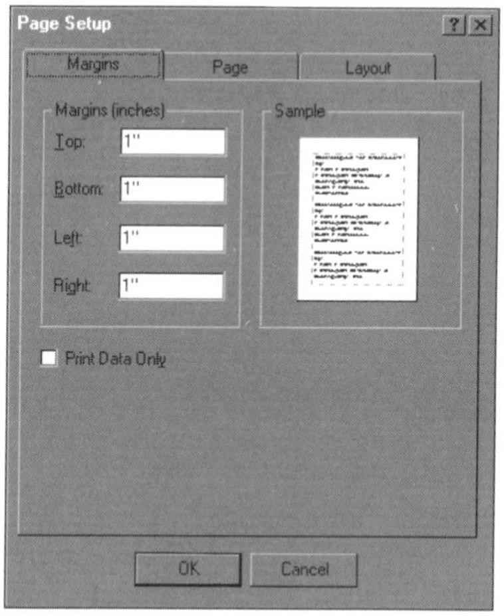

Figure 17-13:
The Margins tab controls the space between the edge of the page and the start of your data.

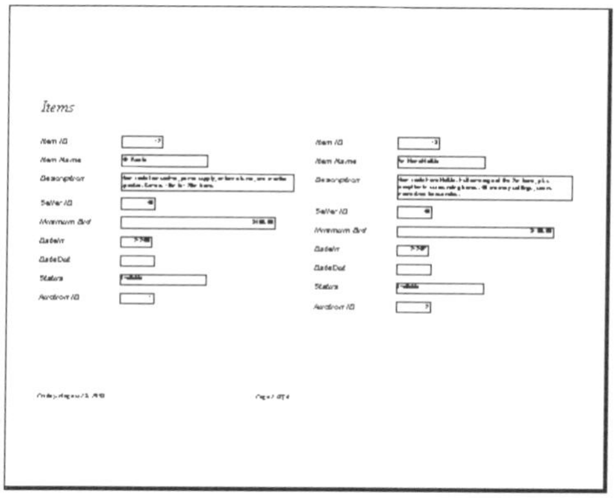

Figure 17-14:
To fit the columns on the page, I changed the left and right margins to .5"; to center the data, I changed the top and bottom margins to 1.5."

The last item on this tab is the Print Data Only check box. If you click on this option so that a check is showing, Access 95 prints only the data in your records; row headings won't appear on the printed document.

Now, wasn't that easy?

There is a short-cut to creating a Columnar AutoReport from any screen. All you have to do is click on the New Object button and select AutoReport from the menu. After your computer considers your request, Access 95 opens a Print Preview screen of a Columnar AutoReport for the table or query that you requested the report from. You still have to fix things in Page Setup, but you can bypass the New Report dialog box. You're welcome.

Using Tabular AutoReports

Once you know how to put together a Columnar AutoReport, you also know how to do a Tabular AutoReport — because the tools are identical. The only real change in doing a Tabular AutoReport is the direction in which you look at your information. Figure 17-15 shows you a Landscape-oriented view of the Items table formatted as a report.

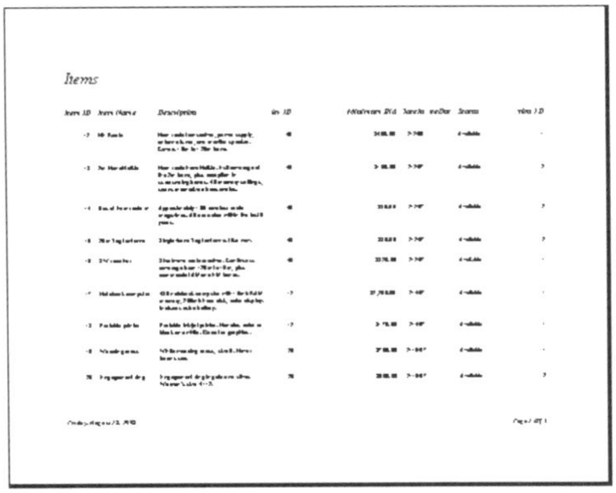

Figure 17-15:
The Tabular
AutoReport
organizes
records to
run across
the page
in rows.
Columns
represent
the different
fields.

The Tabular AutoReport most closely resembles the Datasheet view for your data. It is most useful when you have many records and your fields are restricted in size, as with a series of numbers or one-word text. All of the tools that you used in Columnar AutoReports work identically in Tabular AutoReports.

Labelling the Wizards

Another form of report that I want to cover briefly here is the Label Wizard. The Label Wizard is a tool to create labels for any number of uses. You may need to create a series of labels for your mailing list (probably sorted by postal code), but you may also need to create labels identifying the price and description of the items for sale at your auction. In these cases you want each label to be different, with specific information from your records — and the Label Wizard can do it for you with the waving of a wand.

The first step in using the Label Wizard is to know what data the labels will produce. You may need to create a query to sort through your data before starting on the labels. Using the auction database, suppose that I decide to send a mailing to the sellers who are located only in Indiana and Illinois, so I create a query to select only those records.

You can get the Label Wizard to work for you through the New Report dialog box. From the Reports tab of your main database, click on the New button and select Label Wizard and the table or query that you have created for your labels. After you click OK, you will see the dialog box shown in Figure 17-16.

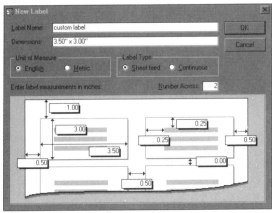

Figure 17-16: The first Label Wizard dialog box determines the size of your labels.

Access 95 has been designed to make this process as painless for you as possible. If you are using Avery labels, the Label Wizard has them listed by number. Just scroll down the list until you find the number that matches what is on your label box, highlight that row, and click Next.

If you are not using Avery labels, then it's a little harder to set things up. To use the Label Wizard for labels other than Avery labels, first click on the Customize button in the Label Wizard dialog box. This opens the New Label dialog box, where you can pick from any types of labels that you've used previously. If you are using a new label type, you will have to input some information so that Access 95 knows what's going on. Click on the New button to see the screen shown in Figure 17-17.

Figure 17-17: The New Label dialog box lets you use nonstandard labels if you supply the measurements. You may need a ruler to do this.

You can tell Access 95 to use metric measurements in the Unit of Measure section of this dialog box; in the Label Type section, you can tell the program to expect labels either on sheets of paper or as a continuous feed. Then you fill in the lower half of the dialog box. To do this, you need the measurements of the physical labels to tell Access 95 the size of the label, the margins around the outside of the label, and the interior margins before the text begins. Just look at the arrows in the dialog box to determine which dimension is being measured, make that measurement on the physical label, and type in the result next to the arrow. When you are finished, click OK to see the New Label Size dialog box shown in Figure 17-18.

If you make a mistake, you can correct it by clicking on the Edit button, which returns you to the previous screen. If you change your mind and want to get rid of that type of label, click on Delete. If, the next time you want to make labels, you are using a style that is close to but not the same as your customized label, click on Duplicate and make the changes you need. Finally, if you are happy with the results of your labors, click on Close to save these settings and return to the Label Wizard. (It's still easier to just use Avery labels. I wonder if Microsoft is going to buy Avery next?)

Notice on the Label Wizard that there is a check box called Show custom label sizes. If you remove the check from that box, you see the listings for Avery labels. If you put the check in that box, you see your customized label settings.

After finding the label you want to use, click on the Next> button in the Label Wizard dialog box to see the screen shown in Figure 17-19.

This screen of the Label Wizard lets you change the format of your label. You can choose the font name, font size, font weight, italics or underline, and even the text color (if you have a color printer) for your labels. Unfortunately, the formatting you choose will apply to *all* the text on your label. You can't choose to italicize one field and not the others. When your formatting is complete, click on the Next> button to see the next screen of the Label Wizard, shown in Figure 17-20.

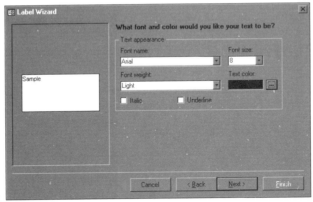

Figure 17-19:
Formatting
your labels
can be a
snap with
this dialog
box.

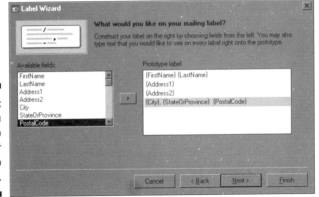

Figure 17-20:
At last, you
are ready to
insert your
data onto
the label.

OK, so it's taken a while, but you're almost finished. At this point, the wizard asks you to tell it how to place your data on the labels. You've seen this drill before: Select the fields from the list on the left and click on the > button to transfer the field to the label. However, this procedure has one slight twist. The Label Wizard prints your fields *exactly* as you tell it to.

If you want fields on separate rows, press Enter or use an arrow key to move to the next row. When you double-click on a field (or click on the > button), that field is always transferred to the highlighted line in the Prototype label box. Access 95 figures out how many lines can print on your label based upon the label's size and the font size you are using.

If you want a consistent character on your labels, type in that character next to the field that you want it to go with. If you're putting more than one field on the same line, you can use this to put punctuation between the fields. For example, to insert a comma between the city and state or province on your mailing labels, enter the City field, type in a comma, press the Spacebar, and enter the State/Province field.

When you have entered your fields to your satisfaction, click on the Next> button. Your next screen, shown in Figure 17-21, lets you sort your labels by any field you choose. Typically, you want to sort a mailing list by postal code.

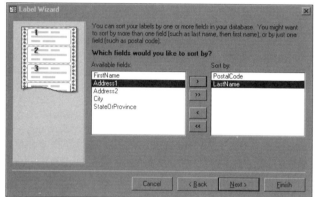

Figure 17-21:
Put in the
fields you
want to
sort by.

The last screen (finally!) of the Label Wizard lets you give your report a name for posterity and determine if you want to see a preview of your labels (which I recommend) or go back and modify your design.

Using the Chart Wizard in Your Report

Generally, reports are a collection of words and numbers organized to allow you to make sense of the information. But there are times when words and numbers are simply not enough. In those instances, a picture is the answer. After all, everybody knows that a picture is worth a thousand words (which is a lot of pages on a single report). The solution for adding a picture within Access is to create a chart using the Chart Wizard.

To get started, simply move to the Report tab and click on the New button. In the New Report dialog box that appears, select Chart Wizard and, from the drop-down list, select the table or query that you wish to use.

To start designing a chart or graph (Access uses the terms interchangeably), you need to select the fields that will be used in the chart. You must select at least one numeric field for Access to use as the data, but you can include more than one if you want. The only limitations are that all of the fields must be from a single table or a single query, and no more than six fields can be used for any single chart. The purpose of your chart determines what you include; for example, if you want to create a Column chart comparing the MinimumBid for each item to the ActualPrice, you need to include both of these fields so that Access can use them as data. You also need to include any fields that you are going to use to organize your data into groups.

Once you select the fields, click on the Next button to select the type of chart you are creating. Five major types of charts are represented — line charts, bar or column charts, pie and donut charts, area charts, and XY charts.

When you click on a chart button, the area to the right of the dialog box provides a brief explanation of how you use that chart. Once you pick the chart type, click on the Next button to reveal a third screen, which lets you organize the chart. This third screen varies depending on the type of chart you select, but some elements are consistent.

The Data area in each screen tells Access which fields to display in the chart. Some of the chart types also have a slot labeled Series that is used to tell Access what field should be used to create the groups that are represented by the various colors on the chart.

Finally, some types of charts have a third slot labeled Axis. The Axis slot is most commonly used in a bar or column chart to identify the field that will be used to create the various clusters of objects in the chart.

The next dialog box lets you provide a title for your chart and control various other aspects of the way the chart is organized. After you make these choices, you can go back and make changes or click on the Finish button, with the option to Open the report with the graph displayed on it, to see the chart displayed on the report.

Chapter 18

Wizardly Control and Multilevel Reports

---

*A*utoReports are just the tip of the report iceberg. If you have the inclination you can use Access 95 to generate much more complex reports and format them within an inch of their lives. I cover formatting your reports in the next chapter, but for now I'll focus on developing a multilevel report.

Anatomy of a Report

The AutoReports Wizard (discussed back in Chapter 17) creates reports where a record stands alone — as a set of labels and entries, as a row, or as a label. But what if you need a report that lists all the items for sale at each auction, who the seller is, and what the minimum bid is supposed to be?

If you want a more complex report with more levels of organization or with information from more than one table, seek help from the Report Wizard. It lets you add fields from as many tables as you wish and organize those fields into as many levels as you wish. Each new level creates its own section of the report with its own header and footer wrapped around the Details line.

Using the auction example started back in Chapter 15, imagine that I want to create a report summarizing the items for sale at the auctions. The fields are Site (from the Auctions table), LastName (from the Customers table), ItemName, and MinimumBid (from the Items table). I want this report grouped by the auction, so for this report, the Site field is my first level of organization.

But I also what to keep track of the folks who have contributed items to the auction (so that they can get paid, of course); so the second level of organization is by the last name of the seller. This way, when the report is printed, it will first divide all items for sale according to which auction they are going to, and then, within each auction listing, it will group the items by the seller.

The Wonderful Report Wizard

To start a new report using the Report Wizard, click the New button from the Reports tab of the Database window. The New Report dialog box pops onto the screen just like in Figure 18-1.

Figure 18-1:
The New Report screen is where you tell Access 95 that you need wizardly advice with your reports.

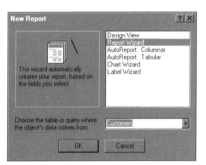

If you were using an AutoReport, you would select a table or query for your report from this screen, but with the full Report Wizard, there's no need to do that. Instead, start by clicking on the Report Wizard and then click OK. After a moment, you see the new dialog box (Figure 18-2), which allows you to add fields from any or all your tables and queries to the report structure.

This dialog box might look familiar because it is almost identical to the first dialog box of the Select Query Wizard (discussed in Chapter 12). In the Tables/Queries drop-down list, you pick a table (or query) that contains some of the fields that you want to use. Once the fields in that table (or query) appear in the Available Fields box, you can start transferring the ones you want to the Selected Fields box on the right. After getting all of the fields from that source, just select a different table or query from the drop-down list. I suggest starting with the fields that you want to have appear on each detail line of your report.

Probably the easiest way to move a field from one side to another is by double-clicking on it. No matter which side you start on, if you double-click on a field, it moves to the list on the other side.

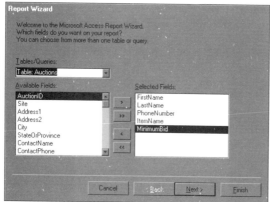

Figure 18-2:
The Report
Wizard lets
you add
fields from
any table or
query in your
database.

Once you have all the fields you could ever possibly want listed on the Selected
Fields side of the dialog box, click on the Next> button to progress to the next
screen, shown in Figure 18-3.

You use this screen to pick the field Access 95 should use to organize the data.
If the first field that you select can be used to group the information in your
report, the Report Wizard assumes that you want to organize your information
using that field and skips this dialog box. On the other hand, if the first field you
selected is intended for the Detail lines and can't be used for grouping the
information, Access 95 starts by listing all of the fields in one group as shown in
Figure 18-3.

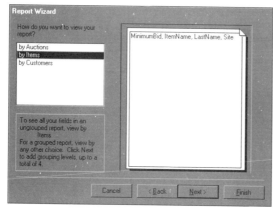

Figure 18-3:
This screen
lets you
decide how
you want
your
information
grouped.

Access 95 may or may not have guessed correctly about what you want. Examine each of the choices carefully and decide which you want to use as your most important level of organization. Once you decide, simply double-click on the field to move it to the list on the right. (If you just single click on the field, Access 95 uses the bottom portion of the dialog box to describe how it will use that field to organize the information.)

Once you select a field, that field is separated from the others and placed at the top of the page. This indicates that all of the information in the Details section of your report (the main body) will be organized based on that field. In other words, the records will be sorted using that field, and records within the same entry in that field will appear together in the report. In the auction example, this means that the records are sorted into two groups — The Ranch and Exposition Hall.

If you don't want the records sorted into groups, that's okay. Access 95 usually includes a field (in this case, Items) that you can select to indicate that the records should be lumped together.

More groups! More groups!

Up to this point, all of the steps are the same whether you built a single-level or a multilevel report. It's only with the next step that things start to get interesting. Click the Next> button to see the screen shown in Figure 18-4.

Access 95 recognizes that fields other than the one specified can be used to organize the information in my report. The program lists all of these fields at the left of the dialog box and lets you pick as many as you like. If you want to organize your report within your main group, select the field to use for grouping the records and double-click on the field name to add it to the list at the right.

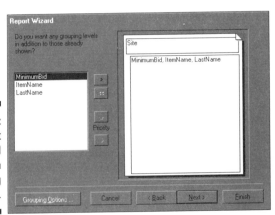

Figure 18-4:
The Report
Wizard
takes an
interesting
turn.

In the Auction database, it is possible to group the information by the site, the seller ID, or even by the type of item. Of course, if you want to use more than one level of grouping, you have to tell Access 95 which groups are most important.

I've decided that it is most important that my report be based upon the site at which an item is being sold, and I've used the Site field to set this up. But I also know that a number of families have contributed more than one item to the auction, and I don't need each family listed multiple times, so I create a subcategory of the LastName field. Doing this means that my report will have two main groups — one for each of the two auction sites — and within each site, the items will be grouped by who donated them. Figure 18-5 shows the dialog box with both of my levels of organization: Site (set with the previous dialog box) and LastName.

If you're feeling daring after you create the first subgroup, you can create reports with more than two levels. In fact, you can create all the subgroups you want until you are left with only one field in the Details section of your report.

What if you realize that you really want to organize the report by last name and then, within last name, by site? All you have to do is rearrange things with the Priority buttons. If you highlight a field and click on the Up Arrow Priority button, the field moves up a level in the organization. If you click on the Down Arrow button, the highlighted field moves down a level.

If you highlight more than one field, the topmost one moves if you click the Up Arrow button; the lower field moves if you click the Down Arrow button. Then if you repeat the click with the same button, the highlighted field next in line moves accordingly, and so on. You can play with this feature to your heart's content until the report is organized exactly as you want it.

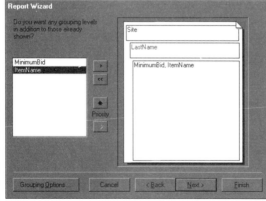

Figure 18-5:
You can create subgroupings in your report using this screen.

Each of the fields you select to organize your report creates a new section. Each of these sections has its own header and footer area that can be used to hold information from your database or information that is added directly to the report (such as labels). I talk about this organization of the report earlier in the chapter in the section "The Anatomy of a Report."

Setting the size of groups

Access 95 first sorts your report information based upon the entries in the first (and most important) grouping level and then continues sorting for each additional level. In our example, this means that the records are sorted first by the Site field and then, within each site, by the LastName field. Left to its own devices, Access 95 creates a new group every time an entry within a field changes. So in this case, there would be two major groups (one for each site) and then a separate group for each different last name.

That works fine for this report, but sometimes you want your groups to contain a range of entries, rather than just one. A good example would be a report that includes zip codes (in the Auction database, the PostalCode field). Figure 18-6 shows the dialog box that appears after you click on the Grouping Options button in a report that has both PostalCode and LastName as groupings.

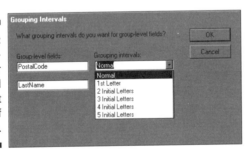

Figure 18-6: The drop-down list for each field lets you set the size of the groups.

For each field that you select, you can set the size of the group. The Normal option tells Access 95 to create a new group every time the entry in the field changes. For text fields, the other choices let you select what must change before a new group is created. For example, if you select 1st Letter, a new group is created only when the first character changes. This is useful for creating groups for each letter of the alphabet.

For other types of fields, you can generally select how many values should be included in each group. For example, in a numeric field, selecting 5 means that 1 through 5 would be the first group and 6 through 10 would be second. In a date field, you can select an option to group by week or by month.

Sorting out the details

Once you picked which fields are going to be used to group the records in your report, click Next> to go on to the dialog box shown in Figure 18-7.

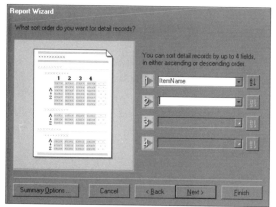

Figure 18-7:
You can
sort your
remaining
fields with
this screen.

Access 95 calls the fields that are not grouped as headers *Detail records.* The screen in Figure 18-7 lets you sort those records by the remaining fields, which you can do in either ascending or descending order. To do that, simply select the field in the drop-down list and then click the button at the right to change the sorting order from ascending (with the letters going from A at the top to Z at the bottom) to descending (with the letters going from Z at the top to A at the bottom). Don't ask me why the arrow doesn't just change directions. (Sorting with more than one field is discussed in more detail in Chapter 10.)

Notice that in the lower left of this dialog box is a button labeled Summary Options. You can click on this button to see the dialog box shown in Figure 18-8. This dialog box allows you to tell Access 95 to summarize your data with a number of statistical tools, including totals (Sum), averages (Avg), minimums (Min), and maximums (Max). Check the boxes that you want included in your report to get these features.

On the right of this dialog box is an option called Show value details. If you want to see both the data and the summary, click on the Detail and Summary button. If you need to see only the summarized information, click on the Summary Only button. The last check box on this dialog box is Calculate the percent of total for sums. If you click this button, Access 95 calculates the total amount of the field and tells you the percentage of each record's contribution to that total.

Figure 18-8:
The
Summary
Options
dialog box
gets Access
95 to do
statistical
calculations
for your
report.
Better it
than me.

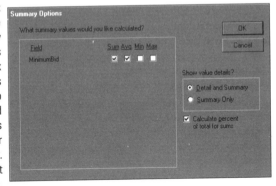

The home stretch

After you OK the Summary Options and return to the Report Wizard, click Next> to move along to the next screen (see Figure 18-9).

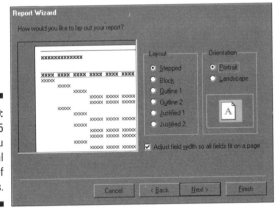

Figure 18-9:
Access 95
gives you
several
choices of
layouts.

You can use the Layout page of the Report Wizard to organize your data on the page in any of the organizational styles that Access 95 is programmed to give you. If you click on one of those styles, the window to the left shows you the basic structure of that style. Your choices here vary depending on the data you're trying to present and your personal preference.

The Orientation page lets you decide between having your report printed in Portrait (long edge along the side) or Landscape (long edge across the top and bottom) orientation. Again, this is a matter for your specific circumstances and preference, but generally, if you have a lot of fields or the fields are large, you may want to consider the Landscape orientation.

The check box labeled `Adjust field width so all fields fit on a page` is important. If this box is checked, Access 95 force-fits all of your fields onto one page, even if it has to squish some of them to do it. This is a dandy feature but it has a little, tiny drawback that you need to understand. During the highly scientific squishing process, the field might end up being too small to display all of the data it contains. For instance, a field holding the name *Harriet Isa Finkelmeier* might only display *Harriet Isa Fink* after it gets squished. The rest of the name isn't lost — it just doesn't appear on the report. If you *don't* check the box, then Access 95 packs as many fields onto the page as it can *without* changing any of the field widths. Fields that don't fit are left off the page, but the fields that *are* printed appear in their normal, glorious size.

Click Next> one more time to see a dialog box that lets you choose from six predetermined styles for your report. The window at the left gives you a basic idea of what the style looks like. Again, this is a matter of taste, not what is "correct." Pick the one you like the most and move on.

Finally, you're ready to click Next> for the last time. In the final screen, you give your report a name. This saves your report and provides it with its title. You also have the choice of previewing your report in Print Preview, of modifying your report, or of screaming for help. If you think that you are satisfied with what you've done, go ahead and preview your report. You should see something like the one shown in Figure 18-10.

If you know that you are going to want to make changes to the design of your report, you can click on the Modify the report's design button before you click on Finish. If you do, Access 95 opens the Design view of your report, and you can tinker with the report to your heart's content. Chapter 19 explains how to modify and format your reports to create your own unique look.

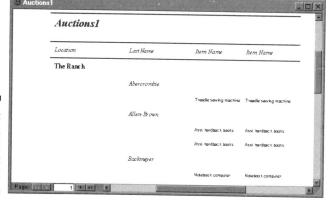

Figure 18-10: Wow! A professional report in just moments!

Chapter 19

It's Amazing What a Little Formatting Can Do

Access 95's Report Wizard is a pretty swell fellow. After a brief round of 20 compu-questions, he sets up an informative, good looking report for you automatically. Well, at least it's *informative* — just between you and me, I think the wizard could use a little design training.

Although the Access 95 wizard tries to do the best job it can, its results aren't always exactly what you need. Those clever engineers at Microsoft foresaw this problem and left a back door open for you. That door is *Design view*.

Thanks to Design view, you can change anything — and I mean *anything* — in a report design. This chapter guides you through some popular tweaking and tuning to make your reports the envy of the office. (I *would* say that they'll turn emerald green with envy, but my better judgment suggested I make it a parenthetical comment instead.)

Strike Up the Bands

After creating a report with the Report Wizard, you get the choice of either previewing the report or modifying its design. If you decide to modify the design, Access 95 sends you (and your report) to the Design screen shown in Figure 19-1.

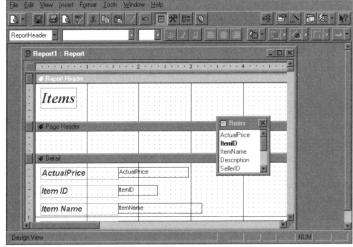

Figure 19-1:
The Design view gives you all the tools you'll need to modify your reports.

✔ If you're already previewing the report, you can get into the design screen by clicking on the Close button on the toolbar at any time.

✔ To get into Design view from the Database window, click the Reports tab, then click the name of the report you want to work with. Click the Design button to open the report in Design view.

Each of the entities that appear on your final report is represented in the design with a marker. These markers indicate where Access 95 is supposed to put the various items and how everything should be formatted.

The markers are grouped into sections (or *bands*) that represent the different parts of your report. The report design in Figure 19-2 has the three most common bands: Report Header, Page Header, and Detail. These bands are used to organize the elements of your report; how items are positioned in the bands represents how they are printed. The arrows to the left of the band names show you which markers that band contains.

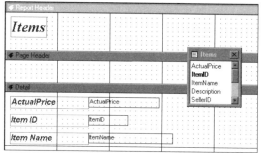

Figure 19-2:
Three basic
bands are
in every
report:
Report
Header,
Page
Header,
and Detail.

The bands work in teams that straddle the Detail line. The teams are pretty easy to figure out (Report Header with Report Footer and Page Header with Page Footer, for example). Figure 19-3 displays the mates to Figure 19-2's bands.

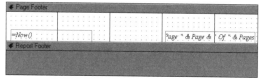

Figure 19-3:
The Page
Footer and
Report
Footer
mirror the
headers of
your report.

I cover how to make these bands appear and disappear on your screen and how to get them to make calculations for you in Chapter 20, "Grouping Ducks and Apples (and Counting Them, Too)." Placing information into the bands is covered in the sidebar "Those pesky controls," later in this chapter.

Anything that appears in the Report Header is printed at the very start of the report. The information prints only once and appears at the top of the first page. Information in the Page Header prints at the top of each and every page. The only exception is on the report's very first page, where Access 95 prints the Report Header and *then* the Page Header.

The meat of the report, the stuff in the Detail band, fill the majority of each report page. It's repeated for every record included in the report. Once each page is nearly full, Access 95 finishes off the page by filling in the Page Footers at the bottom. The Report Footer appears at the bottom of the very last page immediately following that page's Page Footer.

NOTE

Access 95 has a master plan for how it wants to deal with your Page Footers. By default, when you create a report, Access 95 will insert the date that the report was generated on the left side of the footer and the page number and total number of pages on the right of the footer.

Formatting This, That, These, and Those

You can format almost anything in the report's design with the tools on the Formatting toolbar. To bring the tools to life, click on a field, text box, or anything else in a report band. Figure 19-4 shows the Items field selected. In the Figure, the toolbar selections are alive and available.

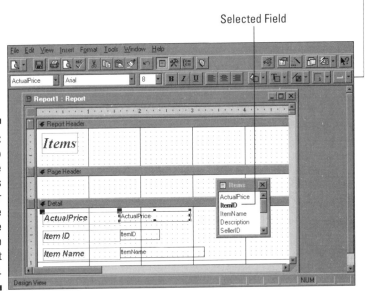

Figure 19-4: The tools to format the features of your report are available only when you select a field.

When you have the wizard generate a Columnar Report for you, each entry in the record is represented with two parts: a marker for the label and the marker for the field's contents. Which of these two you click on determines whether the label marker or the field marker is selected. Back in Figure 19-4, the marker for the field information was selected. In Figure 19-5, the marker for the label information is selected. It's very important to make sure that you select the right part of the field before you begin formatting.

Those pesky controls

Of course, there are other things besides labels and simple rectangular fields that can go onto your report. All of the various items together are referred to as *controls*. You can use certain types

The Control Wizards Button

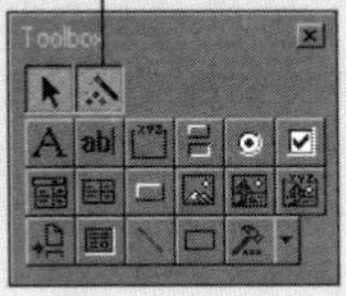

of controls for specific types of fields; for example, you might use a check box with a Yes/No

field. These various controls are all added using the Toolbox.

Some of these controls (the Line, Box, Page Break, and those for inserting a picture) are discussed later in this chapter. Using controls to get summaries of the values in your report is covered in the next chapter.

The most important thing to know about the Control Wizards is that using them makes your life much easier. A Control Wizard is active when its button has been pressed. Whenever you create a control, the appropriate wizard appears and guides you through the steps.

Figure 19-5:
Here the field marker for the label information is selected.

You have another way to indicate the field or label that you wish to format. Rather than clicking on the area, you can use the drop-down list to the left of the Formatting toolbar. When you click on the arrow at the side of the list box, a menu drops down listing all the labels and fields included in your report. Simply scroll through the list and highlight the one you want to work with and then click on it. The handles then appear just as if you had clicked on the field or label itself.

Colorizing your report

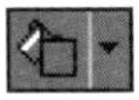

Nothing brightens up a drab report like a spot of color. Access 95 makes it easy with the Color buttons on the Toolbar. To select a color, click on the arrow that forms the right part of the button and then pick a color from the list of colors displayed. To change the color of a field or label on your report, click on what you want to color, then click Color button. Figure 19-6 shows a pair of labels sporting a new gray background.

Figure 19-6:
Shade in the
background
of any text.

 You can use the Fore Color button to change the color of the text in the field or the field's label. This lets you do special effects like making the background color black and the item color white, as shown in Figure 19-7. Be careful when choosing your colors — if you make the text color and the background color the same color, then the field seems to disappear!

Figure 19-7:
Create
different
combinations
by mixing
colors.

Moving things around

You can move just about anything on a report (and it's even pretty easy). Click on the item you want to move, then move your cursor to the edge of the box that appears around the item. When the cursor changes to a hand, press and hold the mouse button, then drag your item to a new position.

 If you want to move a field separately from its label, use the big square handles shown in Figure 19-8. To use these, click on the field, then carefully move your cursor onto the big handle you want to use. When it changes to a pointing finger, press and hold the mouse button, then start moving. Release the mouse button when you're done. If the mouse changes to a double-ended arrow instead of a pointing hand, try moving the mouse onto the big handle again. That means Access 95 thought you wanted to *resize* the item, not move it. (You know how programs get confused sometimes.)

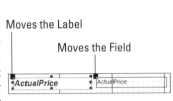

Figure 19-8:
The big handle in the upper-left corner of a box will move that marker independently of the other marker.

Other types of reports, such as Tabular Reports and Labels, do not combine the label and the field together. Either there is no label or the label appears only once in the Page Header section. When labels aren't linked to their respective fields, they each appear separately without the special larger handles shown in the figure.

You use the smaller handles around the edge of the field to change how much space the field takes up on the report. If you discover the information in one of your fields is being cut off, you can click on the field and use the handles to make that field somewhat longer; or if there is a lot of information in a text field or a memo field (any field where the information is broken into words), you can make the field taller, and Access 95 will wrap the information to more than one line.

The amount of space between the markers controls the space between items in the report. Increasing that spacing gives your report a more spacious look; decreasing the space lets you put more on the page.

On the border

 The Border Color button changes the color and type of line used for a field's border. It works just like the Back Color and Fore Color buttons. Click the arrow next to the button to drop down a display of your color choices (see Figure 19-9). Click the button itself to color the border of the highlighted field.

Figure 19-9:
Choose from an entire palette.

You can also control the width of the border line by using the Border Width button. Your choices for this are actually represented in terms of points, with options on the menu for a hairline (half-point) line, 1 point, 2 points, 3 points, 4 points, 5 points, and 6 points. A 6-point line is $1/12$ of an inch thick and actually appears quite heavy on a report.

 Finally, you can change the style of the marker's border by using the Special Effects button. Six choices are available under this button. Figure 19-10 gives you the official names of the different options.

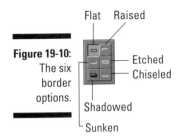

Figure 19-10:
The six border options.

The Sunken and Raised options change the colors for two sides of the field. If you select your colors appropriately, giving a sunken border makes the label or field appear as though it is pushed into your text; a raised border makes it seem as though your field is coming out of your text. Figure 19-11 shows an example of a raised border and a sunken border for duplicates of the same field.

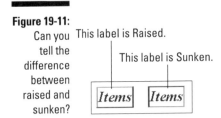

Figure 19-11:
Can you tell the difference between raised and sunken?

The Chiseled option gives the field the appearance of having the bottom portion of its border raised upward, and the Etched option gives the effect of the border being etched into the background around the field. The colors of your field and your report background affect how these borders look. Figure 19-12 shows examples of these two types of borders.

Figure 19-12:
You can't
miss the
difference
between the
chiseled and
etched
effects.

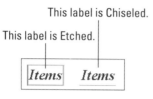

You can also select the Shadow option, which just puts a shadow to the lower right of the field; or the Flat option, which simply puts a standard, single-line border around the entire field.

If you have trouble reaching all of the buttons on the drop-down list, you can tear it off of the menu bar. To do that, click the arrow to display the list and then continue to hold the mouse button down. If you drag the pointer down and to the left (outside of the border of the list), a dotted rectangle the same size and shape as the list begins following the pointer. When you can see all of the rectangle, release the mouse button. This creates a floating toolbar of those choices on your screen.

Terribly terrific text

You can also change the style of text used within a field by using the tools on the left portion of the toolbar. You can select the font (the actual shape of the characters used for the information); the size of the font; and whether the font is bold, italic, or underlined by using the buttons shown in Figure 19-13.

Figure 19-13:
These
buttons can
make your
actual text
look
different.

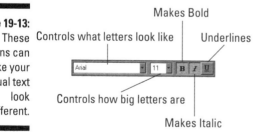

To change the font or the font size, simply click on the arrow to the right of the Font or Font Size control and select from the list. To turn on or off the bold, italic, or underline characteristics, simply make sure the correct field is se-lected and click on the button. If the feature is off, clicking on the button turns it on. If the feature is on, clicking on the button turns it off. When one of these features is turned on, it appears as though the button is pressed into the surface of the toolbar.

You can also control the alignment of the text within your labels and fields. One approach is to left-align your labels, so that they appear at the right edge of the label box, and right-align your fields. This means the text appears to come out from a common center point, as shown in Figure 19-14.

Figure 19-14:
You can
change the
alignment
of text for
each label
and field.

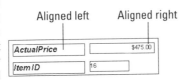

To change the alignment of the text for a marker or a field, you simply select the marker and then click on one of the three alignment buttons on the toolbar. The alignment buttons are shown in Figure 19-15, with a label indicating to which edge of the text they align information.

Figure 19-15:
These
buttons
align your
text.

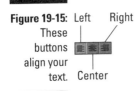

Taking a Peek

Eventually, with every report, a time comes when you want to look at the actual report rather than the technical magic being used to create it. No matter how good your imagination is, it's difficult to visualize how the various sections will repeat and how the information will actually look at the report. Access 95 provides two distinct tools for previewing your report.

The first of these is the Layout Preview. When you select the Layout Preview, Access 95 takes a portion of your data and arranges it to give you an idea of what your data will look like in the finished report. The preview shows only a sampling of your data without performing any final calculations you included.

The whole goal is to see what the report *looks like,* not to review your calculations. You can get to Layout Preview by clicking the down arrow next to the Report View button and then selecting Layout Preview from the drop-down list, as shown in Figure 19-16.

Figure 19-16:
Choose
Layout
Preview
from the list
under the
Report View
button.

 If you want to see a *full* preview of your report, complete with the calculations and all of the data, select Print Preview. Select Print Preview by clicking on the Print Preview button or by clicking on the down arrow next to the Report View button and then selecting Print Preview from the drop-down list (refer to Figure 19-16).

Regardless of which system you use, you get a screen similar to the one shown in Figure 19-17, with the various items of your report filled in the way they will actually appear when the report is printed. You can then use the controls at the top of the screen to change the way in which you are looking at your report.

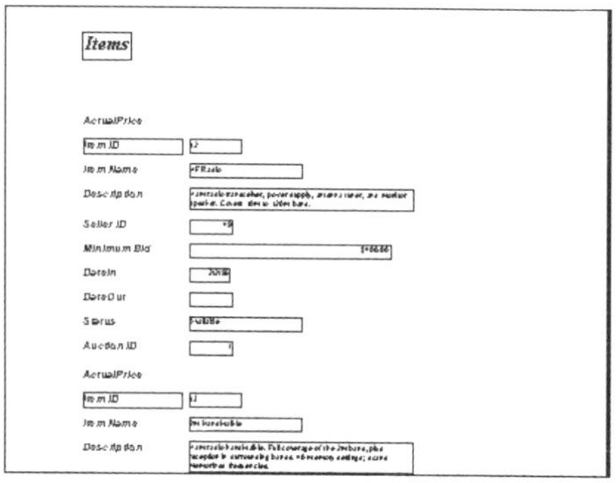

Figure 19-17:
Print
Preview lets
you see
what your
report will
look like
when you
print it out.

For more information about using Print Preview and Layout Preview, see Chapter 17, "The Model-T Report: It's Clunky, but it Works."

AutoFormatting Your Way to a Beautiful Report

 You can use the AutoFormat button to start the Report Wizard in its final dialog boxes, where you can select a general look using the dialog box shown in Figure 19-18. In the dialog box shown, the Options button has been clicked to display the Styles to Apply choices at the bottom of the dialog box. These choices let you determine which elements from AutoFormat are actually applied to all of the controls in your report.

Figure 19-18: Remember this screen from the Report Wizard? Some additions have been made to give you greater control.

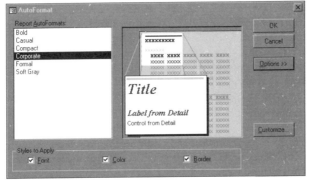

 You can use the Customize button to create your own formats, which will be stored on the AutoFormat page. Simply format your report using a consistent set of fonts, colors, and borders for the same types of controls; then open the AutoFormat dialog box and click on the Customize button. The options let you choose to just add the new format to the list or to replace one of the existing formats with your new definition. You can also remove formats from the list using this feature.

Everybody Get in Line!

Once you start moving various items around on you report, it can become difficult to make sure that things in different sections line up with each other. You may have put the column headings in the Page Header and the actual information farther down, in a Detail line. You want those two to line up, and that may be more than you can do by moving them by hand.

The grid in the background of the screen can be useful to help position things by aligning them with the vertical lines or with the various dots that appear. The Snap to Grid command on the Format menu lets you control whether, when you move an object, the object moves from being lined up immediately with these dots snapped to the grid, or whether you can move the object freely between the dots.

When you move an object with Snap to Grid turned on, the object's upper-left corner always aligns with one of the dots of the grid. Resizing an object causes the side that is being moved to align with one of the dots on the grid. Figure 19-19 shows several objects that have been positioned on the screen. Those on the left half were positioned with Snap to Grid on; those on the right hand were positioned with Snap to Grid off.

Figure 19-19:
The Snap to Grid feature lets you keep your reports neat without having to drive yourself crazy.

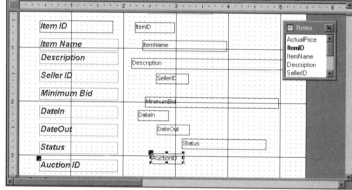

There are other commands on the Format menu that are useful for arranging things, too. One of the most popular is the Align command, which lets you take two or more objects and align them either to each other or to the grid. Figure 19-20 shows the Align submenu with the various choices available on it.

Figure 19-20:
The Align submenu controls how your fields position themselves.

Selecting <u>L</u>eft, <u>R</u>ight, <u>T</u>op, or <u>B</u>ottom causes the selected items to align along that side. For example, if you have three objects selected and you select Format⇨Align⇨<u>L</u>eft, the left edges of the three objects are moved so that they line up. In general, Access 95 moves the objects to line up with the one that is the furthest to the left.

You can also change the size of a group of objects by selecting all of them and then selecting a choice from the <u>S</u>ize submenu. The choices on the Size submenu allow you to select <u>S</u>ize⇨to <u>F</u>it, which adjusts each of the controls so that it is just large enough to hold the information within it; <u>S</u>ize⇨to <u>G</u>rid, which causes each of the controls to adjust so that all of its corners are positioned on grid points; or adjust the controls relative to each other.

If you select the <u>S</u>ize⇨to <u>T</u>allest, <u>S</u>ize⇨to <u>S</u>hortest, <u>S</u>ize⇨to <u>W</u>idest, or <u>S</u>ize⇨to <u>N</u>arrowest options, all of the boxes in the selected group are adjusted to those characteristics. In other words, if you have a group selected and you select <u>S</u>ize⇨to <u>T</u>allest, all of the selected controls are made the same height as the tallest control in the existing group.

Hori<u>z</u>ontal Spacing and <u>V</u>ertical Spacing commands can be used to select a group of objects and space them equally. This can be very useful when you are trying to spread out the title items for a report. Simply select the items in your group, and then select Make <u>E</u>qual from the <u>V</u>ertical Spacing submenu of the F<u>o</u>rmat menu to have Access 95 take the items and distribute them equally.

Figure 19-21 shows four labels and fields in the top of the figure that are some-what mushed together, and a duplicate set of four labels and fields lower down on the page that have been distributed with Make <u>E</u>qual. Make <u>E</u>qual adjusts the horizontal spacing of your controls, not the vertical spacing.

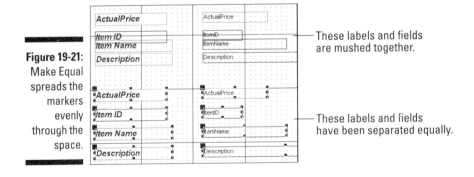

Figure 19-21:
Make Equal
spreads the
markers
evenly
through the
space.

These labels and fields
are mushed together.

These labels and fields
have been separated equally.

Creating your own lines

 One of the things that you may want to do to your report to make it a little bit easier to read is to add lines to it to divide the various sections. In order to do that, you need to turn on the Toolbox by clicking on the Toolbox button shown to the left. You can then use the Line tool toward the bottom of the Toolbox to draw a line on your report. When you select the Toolbox, it is first displayed as a toolbar running up and down your screen. Notice in Figure 19-22 that I've adjusted it so it runs left to right.

Line tool

Figure 19-22:
The Toolbox
is a
handyman's
treasure
trove.

With the Line tool selected, your cursor changes to a cross-hair with a line trailing off to the right. You can simply click where you want to start the line and drag to the location where you want to end the line. When you release the mouse button, Access 95 adds a line following the path that you took.

You can then use the various toolbar buttons discussed previously to change the line's color, thickness, and special effect by using the Border Color, Border Width, and Special Effects buttons. You can also use the Box tool, located to the right of the Line tool, to draw boxes on your report around separate items. Most of the remainder of these items are used to add controls to your report, which is a topic more for a programming book than for this one.

Breaking pages

 There are, however, still a couple of buttons that are worth mentioning. You can use the Page Break button to add a page break to your document. The cursor for drawing a page break looks a lot like one for drawing a line, except that instead of a line trailing off of it, you see a little tiny picture of a page. A page break is represented on-screen by a series of six small dots. To remove a page break that you've added manually, simply click on it with the Arrow tool and then press delete. It's outta there.

Sprucing Up the Place with a Few Pictures

 Another thing that you may wish to do is add an image to your report. You can use the Image button, shown to the left of this paragraph, to create a box to paste in an image from your clip art collection. This can add a little bit of jazz to your report, although I strongly encourage you to add images only to the Report Header or Page Header. Otherwise, the images repeat so frequently that they can become distracting.

 If you do not have an image that you are ready to use, but instead have one that you are working on, you may choose to use the Unbound Object Frame to add an *OLE object.* An OLE object allows you to put the object onto the page, but retain its link back to its original file. Any changes to that original file are reflected in the report. You can link to an image or to any type of file that supports OLE.

With both tools, when you activate the button you get a plus-sign pointer with the button's image to the lower right. You can then use this tool to draw a box onto your screen. With the static image, you draw a box and then Access 95 opens the Insert Picture dialog box, which can be used to locate the image to be inserted. With the Unbound Object Frame button, Access 95 opens the Insert Object dialog box so you can select the type of object to insert. This option lets you insert objects ranging from graphic images to digital sound files — you could even include a whole Microsoft Excel worksheet! (For more about the magic of OLE, see *Windows 95 For Dummies* by Andy Rathbone.)

 You can also add an image to your report by cutting it or copying it from another program, storing it on the Clipboard, and then pasting it onto your design. This is the only easy way available for including part of an image from a file.

Passing Your Reports around the (Microsoft) Office

You can do an awful lot with Access 95, but there are times when another program might make your life a little easier. The engineers at Microsoft were aware of this, so they gave Access 95 the ability to send information directly to other programs when you need to. Which other programs? Why, other Microsoft programs, of course! (Why does this not surprise me?)

 On several toolbars, you see the Publish It with MS Word button. This button takes whatever you are working with and formats it as a Word document. In general, the various items in your report are formatted with tabs in a new Word document. In fact, Access 95 even gets Word to display the document for you without your having to do a single thing. (That's assuming that you own a copy of Word and that you have enough memory in your computer to run both programs at the same time.)

In reality, the file that is created is in a format that can be read by most word processors. If you don't own Word, the only problem you might encounter is trying to figure out where Access 95 stored your file.

The button that you use to move information out of Access 95 is actually called the OfficeLinks button and is the same as the Tools➪OfficeLinks command. Just as the submenu for the OfficeLinks command has three choices, its button on your toolbars has three different faces.

The Analyze It with MS Excel choice takes your report (or whatever you were working with in Access 95), creates a datasheet, and then formats it as an Excel worksheet. Each line of the report is placed in its own row, and the information that forms columns in your report becomes separate columns on your worksheet. Your system then runs Excel and displays your newest creation. You can then use any of Excel's tools (including charting) to analyze, interpret, and generally abuse your data.

The Merge It button is available only when you are working with a table or datasheet. Unlike the other buttons, which just take your information and run with it, clicking the Merge It button (or selecting the Merge It command) starts the Mail Merge Wizard. This wizard guides you through the steps of linking your database with a Word Mail Merge document. If you don't already have a Mail Merge document, the wizard helps you create one.

The 5th Wave By Rich Tennant

"...AND TO ACCESS THE PROGRAM'S 'HOT KEY,' YOU JUST DEPRESS THESE ELEVEN KEYS SIMULTANEOUSLY. HERB OVER THERE HAS A KNACK FOR DOING THIS THAT I THINK YOU'LL ENJOY—HERB! GOT A MINUTE?"

Chapter 20

Grouping Ducks and Apples (and Counting Them, Too)

. . . .

In This Chapter

▶ The components of the Design view

▶ Grouping and sorting your records

▶ Adjusting the sections' size

▶ Fine-tuning the layout of your report

▶ Controlling your headers

▶ Personalizing footers

▶ Putting Expressions into your footers

▶ Adding page numbers and dates

. . . .

*W*izards can only do so much of your work for you. A time may come when you need to change the organization or fine-tune the components of a report to make it more closely fit your needs. Unfortunately, there isn't a magic wand that you can wave to fix it. You need to go into the Design view and make the changes you want manually. Even when you're working with the Wizard, you need to know some things about how to group the fields of your report to get the optimum result.

Don't despair! This chapter is designed to help you through those thorny issues. It explains the logic behind grouping your fields in a report and shows you several options for your groups. It also walks you through the Design view thicket — a thorny place if ever there was one. With this chapter's help, your reports will make you proud.

Everything in Its Place

The entire secret to the organization of a report lies in the way you position the controls for the labels and fields within the report design. Each and every report design is separated into *sections* or *bands,* that identify different portions of the report. Figure 20-1 shows the first few bands for a Columnar report. Notice that for this type of report the headings for the page and for the section contain the labels for the field.

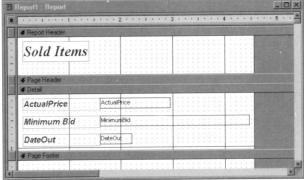

Figure 20-1: The bands in the Design view. In a Columnar report, the labels are to the left of the fields and repeat for each record.

Figure 20-2 shows the design for a Tabular report. In this case, the labels hang out in the Page Header, but the fields appear in the report's Detail section. These two different organizations of markers lead to the two different styles of reports.

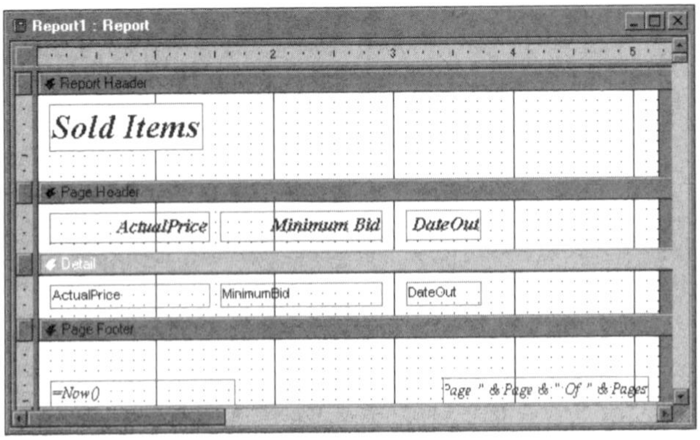

Figure 20-2: In a Tabular report, labels are used as column headers for the fields and appear only once.

Before performing any serious surgery on your report (or running off to build a report from scratch), you need to have a *really* good understanding of the whole *section* thing and how it works. Otherwise, your report groupings won't work right, things will be out of place, and life will be generally non-fun.

The most important thing to understand is that the contents of each section are printed only when certain events occur. It's easiest to understand this looking at the innermost section and working your way outward. At the center of every report is the Details section. Access prints items in this band each time it moves on to a new record. You have one printout of the Details section for each and every record in the table used for the report.

Moving outward from the Details section, you may have one or more *grouping sections*, such as the one shown in Figure 20-3. Notice that the grouping section identifies what field is used for grouping, and that the arrow on the bar identifies which section goes with that grouping.

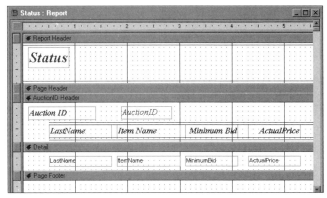

Figure 20-3:
Grouping records by AuctionID.

Items in the grouping section only print when the contents of the field used to create the section change. In this example, this section is the header for the Auction ID group and only appears immediately before a record in which the contents of the AuctionID field have changed.

The next section out from the groups is the Page Header. This section appears at the top of each and every page and is one of the few sections that are not controlled by the contents of your records. The information in this section is used to identify the pages of your report.

The outermost section is the Report Header, which appears at the start of your report. The Report Header is one of two sections that can only appear once in a given report. The information in the Report Header generally appears as the first thing in your report. (You decide whether the first page has the Page Header appear upon it.)

When Access 95 produces a report, it begins by printing the Report Header. Since this is a new page, it prints the Page Header next (and reprints the Page Header at the top of every succeeding page). If your report has some groups, the Section Headers come next. When all of the headers are in place, Access 95 finally prints the Detail lines for each record that's part of the first group. So far so good, but that's only half of the story.

Once it's done with all of the Detail lines, Access 95 prints the group's footer. Then, it starts the process over again by printing the next group header. When it's done with the last group, Access 95 prints the Report Footer.

Having all of these headers and footers is great, but what do you *do* with them? The header sections usually identify general information about the report, the contents of a particular section, and the field names. Section footers contain summary information, like counts and calculations. The footer for the Auction ID section in this example might hold a calculation that totals up the Minimum Bids. The Page Footer, which appears at the bottom of every page, traditionally holds the page number and report date fields.

A section of your own

When the Report Wizard creates a report for you, it automatically includes a section header and footer for each group you want. If I tell the Report Wizard to group my information by AuctionID, it automatically creates both the AuctionID Header and the AuctionID Footer sections.

If you're adventuresome, you can create sections in a report of your own by using the Sorting and Grouping command on the View menu. When you select this command, you see the dialog box shown in Figure 20-4. The most obvious thing that this dialog box controls is the order in which the records in your report are sorted. If you have a section listed in your report, it is automatically included in your sorting and grouping list. You can also have additional entries that sort the records, although these do not generate their own section headers.

Figure 20-4:
You can adjust the organization of your report without going back to see the wizard.

Grouping icon

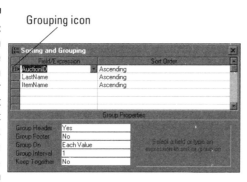

Notice that the first entry in Figure 20-4 has a special symbol to the left of it. The symbol indicates that this field is used for grouping levels. If you group by more than one field, this symbol is repeated in the list for each of the grouping fields.

The properties for the currently selected group are displayed at the bottom of the dialog box. The first two properties, Group Header and Group Footer, control whether or not a section is created for that group. You can have a Group Header, a Group Footer, or both in your report.

The Group On determines how Access 95 will create the groups for that value. For more about this feature, check out the "Groovy grouping" sidebar.

TIP

Groovy grouping

Groups are one of the too-cool-for-words features that make Access 95 reports so flexible. But wait — there's still *more* untapped power in groups, thanks to the Group On setting in the Sorting and Grouping dialog box. This setting tells Access 95 when to begin a new group of records on a report. The dialog box contains two settings for your grouping pleasure: *Each Value* and *Interval.*

The Each Value setting tells Access 95 to group identical entries together. If there's *any* difference between values in the grouping field, Access 95 puts them into different groups. This is a great setting if you're grouping by customer numbers, vendor numbers, or government identification numbers. It's not such a great choice if you're working with names, since every little variation (*Kaufield* instead of *Kaufeld,* for instance) ends up in its own group.

The Group On Interval setting works a little differently. It tells Access 95 that you're interested in organizing by a *range* of entries. Exactly how Access 95 interprets the Interval setting depends on whether you're grouping with a number or text field.

If you're grouping with a number field, Access 95 counts by the Interval setting when making the groups. For example, if your Interval is 10 then it groups records that have values from 0 to 9, 10 to 19, 20 to 29, and so on.

Before explaining how the Interval setting works with a text field, I have a quick question for you: Do you remember how you were taught to alphabetize things? The teacher said to start with the first letter of the word and put the A's first, followed by the B's. If two words started with A, you used the second letter in each word to break the tie. If those letters were identical too, you tried again with the third, and so on until everything was in perfect order or it was time for recess.

So what do blissful memories of childhood grammar lessons have to do with how the Interval setting works with a text field? To make a long story short (too late!), the Interval setting is the number of characters Access 95 reads from each record when it's grouping them. An Interval of one makes Access 95 group the entries by the first letter only; an Interval of two tells Access 95 to consider the first and second letters of each entry.

For example, the words *abandon* and *abalone* would land in the same group if the interval setting was one, two, or three, because they start with the same three letters. An interval setting of four or more would *finally* split them apart.

The last property, Keep Together, controls whether all of the information within that group must be printed on the same page, whether the first Detail line and the headings for that group must be printed on the same page, or whether Access can split the information any which way it wants, as long as it all gets printed on one page or another. The choices within the Keep Together option are No, which lets Access do whatever it pleases; Whole group, which means that the entire group, from Header to Footer, must be on the same page; and With first detail, which means that all the information in the Header for the group down through the Detail section for the first entry in that group must be printed on the same page. This means that each of your pages starts with a set of headings.

If you are designing a report from scratch, you can use this dialog box to create your groupings and control how they behave. Perhaps more importantly, however, if you use a wizard to create a report for you, you can then use this dialog box to control how that report behaves, and where information appears.

Changing the section's size

One thing that can be a problem with designing your own report is controlling how much space appears in a section. When a section is printed, whether it is the Page Header, a Section Header, or the Detail line, it normally takes up the same amount of space as shown on the Design screen. This means that you generally want to tighten the space within the group so that there is not a lot of wasted space on your page, but your section needs to be large enough to contain all of the elements that go into it. (How to create sections that change size based on the information in them is discussed in the next section, "Fine-Tuning the Layout.")

Fortunately it's quite easy to change the size of a section. Figure 20-5 shows the Resizing cursor that appears when you position your pointer over the top portion of the bar representing the section. This works a bit oddly in that the bar you move increases or decreases the section *above* it, not the section for which it is labeled.

If you place your mouse pointer to the left of the section, you get an arrow pointing into your report. You can use that arrow to select all the items within that section. Double-clicking in the bar at the left of the report selects every object within that section and displays a Properties dialog box for all of those items.

When your cursor looks like this, you can drag the band up or down.

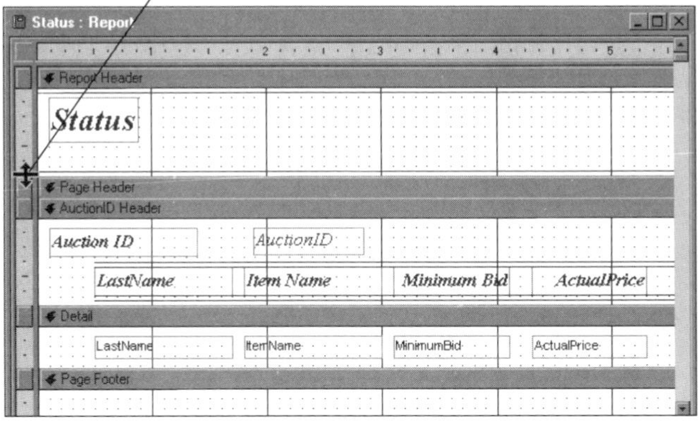

Figure 20-5:
The Resizing
cursor
allows you
to change
the size
of your
sections for
headers,
footers, and
details.

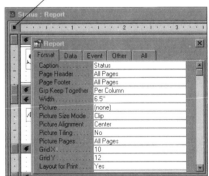

Fine-Tuning the Layout

Most of the control that you have over your report comes from setting the report's Properties. Although this is a formatting topic, it only becomes useful once you start dividing your report into sections. In order to get into the Properties dialog box, simply double-click on the item that you want to use, whether it's a field, a label, something that you've drawn on your report, or a Report Header itself. To see the dialog box for the report itself, double-click in the small box in the upper-left corner of the report window. When you do so, you display the dialog box shown in Figure 20-6.

Figure 20-6: Double-click here to see the Report Control.
Double-
clicking on
the box in
the upper-
left corner
in the
Design view
of your
report
opens the
Report
Control
dialog box.

Of particular interest in the Report Control dialog box are controls for whether the Page Header appears on every page in the report (the default setting) or if it should skip the first and last pages (where the Report Header and Report Footer are printed) and appear on all of the others. There's also an option that affects the Keep Together control discussed earlier that determines whether it is controlled by the page or — in a report with multiple columns — by the columns.

Double-clicking on the Page Header bar shows a dialog box similar to the one in Figure 20-7. You can use this dialog box to control whether the Page Header appears at all (with the Visible setting) and — if you wish — to control the color and height of the background. There are easier ways to do this, however. (*Hint:* You can click on just about anything and change its color by using the drop-down lists on the Formatting toolbar.)

Figure 20-7:
You can control how your Page Header looks with the Page Header Control dialog box.

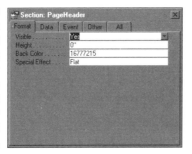

Double-clicking on a Section Header gives you the dialog box shown in Figure 20-8. Notice that there are more available options in the dialog box.

Figure 20-8:
Yet a third Control dialog box lets you manage an entire section of your report.

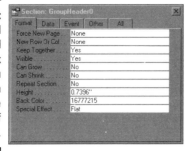

You can control whether or not the change for that group automatically forces the information to start on a new page by setting the Force New Page option. When you set this option, you can determine whether this occurs only before the header, only after the footer, or in both places. Similarly, you can control the way in which section starts and endings are handled for multiple column reports (such as having the group always start in a separate column). As with the previous dialog boxes, you can control whether or not the group is kept together and whether or not the section is visible.

Perhaps the most important settings are those for Can Grow, Can Shrink, and Repeat Section.

✔ When the *Can Grow* option is turned on, the section can expand as necessary based upon the data within it.

This is particularly useful when you are printing a report that contains a Memo field. You set the width of the field so that it is as wide as you want. Then you can use the Can Grow property to allow Access 95 to adjust the height available for the information.

✔ With *Can Shrink* turned on, the section can become smaller if, for example, some of the fields are empty. In order to use the Can Grow and Can Shrink properties, you need to set them both for the section and for the items within the section that are able to grow or shrink.

✔ You can use the *Repeat Section* option to control whether or not, when a group is split across pages or columns, Access 95 repeats the heading on the new page (or pages, if the section is so big that it covers more than two pages).

Filling in Those Sections

Although Access has several default settings for headers and footers, those aren't very personalized or imaginative. You can do a whole lot more with headers and footers than simply display labels for your data. You can build expressions or insert text into these sections that can be used to introduce or summarize your data and impress your friends and influence your co-workers.

Perhaps the most important thing to keep in mind is that you can use the Formatting toolbar to change the look of the various controls.

At the head of the class

How you place the labels within the report's Header sections controls how the final report both looks and works, so it's a good idea to put some thought into your Headers. You want to make sure they're easy to understand, and that they actually add some useful information to the report.

When you're setting up a report, feel free to play around with the header layouts. Experiment with your options and see what you can come up with — the results may surprise you. For example, Figure 20-9 shows a common header configuration in Design view. Figure 20-10 shows the same report in action.

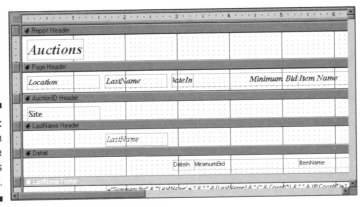

Figure 20-9: The Design View of the Auctions report.

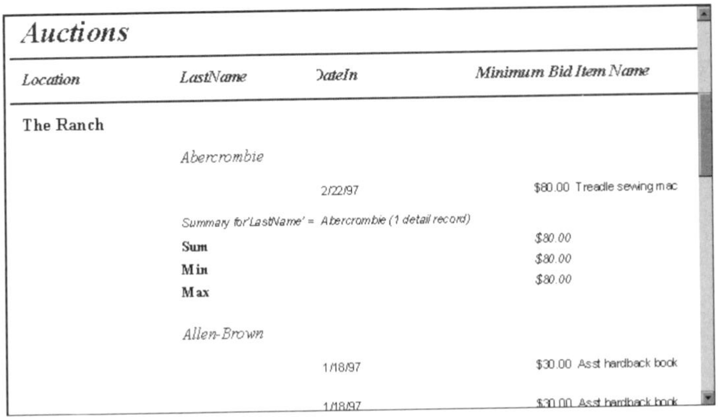

Figure 20-10: What the Auctions Report actually will look like.

In this case, the headings for the columns are printed above the site name. The information for the column headings appears at the top of each and every page (because it's in the Page Header). It's certainly not a bad layout, but there are other ways of accomplishing the same goal.

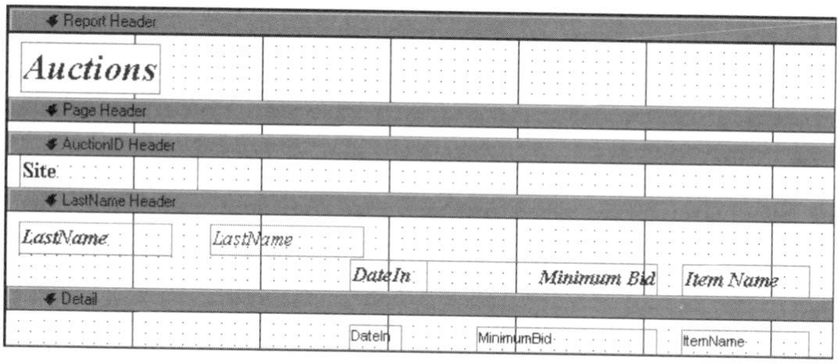

Figure 20-11:
Another arrangement for the Auctions report. Notice the new position for the headers.

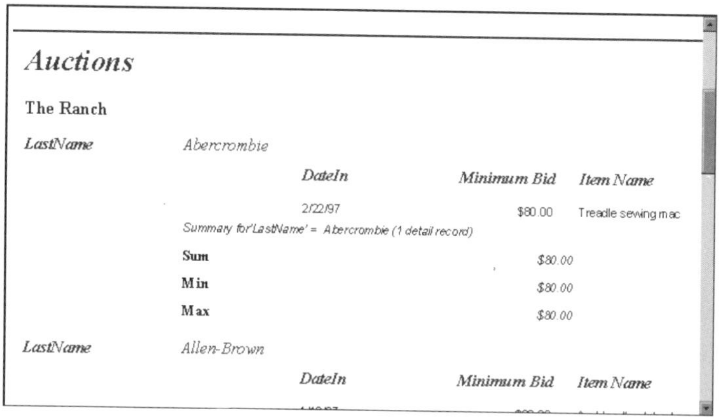

Figure 20-12:
How the new arrangement looks in Print Preview. Compare this to Figure 20-10.

Take for example the alternate arrangement shown in Figures 20-11 and 20-12. In this case, the heading repeats every time the LastName Header is printed. In this example, the column headings appear along with the actual information in the Detail row; rather than appearing at the top of each page, they appear within each group. This means that every time you see the Detail Record column, the information identifying what those columns are will appear immediately before the first record in the group.

In comparing the figures, you may notice that some of the labels (such as Last Name) were also moved, and the various sections were resized. In addition, the pair of lines used to mark the top and bottom of the Page Header were removed in order to close that space.

Controlling the words

Footers are most often used to produce summary statistics and general information. Figure 20-13 shows some of the footer fields that might appear in a simple Auction report.

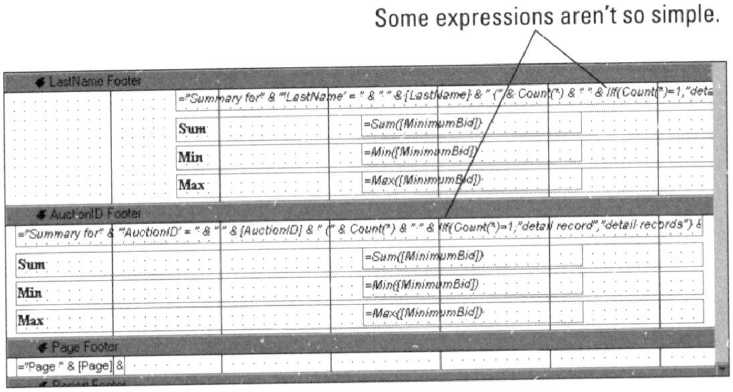

Some expressions aren't so simple.

Figure 20-13: You can select from a plethora of footers to include in your reports.

In many of these cases, the field simply prints text and is a normal label. However, notice the first field in each of the footer sections. These fields involve a somewhat complex looking formula. This formula combines text with the current value of a field in the report. Figure 20-14 shows the results of this complicated bit of computer wizardry.

In the example, the actual last name is inserted along with some standard text ("Summary for"), and a function is used to count the number of records being reported in the group. The expression at the end is just used to determine whether the sentence ends with "record" or "records." In order to help you better understand the formula used for this last bit of magic, Figure 20-15 shows the expression in the Expression Builder.

Remember that the names controlled in square brackets represent fields from the database. The last portion of the expression, starting with the If, controls whether the sentence ends with the singular *detail record* or the plural *detail records*, and it does this by determining whether or not the count of records is equal to one or to some other number (that is, more than one). If there were no records, the section wouldn't have been printed at all, so there would be no summary for it.

Complex calculations build these sentences.

Figure 20-14:
The results
of the work
shown in
Figure 20-13.

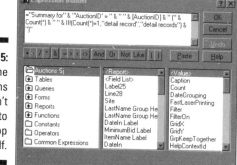

Figure 20-15:
Some
expressions
you don't
want to
develop
yourself.

These feet were made for summing

Access 95 contains a *lot* of functions, but the ones listed in Table 20-1 win the award for Most Likely to Be Used in a Normal Human's Report. These functions create different summaries of the fields in your report.

Table 20-1	**Summary Functions**	
Function	**Description**	**Example**
Sum	Adds up all of the values in the field.	Sum([MinimumBid])
Maximum	Finds the largest value in the values listed in this section for this field.	Max([MinimumBid])

(continued)

Table 20-1 *(continued)*

Function	Description	Example
Minimum	Finds the smallest value in the values listed in this section for this field.	Min([MinimumBid])
Average	Finds the average value of all of the values listed within this section for this field.	Avg([MinimumBid])
Count	Counts up how many values are listed in this section for this field.	Count([MinimumBid])

Figure 20-16:
The
Properties
dialog box
that lets you
control more
things than
you ever
thought
possible.

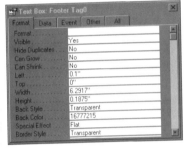

By double–clicking on a calculated field in a report, you open the Properties dialog box like the one shown in Figure 20-16. You can use the first line of the Format tab to select a format for displaying the information in the field. This is the most useful control for setting the look of your report. You also have options for whether duplicates are shown within the field or whether the fields after the first are left blank. These are most useful in the Detail section, where you may wish to show only the first record of several records with the same entry in a field.

The Data tab contains four entries, one of which is the Control Source that provides the calculation's information. The easiest way to get to this card is to double-click on the field itself, which brings up the Properties dialog box, and then click on the Data tab.

At the bottom of the Data tab is an option for whether or not the entry is a Running Sum. This feature controls whether or not the value is reset at zero each time the corresponding Header appears, or whether the value from the previous group is carried through. If this is set to No, every time the Header for the group is printed (every time the entries in the grouping field change), then the total is reset to zero.

If Running Sum is set to Over Group or Over All, then the value from the previous group is carried forward across all of the groups. This can be useful for giving a grand total or a grand average of a group of records; it's used to obtain such things as the average across regions in a report summarizing information about regions.

With the Over Group option, the calculation is continued across all of the groups contained within that section (any sections that fall between the header for the group and the footer for the group). With Over All, the calculation continues no matter how the group changes.

Page numbers and dates

You can have Access insert certain types of information for you in either the Headers or the Footers. Most specifically, Access has the Page Number command as well as the Date and Time command under the Insert menu.

Selecting the Page Number command from the Insert menu displays the dialog box shown in Figure 20-17. You can select between having the page number displayed as simply following the word "Page," or have Access count the total number of pages in the report and display what page you are on currently (as in Page 2 of 15).

Figure 20-17: To fiddle with how your reports generate their page numbers, this is the place.

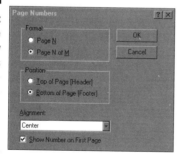

Using Properties dialog box, you can also determine whether page number appears in the Header or Footer and the position of it as far as whether it is centered or aligned to one edge of the page. The alignment list may appear to only contain a single value. If this happens, try clicking at the right edge of it to scroll through additional options. The Inside and Outside options control how the material appears on repeating pages.

✔ If you want to add a page number to a report that already has one, first manually delete the existing page number by clicking on it and pressing the Delete key.

✔ You can also use the check box at the bottom for Show Number on First Page to control whether or not the page number appears on the first page.

The command to insert the date and time displays the dialog box shown in Figure 20-18. The most important thing you need to determine is whether or not you select Include Date, Include Time, or both.

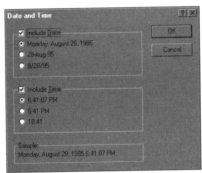

Figure 20-18.
You can even tell Access how you want the date displayed on your report.

You then can select the format for both the date and the time from a somewhat limited set of choices. When you insert the date and time, for some reason, they always appear at the very top of the report. You can use the Cut and Paste commands, however, to move the date and time to the section where you want to place them and then format the fields according to your desires.

Part V
Wizards, Forms, and Other Mystical Stuff

The 5th Wave   By Rich Tennant

"NO, YOU'RE IN THE CASTLE COMPUTER ROOM. THAT'S THE 'WIZARD OF NERD'. YOU WANT 'OZ'—TWO DOORS DOWN ON YOUR RIGHT."

In this part . . .

Part V defies rational explanation. (How's *that* for a compelling tag line?) Its three chapters introduce a wide range of stuff that's all individually useful, but collectively unrelated. When you get down to it, the only thing tying these topics together is the fact that they're not related to anything else.

Be sure to check out Chapter 21 to find out all about forms in Access 95. (Uh oh — my *inner nerd* is starting to get excited...) They're really powerful and flexible... and fun to make — yeah, really fun. And you can have more than one form for a table. Did you know that?

(Perhaps you should just go ahead and read the part while I try to get the nerd back under control before it's too late.)

Chapter 21

Making Forms That Look Cool and Work Great

*P*aper forms are the lifeblood of almost every enterprise. If they weren't, life would probably be simpler, but that's beside the point. Because real life is the mirror that software engineers peer into (and frequently faint while looking at) when they're designing programs, Access 95 includes the ever-cherished ability to view and work with forms.

The electronic version of the dreaded PBF (*paper-based form*) is a much friendlier fellow than its analog counterpart. In fact, you may even discover that you *like* messing around with forms in Access 95. (If that happens, I wouldn't tell anyone if I were you.) This chapter looks at what forms do for you, explores a couple different ways to make forms, and tosses out some tips for customizing forms so they're exactly what you need.

Tax Forms and Data Forms Are Very Different Things

All forms are *not* created equal. Paper forms make cool paper airplanes, take up physical space, are hard to update, and (depending on the number of forms involved) can constitute a safety hazard when stacked. Access 95 forms, on the other hand, are simple to update, safe to store, and are rarely a safety risk (although designing a form *can* be hazardous to your productivity, because it's kinda fun).

Forms in Access 95 are something like digital versions of their paper cousins, but that's only the beginning:

- **Escape the clutches of Datasheet view:** Instead of scrolling back and forth through a datasheet, focus on one record at a time with all the data pleasantly laid out on a single screen.

- **Modify at will:** When your needs change, take the form into Design view and update it. And, unlike with their paper cousins, you don't have to worry about recycling 10,000 leftover copies of the old form, either.

- **See your data any way you want:** Access 95 lets you have as many forms as you want. Create a special form for the data-entry folks, another for your analysts, and a third for yourself. Well-designed forms give the right information to the right people *without* revealing things they don't need to.

- **View the entries in a table or the results of a query:** Forms pull information from tables or queries with equal ease. Forms based on queries are especially flexible because they always display the latest information.

- **Combine data from linked tables:** One form can display data from several related tables. Forms automatically use the relationships built into your database.

Like reports and queries, forms are stored in the database file under the Forms tab, as Figure 21-1 shows. They're full-fledged Access 95 objects, so you can do all kinds of cool tricks with them.

Depending on your needs, you can use three ways to make forms. The *Form Wizard* offers a take-you-by-the-hand approach, walking you through a series of questions and then proudly producing a rather bland-looking form. The three *AutoForm* tools make the same forms as the Form Wizard but don't ask any questions. Finally, there's the *by-hand* approach, where Access 95 sets you up with a blank form and a toolbox full of form-related goodies, shakes your hand, and wanders off to do something fun while you make something from scratch.

Figure 21-1:
It's nice to know the forms are just where I left them.

There's no reason to do any more work than necessary, so this chapter explains how to use the Form Wizard and the AutoForm tools to make the software build basic forms for you. The chapter closes with tips and tricks for manually tweaking these Masterpieces of Vanilla into Truly Cool Forms.

Creating a Form at the Wave of a Wand

The easiest path to the best in computer-designed forms (notice that I didn't say *stunning forms* or *especially useful forms*) is through the Form Wizard. As with all of the other Access 95 wizards, the Form Wizard steps you through the creation process, peppering you with questions to the point that you sometimes want to tell him to grow up and start making his own decisions.

To get the Form Wizard up and running, follow these steps:

1. **Open your database file and click the Forms tab.**

   Access 95 displays a list of the forms currently in your database. Don't fret if the list is currently empty — you're about to change that.

2. **Click New.**

   The New Form dialog box appears.

3. **Double-click the Form Wizard choice in the dialog box (see Figure 21-2).**

   The computer's hard disk sounds like it's having a massive fight with itself, and then the Form Wizard poofs into action.

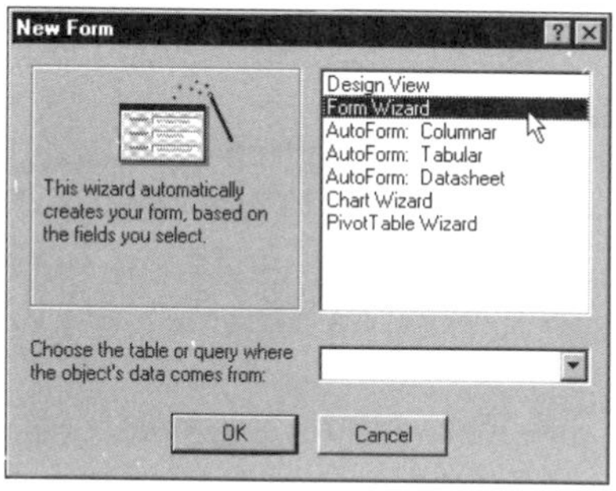

Figure 21-2:
Ringing
the Form
Wizard's
bell.

4. **Click the down arrow in the Tables/Queries box to list the tables and queries in your database, and then select the one that contains the fields that you want to view with this form.**

   The Form Wizard lists the available fields. Now it's time to tell the wizard what you want to display in the form.

5. **To include a field in your form, double-click on the field's name in the Available Fields list.**

   If you want to see *all* the fields, click the >> button in the middle of the screen.

   To remove a field that you accidentally picked, double-click on its name in the Selected Fields list. The field jumps back to the Available Fields side of the dialog box.

6. **Repeat the process on each field destined for the form. When you're done, click Next (see Figure 21-3).**

   Remember that a form can include fields from related tables? If you want to do that, select the fields from the first table (which you just finished doing). When you're done, go back to Step 4 and choose the related table, and then pick the fields you want to include. Is this easy or what?

Figure 21-3:
The fields are ready, so it's time to move along.

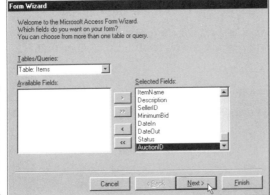

7. **The Form Wizard wants to know how you want the data displayed on the form. Leave it set to Columnar (the default) and click Next.**

   The other formats (Tabular and Datasheet) are interesting, but they create much more complicated forms that frankly aren't easy to work with or customize.

8. **In the name of sprucing up a bland form, the wizard offers to use some interesting color and background combinations to display your data. For now, click the Win95 option and click Next to continue (see Figure 21-4).**

   Most of the color and background combinations *really* slow down the performance of your forms. If you absolutely *must* have some color in your forms, try the Colorful1 and Colorful2 settings. They provide some lively highlights without affecting your form's performance.

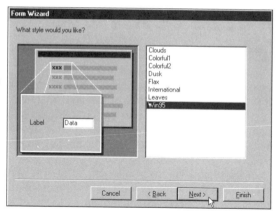

Figure 21-4:
Even though
the options
are
tempting,
stick with
simplicity.

9. **Type a descriptive title for your form in the cleverly named box at the top of the Form Wizard screen.**

   By default, the Form Wizard offers you the name of the table that you used to feed the form, but *please* use something more descriptive than just that.

10. **Click Finish when you're done.**

   After a few moments (or a few *minutes,* if you have a slow computer), your new form appears on-screen, ready for action (see Figure 21-5).

   The Form Wizard automatically saves the form as part of the creation process, so you don't need to manually save and name it. (That's why the wizard asked for a form name — so it could save the form in the database.)

Figure 21-5:
It's no *Mona
Lisa,* but it's
not finger
painting,
either.

Mass Production at Its Best: Forms from the Auto Factory

When I was a kid, I became fascinated with business and how it worked. The move from hand-built products to Henry Ford's automated assembly line particularly amazed me. (Yes, I *was* a little different. Why do you ask?) The assembly line had its good and bad points, but the quote that always defined it for me was, "You can have any color you want, as long as it's black."

With that thought in mind, let me welcome you to the AutoForm Factory. Our motto: "You can have any form you want, as long as it's one of the three we make." Ah, the joys of flexible production management....

Access 95 claims that the AutoForms are wizards, but because they're so limited — er, I mean *focused* — I don't think of them as full-fledged purveyors of the magical arts. Semantics aside, each of the three AutoForms builds a different kind of form:

✔ *Columnar* assembles a classic, one-record-per-page form.

✔ *Tabular* makes a rather cool, multirecord-per-page form, but be ready for some cosmetic surgery to grind away the rough edges and make the form truly useful (see Figure 21-6).

✔ *Datasheet* creates (hold on tight for this one) a *form* that looks, acts, smells, and feels just like a classic *datasheet.* Check out Figure 21-7 to see for yourself. Did the world *need* a form that pretends to be a datasheet? Who knows — it's probably a nerd thing.

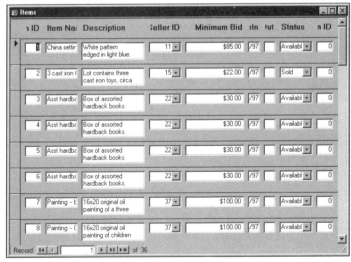

Figure 21-6:
Tabular
forms are
more avant-
garde, but
those
headings
are a mess.

	ItemID	ItemName	Description	SellerID	
▶	1	China setting for 8	White pattern edged in light blue.	11	
	2	3 cast iron toys	Lot contains three cast iron toys,	15	
	3	Asst hardback books (1 o	Box of assorted hardback books.	22	
	4	Asst hardback books (2 o	Box of assorted hardback books.	22	
	5	Asst hardback books (3 o	Box of assorted hardback books.	22	
	6	Asst hardback books (4 o	Box of assorted hardback books.	22	
	7	Painting -- boat on lake	16x20 original oil painting of a thre	37	
	8	Painting -- Children	16x20 original oil painting of childr	37	
	9	Painting -- Convertible	16x20 original oil painting of a 195	37	
	10	Painting -- Old man	16x20 original oil portrait of an age	37	
	11	Mandolin	Mandolin, cherry front with pearl in	14	
	12	HF Radio	Ham radio transceiver, power supp	49	
	13	2m Handi-talkie	Ham radio handi-talkie. Full covera	49	
	14	Box of ham radio magazir	Approximately 100 amateur radio	49	
	15	20m Yagi antenna	Single-band Yagi antenna. Like ne	49	
	16	SW receiver	Shortwave radio receiver. Continuc	49	
	17	Notebook computer	486 notebook computer with 16ml	12	
	18	Portable printer	Portable ink-jet printer. Handles c	12	
	19	Wedding dress	White wedding dress, size 6. New	20	
	20	Engagement ring	Engagement ring in gold and silve	20	

Record: ◄ ◄ | 1 | ► ►I ►* | of 36

Figure 21-7:
Is it a
datasheet
or a form
pretending
to be a
datasheet?
Only its
properties
know for
sure.

Using the AutoForms is a quick process. Despite their alleged *wizard* status, they're more like office temps: Just point them at data, stand back, and before you know it the form is done. Here are the details of the process:

1. **With your database open, click the Tables or Queries tab, depending on where the form should get its information.**

   If you're not sure, click Tables.

2. **Click once on the table or query that's providing fields for the form.**

   The item's name is highlighted, letting you know that Access 95 is *still* in there listening to you, despite what you may think sometimes.

3. **Select Insert⇨Form from the main menu. If you're a toolbar fan, click the down arrow on the far right end of the toolbar and then select New Form from the drop-down menu.**

   The New Form dialog box hops onto the screen, ready to help.

   If you're creating a *columnar* form, here's a shortcut for you: Select AutoForm instead of New Form on the drop-down menu. That choice automatically runs the columnar AutoForm Wizard.

4. **Depending on which look you're after, double-click on AutoForm: Columnar, AutoForm: Tabular, or AutoForm: Datasheet.**

   The appropriate mini-wizard does its focused little job, and your new form appears on-screen in a few moments.

5. If you like the form, preserve it for posterity by selecting File⇨Save from the menu or clicking the Save button on the toolbar. When the Save As dialog box appears, type a name for the form and then click OK.

Unlike the Form Wizard, AutoForms *don't* automatically save the form they create, so you have to save the form manually. The form is added to your database in the Forms tab.

Ultimate Beauty through Cosmetic Surgery

I have a question for you. Tell me the brutal truth, okay? Don't hold back. I want your honest opinion on this. Ready? Would you rather slavishly toil away in the data-entry sweatshop of Figure 21-8 or casually pop a few records into Figure 21-9 between tennis sets? Take your time to answer.

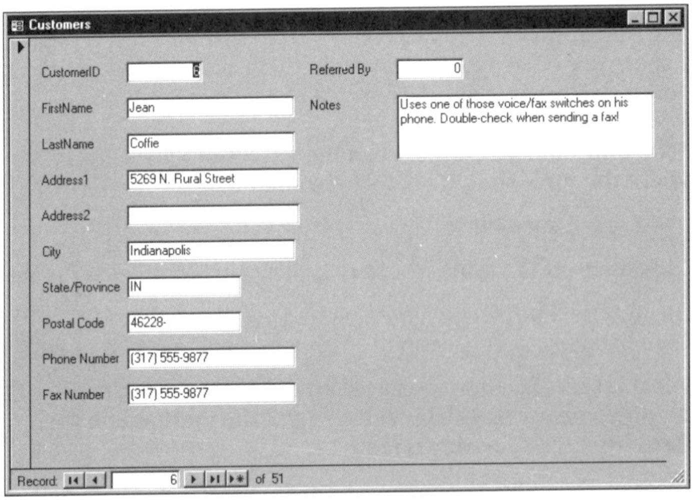

Figure 21-8:
Before: an
unimaginative
form
created by a
mindless
software
automaton.

CustomerID	
FirstName	Jean
LastName	Coffie
Address1	5269 N. Rural Street
Address2	
City	Indianapolis
State/Province	IN
Postal Code	46228-
Phone Number	(317) 555-9877
Fax Number	(317) 555-9877
Referred By	0
Notes	Uses one of those voice/fax switches on his phone. Double-check when sending a fax!

Record: 6 of 51

Believe it or not, those images are the *same form*. Yup, it's true. The *Before* image in Figure 21-8 is a standard columnar form straight from the AutoForm Factory of the previous section. Figure 21-9's *After* image emerged poised, beautiful, and easy to use after just one visit to Dr. John's School for Operationally Inept Forms. To bring about the transformation, I moved the fields around, added some graphics to segment the form, and changed the tab order to make data entry more intuitive.

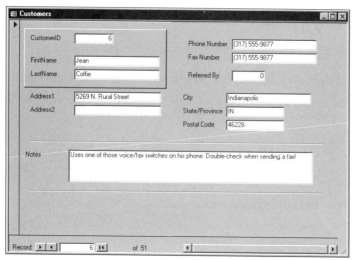

Figure 21-9:
After: the same form rescued from the depths of digital despair, thanks to cosmetic surgery.

Because the school is a small private institution, there isn't enough space for the thousands upon thousands of forms that desperately require this treatment. So instead of sending your forms to my school, I'm sending the school to you. This section outfits you with the basic toolkit used by top form surgeons around the country. In no time at all, your frumpy forms will be sleek data-entry machines, both functionally useful and visually appealing.

Taking a form into Design view

Before you can make *any* of these changes, the form has to be in Design view. There are two easy ways to get there, depending on where you happen to be right now:

> ✔ *From the database window,* click the Forms tab to list the available forms. Click on the form you want to change and then click Design.

> ✔ *From a form window,* click the Design button on the toolbar or select View➪Form Design from the menu.

Don't let Design view stress you out. It *looks* more complicated than normal life, but that's okay. If something goes wrong and you accidentally mess up your form, just select File➪Close from the menu, tell Access 95 No when it asks about saving your changes, and start the design process over again.

Moving fields

To move a field around in the form design, follow these steps:

1. **Put the mouse pointer anywhere on the field that you want to move.**

   You can point to the field name or the box where the field's value goes. Either place is equally fine for what you're doing.

   If the field is already selected (the name has a box around it that's decorated with small, filled-in squares), click on any blank spot of your form to deselect the field; then start with Step 1. Otherwise, Access gets confused and thinks you want to do something *other* than just move the field.

2. **Press and hold the left mouse button.**

   The mouse pointer turns into a hand. That's how Access 95 says it's ready to move something. Strange response, isn't it?

3. **Drag the field to its new location.**

   As you move the field, a pair of white boxes moves along with the cursor to show you precisely where the field will land.

4. **When the field is in position, release the mouse button.**

   The field drops smoothly into place.

   If you don't like where it landed, either move the field again or press Ctrl+Z to undo the move and start over from scratch.

Adding lines and boxes

Two buttons on the form design toolbar are there simply to enable you to add lines and boxes. The buttons are near the bottom of the bar. The Line tool is on the left; the Box tool is next to it. Here's how to use them:

1. **Click on the tool of your choice.**

   To show you it's selected, the tool visually *pushes in,* just like a toggle button.

2. **Put the mouse pointer where you want to start the line or place the corner of a box; then press and hold the left mouse button.**

   Aim is important, but you can always undo or move the graphic if things don't work out quite right.

3. **Move the cursor to the spot where the line ends or to the opposite corner of your box and then release the mouse button.**

   The line or box appears on-screen.

When adding graphics, remember that several different *special effects* are available to you, depending on what you're adding:

- ✔ Lines can be *flat* or *raised*. Even though the other options seem to be available, they don't look any different from *raised* when you're working with a line.

- ✔ Boxes respond to *all* of the special effects options, as you can see in Figure 21-10.

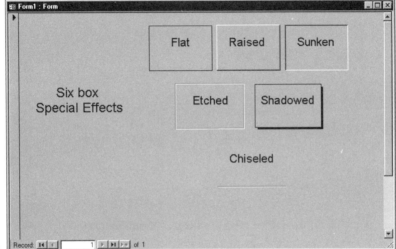

Figure 21-10:
Boxes are
by far the
more stylish
graphic
element.

To use these special effects, draw your line or box and then right-click on it. Select Properties from the pop-up menu and then click the Special Effects box. Choose the effects from the Special Effects box's drop-down menu, and then click the X button to close the Properties dialog box.

Changing the field tab order

Changing the field tab order isn't quite as simple and fun-loving as the other options in this section, but it's even more rewarding. If you move the fields around on the form and then try to use the form, you quickly discover that the fields remember their *old* order when you move from one field to the next with the Tab key. To fix this problem, you need to change the Tab Index property of the fields.

As I mentioned, changing the field tab order is a slightly more technical under-taking than drawing boxes. On a more positive note, it doesn't hold a candle to flying a Boeing 747 aircraft. Now that the issue is in perspective, here's how to change the tab order:

1. **Right-click on the data area of the first field on the form and select Properties from the pop-up menu.**

   The Properties dialog box appears, as shown in Figure 21-11.

   To make this work, you *must* click on the box for the field's values, not the name of the field. If you miss, it's no great loss. Click on a blank area of the form to remove the selection boxes and then try again.

Figure 21-11:
Here's
where the
field's
properties
live.

Text Box: CustomerID	
Format	Data	Event	Other	All
Format	
Visible	Yes
Display When	Always
Scroll Bars	None
Can Grow	No
Can Shrink	No
Left	1.0625"
Top	0.25"
Width	0.7188"
Height	0.1771"
Back Style	Normal
Back Color	-2147483643
Special Effect	Sunken

2. **Click on the Other tab at the top of the dialog box.**

   The display changes slightly. About halfway down the list of properties is one labeled Tab Index. If you don't see it, then Access 95 doesn't think you right-clicked in the data area of the field. In that case, click on the dialog box's X button to close the Properties box and start over.

3. **Click in the Tab Index box.**

   The blinking toothpick cursor pops into the box.

4. **Delete the number that's already there and type 0 (zero) as the new entry.**

   The first field on a form has a Tab Index of 0, the second is 1, and so on.

5. **Close the Properties box by clicking the X button in its upper-right corner and then start again at Step 1 with the next field on the form.**

   Make sure that you work through the fields in the same order you want the Tab key to work.

6. **Once you're done changing all the fields, click the Form View button on the toolbar and test your work.**

   If you accidentally duplicate any numbers in the Tab Index fields, the form won't work right. If any fields are still out of order, note which ones they are and then go back into Design view and look at their Tab Index entries.

Chapter 22

If Love Is Universal, Why Can't I Export to It?

. . . .

In This Chapter

▶ Pulling data into Access 95

▶ Deciding when to import and when to link data

▶ Speaking in foreign data tongues

▶ Pushing your comfortable data into the cold, cruel outside world

. . . .

*T*o achieve true success these days, it's not enough to speak only the tongue of the country that bore you. You need to be comfortable with several languages before the pinnacle of achievement is within your grasp. I, for instance, am fluent in *American English,* a language that the British view as a poor excuse for grunts and knocking rocks together. But to excel at my work, I also studied several variants of the vernacular *Nerd,* including *Windows, DOS,* the pictorial troubleshooting tongue *$%@&#!,* and the esoteric *Macintosh* dialect (which is particularly challenging because all of the words in it look and act alike).

Access 95 is multilingual as well, because its electronic world is filled with more disagreeing tongues than the UN Security Council. It understands a couple of spreadsheets, several competing databases, and even plain old text files. Because of that, you can exchange data with almost any source out there. I have to say that Access 95 is one of the most flexible programs I've ever seen (and I've seen a *lot* of programs).

This chapter looks at the import and export capabilities of Access 95, how they work, and what you can do with them. If you work with Access 95 and almost *any* other program, you need this chapter, because sometime soon some data will be in the wrong place — and guess whose job it will be to move it. . . .

Importing Only the Best Information for Your Databases

Access 95 really has two different ways of sucking data into its greedy clutches. *Importing* involves translating the data from a foreign format into the Access 95 database file format (which, according to Microsoft, all the world's data should be stored in). The other method is *linking*, where you build a temporary bridge between the external data and Access 95.

If you worked with older versions of Access, *linking* used to be called *attaching*. The concept is the same; only the name has been changed to confuse the innocent.

Translating file formats

Regardless of whether you import or link the data, Access 95 understands only certain data formats. Table 22-1 lists the most common file types that the program interacts with. Believe it or not, the few entries in that table cover the majority of data stored on PCs around the world.

Table 22-1	Access 95's List of Language Fluencies		
Program	*DOS extension*	*Versions*	*Notes*
dBASE	.DBF	III, III+, IV, V	One of the most popular formats out there; many programs use the dBASE format.
FoxPro	.DBF	2.0, 2.5, 2.6, 3.0	Microsoft's *other* database program; not *directly* compatible with dBASE in some cases.
Paradox	.DB	3.*x*, 4.*x*, 5.*x*	A competing database from Borland.
Excel	.XLS	2.0, 3.0, 4.0, 5.0, 7.0	Although it's a spreadsheet, lots of people use it as a simple flat-file database manager.
Lotus 1-2-3	.WKS, .WK1, .WK3	1.*x*, 2.*x*, 3.*x*, 4.*x*	The most popular DOS spreadsheet is also the home of many tortured flat-file databases.
ASCII	.TXT	N/A	The "if all else fails" format; Access 95 understands both delimited and fixed-width text files.
SQL	N/A	Sybase, Oracle, Microsoft	This is nerd country, but you might run across it when working with the company's *big* databases.

Although Access 95 is pretty intelligent about the translation process, there are some quirks to watch out for. Here are some specific things to keep in mind as you play The Great Data Liberator and set the imperiled information free to enjoy a new life in Access 95:

✔ When working with dBASE and FoxPro files, make sure you keep careful track of the associated index files. Access 95 needs the index to work with the table. If it can't find it or if the index is corrupt, your table is gibberish to Access 95.

✔ Access 95 has problems linking to Paradox tables that don't have a primary key. Specifically, it can't write changes to the unkeyed Paradox table. To fix the problem, use Paradox to create a primary key in the table and *then* link the table to Access 95.

✔ Remember that data in Paradox tables *isn't* stored in a single file. It's common to have a .PX (the primary index) and a .MB (memo data — I don't know what the *B* is supposed to stand for) file lurking around the .DB file. If you copy a Paradox table from one computer to another, take care to copy *all* of the associated files!

✔ Double-check information coming from any spreadsheet program to be sure it's *consistent.* Above all, ensure that the data on each row of a column (field) is the same type. Otherwise, the import won't work right (and you know how forgiving software is of such "little" problems).

✔ For ASCII or SQL data, it's probably best to get a guru's help the first (and possibly the second) time. There are a lot of niggling little details that stand between you and a successful data import.

Importing or linking your files

The precise details of importing and linking depend greatly on the type of file you're importing from, but here are the general steps to get you started in the right direction. Although the instructions are written mainly for importing, I include supporting notes about linking as well:

1. **Open the Access 95 database you're pulling the data into.**

   If you're not familiar with this step, *stop* — don't go any further. Flip back to Chapter 1 and spend some time getting comfy with Access 95 before attempting an import.

2. **Select File⇨Get External Data⇨Import from the main menu.**

   The dialog box in Figure 22-1 appears.

To make a link, select Link Tables from the submenu instead of Import. If you do, the dialog box in Figure 22-1 is labeled Link instead of Import, but the choices are exactly the same.

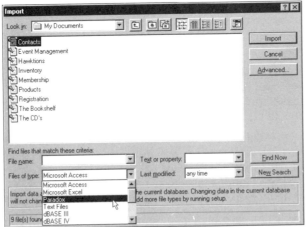

Figure 22-1:
Make sure
you pick
the correct
data type.

3. **Click the down arrow in the Files of type box and click on the kind of data you're importing. If necessary, use the Look in box to navigate your way to the files.**

   The dialog box displays the matching files for your selection pleasure. Make sure you choose the correct file type. Otherwise, Access 95 won't list the file you're looking for in the dialog box!

4. **Double-click on the file you want to import.**

   Here's where the process takes off in wildly different directions depending on the file format you're importing from and whether you're doing a link or an import. The only sage advice I can give is to cross your fingers, follow the instructions on-screen, refer to the tips above, and hope for the best.

One final thought: If you're importing and the process is taking *forever,* Access 95 is probably struggling with errors in the inbound data. Press Ctrl+Break to stop the import process and check the data that's being imported for obvious errors (bad or corrupt data, badly organized spreadsheet data, invalid index, and so on).

To import or to link — the answer is, *It depends*

Because Access 95 offers two different ways to get data in, this brings up the logical question, *Which one should I use?* Because this involves a computer, the simple answer is, *It depends.*

It mainly depends on the other program and its fate within your organization. Are you still using the other program to update the data? Do other people use the program to access the data? If so,

use a *link* with Access 95. This lets you play with the data while keeping it in the original format so everyone else can use it as well.

On the other hand, if the other application was mothballed and you're doing data rescue duty, *import* the data permanently and give it a comfortable new home. There's no sense in preserving a data format that nobody cares about anymore.

Sending Your Data on a Long, One-Way Trip

In the interest of keeping you awake, I'll keep this explanation short. Exporting is just like importing, except where it's different.

Hmm … perhaps that was a little *too* short.

Exporting a table involves reorganizing the data it contains into a different format. Like importing, Access 95 can translate the data into a variety of "languages," depending on your needs. The master list of export formats is the same one governing imports earlier in the chapter.

The main thing to keep an eye out for when exporting is *data loss.* Not all storage formats are created equal (after all, Microsoft didn't come up with them *all,* which is arguably a good thing). Just because the data looked glorious in your Access 95 table doesn't mean a suitable home is waiting when you ship the information off to, say, Paradox or FoxPro. Special Access 95 data types such as *AutoNumber, Yes/No, Memo,* and *OLE* are almost sure to cause problems. Be ready for some creative problem-solving to make things work just the way you want them to.

Likewise, field names can be trouble. Access 95 is very generous about what you can put into a field name. dBASE, on the other hand, is downright totalitarian about it. This can lead to multiple fields with the same name — a frustrating (if slightly humorous) problem. If you export an Access 95 table with fields called Projected1997Sales, Projected1997Net, and Projected1997Overhead, it's distinctly possible to end up with three fields named *Projected1.* This is *not* a pleasant thought. Be ready to spend some time tuning the export so it works just the way you thought it would.

The steps to exporting a table are much simpler than they are for importing. Here goes:

1. **With the database open, click on the table you want to export.**

   As you may expect, the table name is highlighted for the world to see.

2. **Select File⇨Save As/Export from the main menu.**

   The little Save As dialog box in Figure 22-2 bounds merrily onto the screen.

Figure 22-2:
Here's an easy one — click on OK to continue.

3. **Make sure the radio button promising to ship your data To an external File or Database is selected; then click on OK.**

   The little dialog box does its job, and a big honking dialog box takes its place.

4. **Click on the Down arrow in the Save as type box to list the available exporting formats; then click on the one you want (see Figure 22-3).**

   If the format you're looking for is in Table 22-1 but it's *not* in your list on-screen, run the Access 95 setup program again (oh joy, oh rapture!) and install that format on your system. This may require the help of your Information Systems folks, depending on where your copy of Access 95 is stored and who has custody of the installation disks.

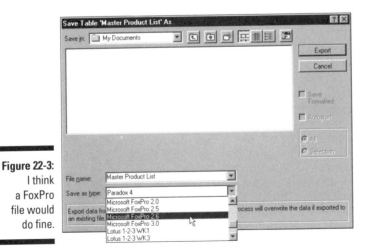

Figure 22-3:
I think a FoxPro file would do fine.

5. **To use a different name for the table, click on the File-name box, highlight the existing table name, and then type a new name.**

   If the table is headed back to an old DOS or Windows 3.x world, remember to limit yourself to eight letters, numbers, or combination thereof. Don't worry about the extension (the three-character part after the period in an old filename), because Access 95 handles that automatically.

6. **If you want to stow the newly exported file in a different folder from the current one, use the Save in box at the top of the window to explain the destination to Access 95.**

   To leave the file in the folder you're in, just skip the step and forge ahead.

7. **Brace yourself and click on Export (see Figure 22-4).**

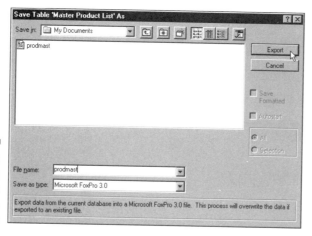

Figure 22-4:
Crossing
your fingers
helps, too.

In true computer style, if the process is a success you get absolutely *no* feedback from Access 95. You only hear about it if something dreadful goes wrong. Luckily, few things ever go wrong with exports, so your computer is probably sitting there looking smugly by at you even as you read this.

Chapter 23

The Analyzer: Your Data's Dr. Freud, Dr. Watson, and Dr. Jekyll

. . . .

In This Chapter

▶ Flat becomes relational with the Table Analyzer

▶ Making the database document itself

▶ Steer clear of the Performance Analyzer

. . . .

1 f I didn't know better, I'd file this chapter under the heading *Oh Sure That's What It Does* (said with heavy sarcasm). After all, the Analyzer promises to do the three things that are nearest to a database person's heart: automatically convert flat files into relational databases; document the database and all its sundry parts (including tables, queries, forms, reports, and more); and analyze the structure of your tables to make sure everything is set up in the best possible way. If it does all that and cooks (or at least orders pizza) too, a nearsighted technoweenie might accidentally fall in love!

Even though technology has come a *long* way in recent years, it's still not as advanced as you suspect. That's true of the Analyzer, too — it promises more than it delivers. On the bright side, it does deliver a *lot.* That's why it earned a chapter of its very own, a place to extol its two virtues and reveal its shortcoming (but I guess one out of three isn't bad).

It Slices, It Dices, It Builds Relational Databases!

Arguably, the Analyzer's biggest promise is hiding under the Tools⇨Analyze⇨Table. This piece of software claims it can turn a flat file table into a relational database with minimal human intervention *and* check for spelling errors in the data at the same time.

Truth be told, the Analyzer *tries* awfully hard to convert the flat file into a relational database. But like most software, sometimes it gets confused and vaults off in the wrong direction. I still recommend giving it a try simply because it *might* work on your table and, if it does, you just saved a lot of time and effort.

With that thought in mind, here's how to inflict — er, invoke — the Table Analyzer Wizard:

1. **With your database open, select Tools⇨Analyze⇨Table from the main menu.**

   After a period of thought punctuated with hard-disk activity, the Table Analyzer Wizard dialog box appears on-screen (see Figure 23-1).

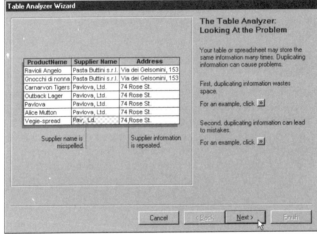

Figure 23-1: So far, so good — the wizard showed up.

2. **The first two screens are interesting, but strictly educational. Read them if you want and then click Next.**

   Stop clicking Next when you get to the screen in Figure 23-2 (which should be precisely two Next clicks from Step 1).

3. **Click the name of the flat file you want to do the relational magic on and then click Next.**

   Although some say it's superstition, I firmly believe in crossing my fingers at moments like this.

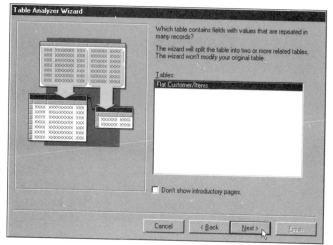

Figure 23-2:
It's time to
do the deed.

4. **The wizard wants to know if he can analyze the table and offer suggestions on how things should work. Click the Yes radio button and then click Next.**

   This is the pivotal step in the whole process. The wizard leaps into the task, displaying a couple of horizontal bar charts to show how things are progressing. When the Analysis Stages bar makes it all the way to the end, the wizard's done.

5. **The analysis is complete, and the results are in (see Figure 23-3). If you like what the wizard came up with, name the tables by clicking on each table and then clicking the Name Table button (the one that looks like a pencil doodling on a table). When you're done, click Next.**

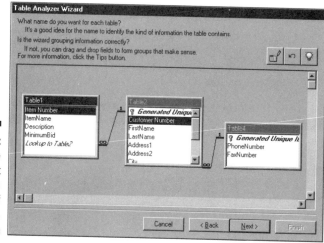

Figure 23-3:
It's a little
odd, but not
bad for a
piece of
software.

If you're not sure about what the wizard wants to do or if it just plain makes no sense, click Cancel and seek human help (see the sidebar "When in doubt, ask a human" for more about that).

6. **The wizard wants your input about key fields for the tables. To designate a key field, click on a field in the table and then click the Key button.**

This step lets you replace many of the `Generated Unique ID` entries that the wizard put in the tables.

Make sure each table has a key field before continuing!

7. **Since the structure is basically complete, the wizard turns his attention to typographical errors within the database. If he finds records that *seem* to be the same except for minor changes, he asks for your help to fix them (see Figure 23-4). Follow the on-screen instructions to effect the repairs.**

Depending on the condition of your data, you may have *many* records to correct. Be patient — the wizard really *is* helping!

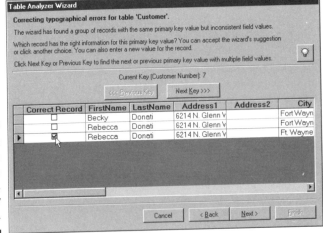

Figure 23-4:
There seems
to be a little
trouble here,
but it's easily
fixed.

8. **Once the correction process is done, the wizard offers to create a query that will look and act like your original table. If you have reports and forms that work with the flat file, let the wizard create the query for you (the default action). Otherwise, click the N̲o radio button. Click F̲inish when you're through.**

You're done. Sit back and take a break. You earned it!

When in doubt, ask a human

Although I mentioned this in the midst of the Great Table Analyzer discussion, it bears repeating out here in the open: It's distinctly possible that the Table Analyzer won't be able to make heads or tails of your table. It will always try, but it might fail rather spectacularly.

If you're trying to split a flat file database into a relational database and don't know where to start, a good place to begin is the snack food aisle at the local food store. Get some goodies (preferably chocolate) and use them to bribe your local database nerd into helping you.

If this database is important to your business or life (and it *must* be, or you wouldn't be haggling with it so much), it's important enough to get some live, human help to put it together correctly.

The moral of the story is to go ahead and try the Analyzer just to see how it responds to your data. It might work fine, it might get confused, or it might go into a great harking fit and attempt to spit your table onto the carpet. The benefits (and possible entertainment value) make it a worthwhile investment of your time. Good luck!

Documentation: What to Give the Nerd in Your Life

Pardon me while I put on my technoweenie hat and taped-together glasses for a moment. There's one thing the world needs more of; can't ever have enough of, in fact. You probably know what I'm talking about. Yes, it's *documentation*. If only life were a little better documented, things would be different.

(I'm taking *off* the technoweenie outfit now. Thanks for your patience.)

In truth, documentation is probably the furthest thing from your mind right now, but it's still important, especially if you're creating something for your business. I know there's barely time to get the database running and tested, but you *absolutely* need to document what you're doing.

Like many problems, documenting your work is a trade-off between a dire need and lack of time. What's a person to do? Call the Database Documentor!

This second piece of the Analyzer puzzle steps through everything in your database (and I do mean *everything*) and documents the living daylights out of it. This thing collects information so obscure that I'm not even sure the programmers know what some of it means.

But the neat part is it works *by itself.* Really. You start it, sic it on a database, and nip off for a spot of lunch. When you come back, its report is done and waiting. {Poof!} Instant documentation.

Here's how to put the Database Documentor to work on your database:

1. **With the database file open, select Tools⇨Analyze⇨Documentor from the main menu.**

   The Database Documentor rises from the hard drive like a digital Phoenix and appears on-screen. (Okay, so I'm in a poetic mood — I'm still giddy about the prospect of the program doing my documentation for me.)

2. **In the Select Objects dialog box, click Select All to document your entire database (see Figure 23-5) and then click OK to continue.**

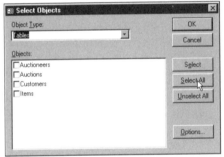

Figure 23-5: One click ensures that everything gets included.

The Documentor begins by examining all of the objects in your database, starting with the tables and moving on to the queries, forms, reports, and so on. During the process, your forms appear on-screen for a moment — that's normal.

The process often takes a while, so this is a good time for lunch or a little coffee break.

3. **When the Documentor finishes, he leaves a report packed with information about your database (Figure 23-6). Click the Print button on the toolbar or select File⇨Print to get a paper copy.**

   If you want to store the information for posterity, select File⇨Save as Table and then give the table a name.

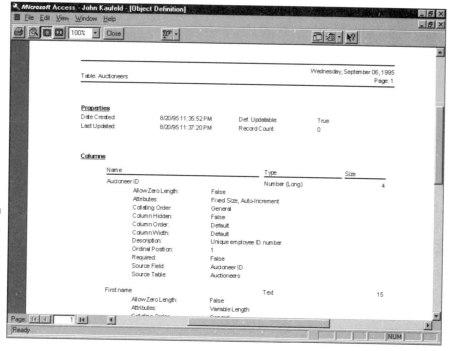

Figure 23-6:
It's all here
in black and
white — and
you barely
lifted a
finger!

Let the Performance Analyzer Work on Someone Else's Tables

I don't usually come right out and drop a great big *hands off* notice in your lap, but I'm afraid that the Performance Analyzer deserves to be the exception to the rule.

Don't get me wrong — this feature shows great promise. After all, who couldn't like something that claims to dig around in your tables, ferret out the technoid tweaks that are the key to better performance, and then implement them for you? But at least for now, forgo the temptation to tinker and instead let someone *else* (preferably someone you don't like) use the Performance Analyzer on his or her data first.

In my tests, the analyzer came up with some pretty lame ideas, such as an ever-present suggestion that I change the phone number field from text to a long integer type. For as smart as the software is, it *certainly* should find something more impressive than that. I tried several combinations, including some with obvious problems in field type. It never *did* come up with anything really useful to say.

Keep this feature in the back of your mind and try it out when Access 96 comes out on the market next year.

Part VI
The Part of Tens

"GENTLEMEN, I SAY RATHER THAN FIX THE 'BUGS', WE CHANGE THE DOCUMENTATION AND CALL THEM 'FEATURES'."

In this part . . .

All hail the traditional Part of Tens, purveyor of numerically organized information, keeper of the sacred decimal count, and upholder of the proud *Dummies* tradition.

Every . . .*For Dummies* book closes with a Part of Tens. I guess it's the *Dummies* version of denouement. Anyway, this book's final part includes stuff you can use today, stuff you might need tomorrow, and stuff for *way* on down the road. I tried to include a little something for everyone, so read every chapter *very* closely and see if you can find the stuff I put in just for you.

By the way, no animals were harmed in the quest to bring you this information. One technoweenie was slightly miffed, but I'm sure he'll get over it.

Chapter 24

Ten Timesaving Keyboard Shortcuts

In This Chapter

▶ Keystrokes to save you time, energy, and hair

*J*ust because Windows 95 is supposed to be the ultimate graphical user environment doesn't mean you won't need the keyboard anymore. In fact, Access 95 has some cool shortcuts up its sleeve that are available only through this special, keyboard-based offer.

This chapter highlights ten cool shortcuts designed to make your life a little easier. Some enter data automatically, some make editing quicker, and others are for fun.

Select an Entire Field — F2

This is particularly handy if you're replacing a lengthy address or description field. Instead of wrestling with the mouse to make sure that you have *everything* in the field highlighted, simply press F2 and *know* that it's taken care of. The keystroke works in both Datasheet view and Form view.

Insert the Current Date — Ctrl+; (semicolon)

This keystroke combination and the one following not only save time but also increase accuracy. Ever mistyped a date because you were in a hurry (or just because the keyboard couldn't spell)? Ctrl+; resolves the issue completely by doing the work for you. The keystroke works in Datasheet view and Form view.

Insert the Current Time — Ctrl+: (colon)

This is another nod to accuracy. To insert the current time, you actually press Ctrl+Shift+; (semicolon), even though Ctrl+: is the keystroke. To get a colon, you have to do the Shift+; (semicolon) routine.

Insert a Line Break — Ctrl+Enter

When a long entry in a memo or large text field feels like it's never going to quit, end the monotony with a line break. Well-placed line breaks make your data more legible, too. The keystroke is available in Datasheet view and Form view.

Add a New Record — Ctrl++ (plus sign)

Delete the Current Record — Ctrl+- (minus sign)

Although they look funny (how *do* you write *plus plus* without spelling it out?), these keys keep you on the go when you're in a hot-and-heavy edit mode. Because you don't have to keep switching between the keyboard and the mouse to insert or delete records, your speed will increase, as will your accuracy. No doubt to your surprise, these two keys work in Datasheet view and Form view.

Save the Record — Shift+Enter

After a long, hard edit, make *sure* the record is saved with a quick Shift+Enter. That signals Access 95 that you're truly done working on this one. The software takes the cue and saves your changes immediately. Use this in Datasheet view or Form view.

Undo Your Last Changes — Ctrl+Z

Everyone should have this one memorized. The Undo keystroke is a golden oldie. With Access 95's propensity to automatically save things every time you turn around, it can really save your bacon. When something goes wrong, don't panic — try Ctrl+Z instead. This keystroke combination works almost everywhere in Access 95.

Open the Selected Object in Design View — Ctrl+Enter

Hey, what's this? Ctrl+Enter does *two* things in Access 95? You're right. When you're editing a table in Datasheet view or Form view, Ctrl+Enter inserts a line break. When you're in *Database* view use Ctrl+Enter to whip open something into Design view. Let the *ordinary folks* use the mouse — instead, be different and do it from the keyboard!

Quit for good — Alt+F4

If you're having a *bad Access 95 day,* reaffirm your power over the software with a good, old-fashioned Alt+F4. Look at Access 95, raise your hand to the keyboard, and wave good-bye as the program goes away and leaves you alone for a while.

Chapter 25

Ten Common Crises and How to Survive Them

In This Chapter

▶ Common hair-raising problems solved (or at least explained)

▶ Misplacing tables

▶ Vanishing files and records

▶ Mysteriously changing numbers

▶ Unasked questions

*W*here there are computers, so also is there software, because a computer is nothing without its software. Where there is software, so also are there problems, because software without problems is obviously outdated and in need of replacement.

Problems are a part of life. When the problems strike in or around your precious data, they seem all the more fearsome. This chapter touches on only ten problems you may encounter while using Access 95. If your problem is covered here, try the solution I outline. If your particular trouble isn't on the list, refer to Chapter 3 for some other spots to seek help.

And good luck. (I mean it!)

You Built Several Tables, but Put Them in Different Databases

Misplacing your tables is an easy mistake to make at first, especially if you have experience with one of those *other* database programs such as Paradox or FoxPro. Those systems store each *table* in a separate file. Working from that experience, it's only natural to start creating databases right and left, each one containing a single table.

Of course, that makes a lot of extra work for you in Access 95, because the confused program can't figure out what you're trying to accomplish. Rather than setting up all kinds of links among a slew of different database files, pull your tables together into a single database, the way Access 95 is designed to work with them.

To do that, open a database file, right-click on the table you want to move, and select Copy from the pop-up menu. Now open the database you're moving the table to. Click on the Tables tab, right-click in the Table list, and select Paste on the pop-up menu. The table hops into the database. Repeat the process for all the orphan tables rattling around in their own database files.

You Type 73.725, but It Changes to 74 by Itself

Automatic rounding can frustrate the living daylights out of you, but it's very easy to fix. By default, Access 95 sets all number fields to accept *long integers* — numbers without decimal places. You need to change the setting to *single*, which is short for *single precision number*, not *hey you swinging text field, let's go party with the forms.*

To fix the problem, open the table in Design view and then click on the field that's giving you fits. On the General tab of the Properties area at the bottom of the screen, click in the Field Size box. Click on the down arrow that appears on the end of the box; then select *single* from the drop-down menu. Save the table and (voilá!) your automatic rounding problem is over.

The Case of the Missing Database

Sometimes it feels like you just can't trust those database files. Here today, AWOL tomorrow. Access 95 knows how slippery the files are, so it offers a very powerful file finder built right into the Open Database window. When one of your database files tries to make a run for it (or if you just can't quite remember where you left it), use the Find File option to track it down. Everything you need to know about it is in the sidebar "Bo Peep needed the Find Files option" back in Chapter 6.

If you're on a network, remember to check the network storage areas too!

You're Almost Completely Sure That's Not the Question You Asked

Remember the old saying, "Kids say the darnedest things"? Well, this problem falls under the heading, "Queries return the darnedest results." Every now and then, one of your queries returns the most *fascinating* answers. In fact, they're *so* fascinating that you begin to wonder precisely what color the sky is in the query's world because the query's world is obviously different than the one you're in.

There's no tried-and-true solution to this one because the actual cause could be any number of things. Generally speaking, first check over your work and make sure there aren't any stray characters anywhere in the query. You might also try closing the query and rebuilding it from scratch — queries *have* been known to simply freak out sometimes (after all, it's *just* a computer). If nothing seems to help, make a backup of your data and call your friendly neighborhood computer guru.

And When You Looked Again, the Record Was Gone

"It was there — right there!" Of course, the key word in that sentence is the verb, because it indicates the record *isn't* there now. Precisely where the record has nipped off to is a moot point because only the computer knows, and machines have a code of silence about these things. (It's a subset of the rules that make all the copiers break at the same time.)

First, *before* doing anything else, press Ctrl+Z (the undo key). If the record comes back, you're done. If nothing seems to happen, you're in slightly more trouble. The best solution is to have a backup copy of the database file and pull the record from there. If you have a paper copy of the data, you can always manually re-enter it into the database. If that was your only original copy of the record, then raise your hand, look at the computer, and wave good-bye because it's gone now (you have my deepest sympathy).

Please, oh *please* keep current backups of your information. You never know when bad things will happen (insert eerie organ music here).

The Validation that Never Was

Validations are one of my favorite things about Access 95. But like anything, validations can cause problems if they're not used properly.

The biggest concern is a validation rule that *can't* be valid. For instance, if I want to limit myself to records between 0 and 100, I might create a validation that says `<0 And >100`. The only problem is that it's wrong. I mixed up the symbols and created a rule that demands that entries be less than 0 *and* greater than 100 at the same time.

The moral of the story: Write your rule, and then apply it to some sample data. Be sure to include examples of both good and bad entries to make sure the rule works just like it's supposed to.

You Can't Link to a FoxPro or dBASE Table

In this bet on the cause of the failed link, the odds-on favorite is a bad index file. Access 95 has a specific problem linking to FoxPro and dBASE tables that have bad indexes. Before getting frustrated — even before panicking — go back to the original program, rebuild the table's index, and then try the link again. Most of the time, that solves the problem.

If this happens to be the one time in 10,000 where the index file *isn't* at fault, pick up a bag of nacho chips at the convenience store and invite the guru over for a snack and some troubleshooting.

Be *really* careful when updating a FoxPro or dBASE file through Access 95. Make sure you attach the index — otherwise, you're crawling around on your knees, begging for trouble.

You Get a Key Violation While Importing a Table

When you get a key violation while importing a table, Access 95 is trying as hard as it can, but there's a duplicate key value in the data you're importing. Because Access 95 can't arbitrarily change the data in question, you need to do the repair. Go back to the master program, find the offending record, and build a good key to replace the duplicated one. Once you're sure the key values are all unique, then try, try again.

Try as You Might, the Program Won't Start

This is often a spectacularly fun problem. After picking Access 95 from the Start menu, the oh-so-cool Access 95 splash screen (the pretty picture that keeps you entertained while the program takes too long to load) flows smoothly onto the screen. Suddenly, the serene moment shatters as a small warning box bursts in. `Can't find ODD_ESOTERIC_FILE.MDB.` The Access 95 splash screen fades and you're left facing the Windows 95 desktop once more.

This really does happen from time to time. Honestly, it's just part of life with computers. I teach my troubleshooting classes a simple mantra to cover precisely this problem: *It's a file. Files go bad.*

Because the error message was kind enough to give you a filename (not all errors are so generous), use the Explorer to look for the file. If it's there, then the odds are that the file is corrupt. If it's not there, well, at least you know why Access 95 couldn't find it either.

Either way, you need to replace the file with a healthy version from your original Access 95 program disks. If you have a CD-ROM copy of Access 95, this process is easy. Just point the Explorer at the installation CD-ROM, find the file, and copy it to the Access 95 subdirectory.

Doing this process from floppy disks is more complicated because the files on floppies are compressed, and you have to use Microsoft's special decompression program to make them usable. Your best bet is (I hate saying this) to call Microsoft's Access support folks and seek their help.

The Wizard Won't Come Out of His Castle

This is a more focused version of the previous problem where Access 95 wouldn't start. Now, the problem is localized to a particular wizard. The solution is the same: Look for the missing file, replace it from the master disks, and then see if that solves the problem. If all else fails (and it might), pick up a bag of nacho chips and call in your favorite nerd for some assistance.

The wizard files usually congregate in the main Access 95 folder, so at least you know where the file goes.

Chapter 26

Ten Tips from the Database Nerds

*L*ike 'em or loathe 'em, the technical experts are always with you. Everywhere you turn, there's someone who might know something more about technology than you do. Sometimes, these folks look funny, frequently act strange, and can often seem amazingly disconnected from reality.

In their more lucid moments, though, the technical experts possess some nuggets of wisdom. This chapter is a distillation of cool ideas that I picked up over the years. Some are very focused, while others are downright philosophical. Such is life with the technical experts (but you knew that already).

Document as if Your Life Depends on It

Yes, it's a pain. Yes, it's a bother. Yes, *I* do it myself (kinda scary when a guy actually listens to his own advice). If you build a database, make sure you document every little thing about it. Here's a list of things to start with:

- ✔ General information about the database. Include file locations, an explanation of what the database does, and information on how it works.

- ✔ Table layouts, including field names, sizes, contents, and sample contents. If some of the data comes from esoteric or temporary sources (like the shipping report that you shred right after data entry), note that in the documentation so people will know.

- ✔ Report names, an explanation of the information on the report, and lists of who gets a copy when it's printed. If you need to run some queries before doing a report, document the process (or better yet, get a nerd to help you automate the whole thing). Documenting who receives the report is *particularly* important. Jot down the job title in the documentation as well as the current person in the position.

✔ Queries and logic. For every query, provide a detailed explanation of how the query works, especially if it involves multiple tables.

✔ Miscellaneous details that keep life together, such as the backup process and schedule, where backup tapes are located (you *are* doing backups, right?), and what to do if the computer isn't working. If your database runs a particularly important business function such as accounting, inventory, point-of-sale, or order entry, make sure there's some kind of manual process that will keep the business going if the computer accidentally breaks down — and remember to document the process here!

One final thought: Keep the documentation up to date. Every few months, review your documentation to see if it's time for some updates. It's only useful if it's up to date and someone *other* than yourself can understand it.

Don't Make Your Fields Way Too Big

When you're building a table, take a moment to make your text fields the appropriate size for the data you're keeping there. By default, Access 95 sets up text fields to hold 50 characters. That's a pretty generous setting, particularly if the field happens to be holding two-letter state abbreviations. Granted, 48 characters of space aren't anything to write home about, but multiplied across a table with 100,000 customer addresses in it, you get 4.8MB of storage space that's very busy holding *nothing*.

Adjust the field size with the Field Size setting on the General tab in Design view.

Real Numbers Use Number Fields

Use number fields for *numbers,* not for text *pretending* to be a number. Computers perceive a difference between the postal code *47201* and the number *47,201.* The postal code is stored as a series of five characters that all happen to be digits, but the number is stored as an actual number. You can do math with it (just try that on a postal code field sometime) and all kinds of fun stuff.

When you're building a table and need to choose the correct field type, ask a simple question when you get to a field with numbers in it: Are you *ever* going to make a calculation or do anything math related with the field? If so, use a number type. If not, store it as text and go on with your life.

Better Validations Make Better Data

Validations work hand in hand with masks to prevent bad data from getting close to your tables. Validations are easy to make, quick to set up, and ever vigilant (even when you're so tired you can't see straight). If you aren't using validations to protect the integrity of your database, you really should. Flip back to Chapter 7 and have another look at them.

Use Understandable Names

When building a table or creating a database, think about the names you use. Will you remember what they mean three months from now? Six months from now? Are they intuitive enough for someone else to look at the table and figure out what it does long after your knowledge of Access 95 puts your career on the fast track?

Now that Windows 95 *finally* offers long filenames, please use them. You don't need to get carried away, but now there's no excuse for files called *97Q1bdg5*. Using *Q1 1997 Budget Rev 5* makes a *lot* more sense to everyone involved.

Take Great Care When Deleting

Whenever you're deleting records from a table, make sure you're killing the *right* record, check again, and — only when you're sure — delete the original. Even then, you can still do a quick Ctrl+Z and recover the little bugger.

Why all the checking and double-checking? Because after you delete a record *and do anything else in the table,* Access 95 completely forgets about your old record. It's gone, just as if it never existed. If that record happened to be important and you don't have a current backup file, you're out of luck. Sorry!

Keep Backups

There is no substitute for a current backup of your data, particularly if it's vital to your company. Don't believe me? Let the phrase *no receivables* float through your mind for a while. How do you feel about backups now? I thought you'd see it my way.

Think First and then Think Again

Apply this rule to any Access 95 step that contains the words *delete* or *redesign*. Think about what you're doing. Then think again. Software makes it easier to handle large amounts of data, but it also offers the tools to screw things up on a scale not seen since the time of P.T. Barnum.

Thomas Watson, Sr., the president of IBM for years and years, simply said it best: "Think."

Get Organized / Keep It Simple

Although they may seem different at first blush, these two tips work together to promote classic nerd values like *a place for every gadget* and *my query ran faster than yours, so there.* By keeping your computer orderly and organizing your entire workspace, everything you need is at hand. Just toss in the Barco-lounger and a remote control, and you'll never need to leave the office again.

But it's also possible to get *too* organized. In fact, it's altogether too easy. Temper your desire to organize with a passion for doing things with as few steps as possible. On your computer, limit the number of folders and subfolders you use — a maximum of five levels of folders is *more* than enough for just about anybody. If you go much beyond that, your organization starts bumping into your productivity (and nobody likes it when that happens, least of all the people who come up with those silly little slogans for the corporate feel-good posters).

Know When to Ask for Help

If you're having trouble with something, swallow your ego and ask for help. There's no shame in saying *I don't know* and then trying to find out. This is *especially* important when you're riding herd on thousands of records in a database. Small missteps are magnified and multiplied, so ask for help *before* the situation becomes dire.

Chapter 27

Ten Sights to See in Your Copious Free Time

. . . .

In This Chapter

▶ Things to look into as your expertise grows

. . . .

*Y*ou won't be a beginner forever. I know it seems that sometimes it seems like you will, but at some point one fateful day, you will look up and realize that Access 95 *makes sense.* Don't worry — you didn't turn the corner into full-bore nerd-dom, you're just comfortable with the program. In fact, it's a good thing.

Now you're ready to look ahead and see what else is out there. Access 95 includes a wide array of powerful capabilities, so there's plenty of room to explore. This chapter gives you ten places to start on your quest, along with resource ideas so you can learn more. Good luck!

Programming for People Who Don't Program

Access 95 has a powerful almost-programming feature called *macros.* You don't need to know a lot of complicated commands or weird-looking functions to use them, but that doesn't mean macros aren't powerful. You can use macros to change a menu, build a toolbar, display dialog boxes, and automate lots of different tasks in Access 95. This is *real* power — and it's within your reach.

To learn more about macros, select Help➪Answer Wizard from the menu. In the Answer Wizard box, type **Tell me about macros** and press Enter. If you want a really good book on the subject, check out *Access Programming For Dummies* from IDG Books Worldwide.

Serious Programming for Techies

Of course, there's a *real* programming language underneath Access 95 as well. It's called *Visual Basic for Applications* and, believe me, it's a real, for-sure programming language, capable of writing real, for-sure applications. If you're already familiar with Visual Basic for Windows, you know how flexible and powerful the language is. This version is specifically oriented toward writing programs that extend the use of Access 95. It's harder than writing a macro, but the rewards are much greater, too. Turn to the Answer Wizard for more about Visual Basic, or check out *Access Programming For Dummies* (it covers *both* macros and the Access 95 version of Visual Basic).

Integrating Access 95 with Other Programs

There are lots of ways to use Access 95 with other Windows applications. Since it's fully OLE2 compliant (that's a fancy way of saying it can easily swap information with other programs), other programs can call Access 95 to do things and vice versa.

A really good example of this is an Access 95 database that works with a World Wide Web page on the Internet. When someone selects a particular item on the Web page, the Web server sends a message to Access requesting information. Access runs a couple queries, then hands the results over to an Access Visual Basic program that writes the answers up as a Web page, complete with all the correct HyperText Markup Language (HTML) tags. Talk about a cool thing!

Although I'm starting to sound like a broken record, the *Access Programming For Dummies* book is a really great place to start getting into stuff like this. If the Internet and the World Wide Web are mysteries, check out *Internet for Dummies* to find out more.

Enlisting the Helpful Lookup Wizard

The Lookup Wizard is another wizard that's just waiting to give you a hand. When you're creating a table, the Lookup Wizard can build a special *lookup field* that pulls data from another Access 95 table. This is a great way to accurately include things like customer numbers or product ID's that are easily mistyped when you're entering things by hand. Using a lookup field ensures that *only* correct data ends up in your table. For more about the Lookup Wizard, consult the Answer Wizard (nothing like getting a wizard referral, is there?).

Advanced Query Wizards Do Esoteric Things

As your databases get more complicated, you need bigger and better wizards to keep things working just right. Two wizards that fill the bill are the Find Duplicates and Archive Wizards.

The Find Duplicates Wizard checks your database for entries that are significantly the same (for instance, the address is identical but the company name is entered differently) and brings them to your attention. The Archive Wizard helps you cull old records from your table, keeping things neat and tidy around your databases.

And where can you learn more? Just ask Mr. Answer Wizard for his thoughts about *query wizards*.

If You Think Forms Are Cool Now, Just Wait Until You See This!

Chapter 21 barely scratches the surface of what forms can do in Access 95. There's so *much* more to know about them that somebody could do an entire book called *The Art of Access Forms*. (Hey — that's a pretty cool idea. I may just do that!)

For instance, forms based on queries provide up-to-the-minute information *every time* you open the form. Combining macros and forms creates powerful data entry, editing, and analysis tools. The possibilities are, as usual, endless.

Check the Answer Wizard for more by asking about *forms* or *forms and macros*.

Go into Desktop Publishing with Access 95 and Word 7

Microsoft thoughtfully built some cool linkage between the new versions of its flagship products — Access and Word. With a mouse click and some Wizard-fiddling, your boring Access 95 table becomes a slick, professional, desktop-published catalog direct from the always fashion-conscious studios of Microsoft Word 7. This is integration that you can *use*, not just imagine.

Check the Answer Wizard Dude for more information about *Word*.

Watch Excel and Access 95 Conspire to Produce Statistics

When your data needs that special touch to produce a complicated statistical analysis, look to the built-in links between Access 95 and Excel 95. Probably the coolest feature of this linkage is the ability to flip an Access 95 table into Excel's Pivot Wizard and look at your data in ways you only dreamed of (and perhaps never dared to hope for). Of course, you need Excel on your computer to do these tricks, but what's a couple hundred bucks compared to the ultimately cool statistics awaiting you?

As you may expect, the Answer Wizard knows all and sees all about using Access and Excel together. Ask about *Excel* and see what he says.

Dancing in the Streets and Shouting "OLE"

I mention the OLE feature earlier, in the section about integrating Access 95 with other Windows 95 programs. But OLE is powerful enough to deserve its own section. Through OLE (or *Object Linking and Embedding)*, you can put an Access 95 database right into a Microsoft Word 7 document or easily add sounds to an Access 95 table. It's *very* flexible — almost mind-bogglingly so.

There's no particular place to just learn about OLE (pronounced "O-Lay" in nerddom), but you can get a reasonable start in *Windows 95 For Dummies* from IDG Books Worldwide.

Mailing Stuff Directly from Access 95

If your company uses Microsoft Mail, you can send someone part of your database *directly* from the Access menu. It's just another example of Microsoft's commitment to leaving you absolutely no choice but to buy their products for everything you do. Instead of worrying about copying, pasting, and generally mucking around with your data, one menu selection and a couple of dialog boxes send a table or form winging on its way through e-mail.

Guess where the info is — yup, that's right. The Answer Wizard, keeper of all knowledge, knows about *mailing database objects.*

Appendix A
Installing Access 95

As great a product as Access 95 is (and it really is a pretty good one), it can't do anything without being installed on your computer. Granted, the box is kinda cute, but it's a little pricey as a decorator item. It looks like installing the software is the only way to recoup your money on the investment. If there were another way out, I'd tell you.

Before installing Access 95, make sure you have everything you need computer-wise. By the way, these are *my* recommendations, not the Official Microsoft Specifications. To make the program work reasonably well, you need

- a 486 (running at 50 MHz or better) or Pentium-based computer
- at least 12MB of RAM, but 16MB or more is a better idea
- Windows 95 (sorry — you can't use Windows 3.1 anymore)
- a floppy disk drive or CD-ROM drive for the installation process

As I write this, the details of how Access 95 will ship are a little fuzzy. According to my sources, it's going to arrive on your choice of CD-ROM or floppy disk, just like the rest of the Office 95 suite. For your sake, I hope you got the CD-ROM, because I figure Access 95 will take something in the vicinity of 30 to 45 diskettes. Even on my most patient days, that's a *lot* of disk swapping.

Enough chitchat — let's install the software so you can get something done today.

1. **If you have the diskettes, find the one marked** Setup **and put it into your disk drive (usually drive A:). If you have the CD-ROM, eject the music disc you're listening to and put the Access 95 disc in there instead.**

   The Moment is at hand. It's kinda like being at the top of the first hill on the roller coaster. The view is great, the prospects are scary, and it's too late to back out now. And to top it all off, you actually *paid* for the privilege of being here.

2. **Click the Start button and then select** <u>R</u>un **from the Start menu.**

   The cute little Run dialog box appears on-screen.

3. **In the Run dialog box, type the disk drive letter, the colon and backslash (:\), and finally the word** setup. **Click OK when you're ready to start the process.**

The command for floppy installations is traditionally A:SETUP. CD-ROM installations are usually D:SETUP.

4. **Access 95 says a few words of welcome. Click Continue to, um, continue.**

Access 95 displays the Name and Organization Information dialog box. It wants to get acquainted. Isn't that neighborly?

5. **Type your name into the Name area and your company into the Organization box. Click OK when you're done, and then click OK again to reassure Access 95 that what you typed is correct.**

This is part of the normal registration process. You aren't signing up for any mailing lists (at least not yet).

6. **The installation program displays your product identification number. Try to look impressed (it's important to humor the software), and then click OK.**

If the Microsoft Product Support folks ever ask you for the number, you can quickly find it by running Access 95 and selecting Help⇨About from the main menu.

7. **The installer takes a brief peek around your hard drive to see what it can find. When it's done, it reports its findings in the dialog box shown in Figure AA-1. Click OK to continue.**

Use the recommended folder names for the installation. Unless there's a *very* good technical reason for choosing something else, leave the folder names alone. This makes future technical support calls *much* easier on both you and the technician helping you.

8. **Figure AA-2 shows the Setup choices dialog box. Click the Typical button for a common installation.**

If you want an *uncommon* installation, use the Custom button. This gives you a wild variety of choices on every niggling little part of Access 95. Don't do this unless you have some very specific needs or are *really* bored.

9. **The installation program takes a few moments to think (while leaving the screen disturbingly blank, I might add), but finally gets around to putting Access 95 on your computer.**

In the name of enhanced entertainment value and shameless propaganda mongering, the screen displays a few advertising billboards during the installation process (see Figure AA-3 for an example).

10. **When the files are all copied, the installer takes one last look around, makes some behind-the-scenes tweaks, and (drumroll please!) announces that Access 95 now resides on your computer (see Figure AA-4).**

Congratulations! Take a celebratory break and then meander back to Chapter 1 for a tour of the software.

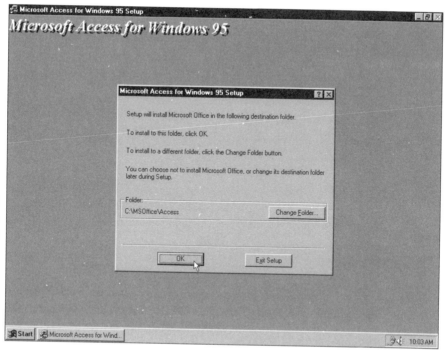

Figure AA-1:
Don't change these settings without a darn good reason!

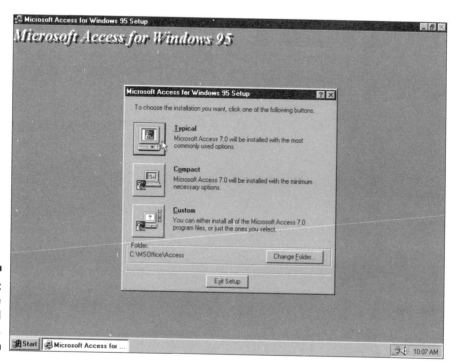

Figure AA-2:
Choose the Typical setup.

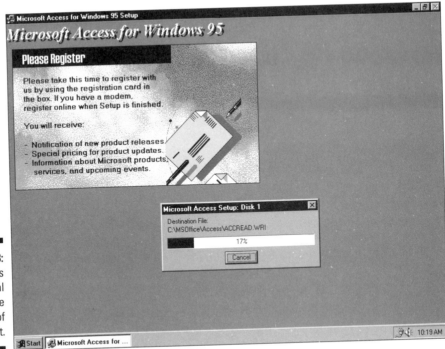

Figure AA-3:
This
commercial
message
courtesy of
Microsoft.

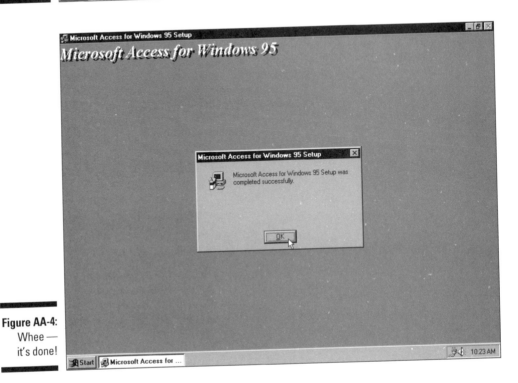

Figure AA-4:
Whee —
it's done!

Appendix B
Problem-Solving Basics

*F*or some reason, the gurus out there think that everybody already knows how to attack problems. Perhaps I missed an early-childhood rite of passage (after all, I *was* sick a lot), but this knowledge missed me. I had to learn it on my own through many trials and *lots* of errors.

That's why I wrote this appendix. It's here to make your life a little easier and problem solving slightly less mysterious. Most of what it says is common sense, something that computers seem to suck out of you the more you work with them.

If you're on the verge of using Access 95 to fix a huge crisis in your business or at home, *stop right now* and read this appendix first. (You can thank me later.)

Pretending There's No Computer on Your Desk

It may sound strange, particularly since this *is* a computer book, but the first step in the march from problem to solution is forgetting all about your computer. Yup, that's right — turn it off, block it out of your mind, and pretend it doesn't exist.

Although computers can be helpful, I believe that they often get in the way of good solutions. You don't need a computer to write notes or discern how a process works. People did all kinds of work like that without personal computers way back in the 1970s, perhaps even earlier than that (although the records are unclear and subject to scholarly interpretation).

As you're brainstorming through the rest of this appendix, I suggest tracking your ideas on a pad of old-fashioned paper with your choice of writing instrument (I'm a fountain pen man, myself). If you do your best thinking with a word processor instead of paper and pencil, you have my permission to use your computer (but keep some paper handy, just in case).

Wining, Dining, and Generally Getting Intimate with the Problem

You're ready to really dig into the problem and figure out how it works. This is an absolutely vital step, but it's one that people sometimes overlook. Instead of looking for a problem, they go merrily off looking for a solution. Luckily, that's not going to happen to you.

Start your analysis by writing down a simple line describing the problem. Keep it short and to the point — a single sentence is all you need. Now that you've captured the problem on paper, loosen up your mind and jot down all the details you can think of. Look beyond the obvious things; peer into the murky depths of the problem itself.

Try some of these questions to get the process going:

- Why is this a problem?
- How long has the problem been going on?
- Has it ever *not* been a problem? What changed since then?
- What information do you need to solve the problem?
- Do you have the needed information available? Is it there, but in the wrong format?
- Who else in your company might be facing the same problem? How did they solve it?

Whatever you do, *don't* ask yourself "What's the best way to solve this problem?" That question comes later. For now, just focus on the problem and let the solution wait.

If the problem is really big, break it down into bite-size pieces. You don't have to solve the whole thing at once, you just need to fix the part that's particularly troublesome. You may discover that what you saw as the problem is actually a *symptom* of the real problem. If that happens, start over with a new problem statement and go from there.

All of this thinking, questioning, and writing isn't mere "busy" work. You can't come up with a good solution unless you know all about the problem.

Actually Solving the Dilemma

Thanks to careful analysis, you uncovered the heart of the problem. Now you merely need to discern a cunning solution, implement it, and you're done. Simple, right? Oh yeah, right...

Actually, this stage isn't as tough as you might think. The hard work (dissecting the problem) is behind you. Compared to that, coming up with the solution is easy. All you really need to do is look at your notes about the problem, decide what information you need to solve it, and come up with a way to store, edit, and generally play with the information.

Want to know the best part of all? You don't have to make a really big, amazing-looking solution. Truly *great* solutions are just big enough to fix the problem. If your problem only requires a pencil-and-notecard solution, then that's all you should create. It's easy to conceive a huge solution for a small problem, but that's not your goal. Don't get carried away with a massive, multi-part system that solves your problem, promises peace to the world, and makes a mean cup of coffee. Instead, focus on the problem you're solving *here and now*. When you're an advanced problem solver, you can try killing two problems at once, but for now, go for one problem and one solution.

Don't get hung up over using Access 95 as part of the solution, either. Business functioned for thousands of years before computers arrived and will arguably survive despite them, too.

Paper forms are often a very good solution to information-oriented problems like mailing lists, inventory systems, or Epicurean cuisine assembly instructions (commonly known as *recipes*). They're easy to create and simple to change — two things that *aren't* usually true of computer-based solutions. It's easy to move from a paper form to Access 95, too, which makes paper a particularly great way to test a new solution. If it doesn't work as a paper form, it probably won't work as a computer form either.

Planning for the Inevitable (Failure)

Have you thought about (insert dramatic pause here) *the future?* Not your future — I'm thinking of your *solution's* future here. What if something catastrophic should happen like a hard disk crash or fire in the building? Even though you may feel uncomfortable talking about disasters and crises, it's far better to be prepared than to wait until (another dramatic pause) *the inevitable* occurs.

When you're solving a problem, think about what you can do when things go wrong. Whether you use paper forms or Access 95, you need a fall-back plan to keep things running smoothly. Don't wait until you *have* the crisis to plan for it.

Here are a few general things to worry about:

- ✔ Does anyone but you *really* understand how everything works?
- ✔ Who takes care of things when you're sick or on vacation?
- ✔ If you suddenly evaporate into thin air, will someone else be able to keep the solution going?

If the solution uses a computer, you also need to wonder about these tidbits:

- ✔ What happens when (not "if") the computer goes down?
- ✔ How important is the information to your business?
- ✔ How long could business go on without the solution in place?
- ✔ What about backups? Do you have any? How recent are they?

I'm not trying to make you paranoid; I just want you to be prepared. It's the Eagle Scout in me.

Organizing, Saving, and Really Saving Your Stuff

Organization is the key to unlocking many problem-solving strategies — especially when you're using a computer. If your disk drive looks like my office, there's trouble brewing. At first, you might misplace an occasional file or spend an extra minute looking for that memo you wrote yesterday. But the more you use the computer, the worse your problem gets. Your files are piled here and there around the disk, and you can't find anything without launching a major expedition — complete with native guides and a couple of elephants.

Before randomly tossing databases here and there around your computer, pause for a moment and get organized. The more comfortable you become with Access 95, the more you'll use it. If you start out with a flexible way to organize your stuff, you won't end up with a digital disaster area on your hands (or, more precisely, on your disk).

Here's the secret: think about what you do with the computer and organize your storage space accordingly. Here are some ideas to get you started:

✔ Use directories to keep your disk neat and tidy. Don't pile all of your files in one directory. Eww — what a mess. That would be like putting all your files in one file folder. Yes, they're there. Yes, you can find them. But where? And when? Look at the section about directories a little later in this appendix for more information.

✔ Organize your data the way your organize your work. Lots of people organize files by type, grouping word processing files with their ilk and so on. But if your work is project-oriented, why not create a directory for each project and store *all* of the project files there?

✔ Keep the things you need most often close at hand. With Windows 95, it's easy to create *shortcuts* for quick access to even the most distant files. You can even make a shortcut that points to a table *inside* an Access 95 database. Just open the database, right-click on the table in the database window, then select Create Shortcut from the pop-up menu. The shortcut automatically lives on your Windows 95 desktop.

✔ If all else fails, make a Safe Place for your stuff. The department secretary at my first job taught me this trick. I have a directory called Safe Place for all of the miscellaneous things that don't seem to fit anywhere else. I know it sounds hokey, but it worked for her and still does for me.

If you're getting dizzy thinking about all this directory and shortcut stuff, pick up a copy of *Windows 95 For Dummies* (IDG Books Worldwide) by Andy Rathbone.

Finding a Home for Your Stuff

Databases have to live somewhere — it's the way of such things. They prefer to make their homes on fancy, spacious hard disks, but there *are* some other places for them to roost as well, such as removable disk drives, floppies, and even optical disks. Directories keep disks organized, which is no small task given the size of today's disk drives.

Start with a disk

Disks come in a variety of shapes and sizes. Your computer probably has at least one floppy disk drive, plus a large-capacity hard disk. You might also have a cool removable disk drive, like the ones from Iomega and Syquest. If you're in an office (or a technologically advanced home), you probably also have access to the hulking disk drives on a network server. Geez — you're awash in storage options.

I have a lot of opinions about disk drives, but in the interest of keeping you awake, I'll only throw in a few of them here:

- Don't *ever* keep the master copy of a database on a floppy disk. Never!

- If something dreadful happens and you can only use a floppy disk for storage, make at least two copies of your database. Don't trust a floppy disk — they'll turn on you at a moment's notice.

- It's fine to put stuff on your local hard disk. After all, that *is* why you have one in there. Just make sure you back up your computer regularly. Please?

- Those of you on a network, I salute you — and suggest that you keep all those database files out on the server. Your company computer guys make sure that everything on the network server is regularly backed up for security. Let them do the backups so you don't need to worry about it.

- If the information in your databases is particularly sensitive, be careful what you say around it (you don't want to offend your files). When security is a concern, consider using a removable disk drive. My personal favorite is the Iomega Zip drive, which holds 100 MB of files on a disk that's just a little larger than a normal 3.5-inch floppy. This is cool technology that you can *use*.

Add some directories

In the beginning, there was a disk. It was empty, but nicely formatted. Then came the software — lots of software. The software begat data files, which multiplied and filled the disk to capacity. And you looked upon the disk and said, "Yeech — what a mess."

Directories are the cornerstone of organized computer storage. They can *also* be a real pain in the neck if you get carried away with them. To find a balance between digital junk piles and subdirectories for every occasion, consider the following tips:

✔ Use enough directories, but not too many. It's easy to get over-organized, particularly on a computer. My rule of thumb is to limit subdirectories to a maximum of *four* levels. That's a directory inside a directory inside a directory inside a directory. (Whew — aren't you glad my limit's four?)

✔ Now that Windows *finally* supports long file and directory names, use names that make sense. There's no excuse for a disk full of directories with names like `C:\MKSNOSNS`. Why make your life more complicated?

✔ To create a directory (or *folder)*, use the Windows Explorer to open a window for your disk drive. Right-click anywhere on the right side of the window (the side with all the files and file folders). On the pop-up menu, select New⇨Folder. A new directory appears, ready to be named. Type a good name, then press Enter to tell Windows you're done. Congrats — your new storage space is ready!

Knowing When to Say "When"

This may sound odd, but you need to watch for the time when your solution is finished and ready to implement. It's possible to get so caught up in solving little side problems or adding *just one more* cool feature that your system never quite gets done; the original problem never quite gets solved.

Figuring out when to send your system into the cold, cruel world can be tough. Remember that old adage about swamps and alligators? (If you don't, that's okay; you probably have more hair than I do.) Keep your eyes on the goal — solving the problem. Don't get sidetracked by the other cool stuff you can do.

And don't worry about getting every little detail right the first time. Put the solution out there and see if it sinks or paddles around the pool. There are *always* things that you can do better. It's more productive to design the solution as best you can and tweak it as experience points out the shortcomings.

Index

• G •

• H •

Notes

Notes

The Fun & Easy Way™ to learn about computers and more!

Windows® 3.11 For Dummies,® 3rd Edition
by Andy Rathbone

ISBN: 1-56884-370-4
$16.95 USA/
$22.95 Canada

Mutual Funds For Dummies™
by Eric Tyson

ISBN: 1-56884-226-0
$16.99 USA/
$22.99 Canada

DOS For Dummies,® 2nd Edition
by Dan Gookin

ISBN: 1-878058-75-4
$16.95 USA/
$22.95 Canada

The Internet For Dummies,® 2nd Edition
by John Levine & Carol Baroudi

ISBN: 1-56884-222-8
$19.99 USA/
$26.99 Canada

Personal Finance For Dummies™
by Eric Tyson

ISBN: 1-56884-150-7
$16.95 USA/
$22.95 Canada

PCs For Dummies,® 3rd Edition
by Dan Gookin & Andy Rathbone

ISBN: 1-56884-904-4
$16.99 USA/
$22.99 Canada

Macs® For Dummies,® 3rd Edition
by David Pogue

ISBN: 1-56884-239-2
$19.99 USA/
$26.99 Canada

The SAT® I For Dummies™
by Suzee Vlk

ISBN: 1-56884-213-9
$14.99 USA/
$20.99 Canada

Here's a complete listing of IDG Books' ...For Dummies® titles

Title	Author	ISBN	Price
DATABASE			
Access 2 For Dummies®	by Scott Palmer	ISBN: 1-56884-090-X	$19.95 USA/$26.95 Canada
Access Programming For Dummies®	by Rob Krumm	ISBN: 1-56884-091-8	$19.95 USA/$26.95 Canada
Approach 3 For Windows® For Dummies®	by Doug Lowe	ISBN: 1-56884-233-3	$19.99 USA/$26.99 Canada
dBASE For DOS For Dummies®	by Scott Palmer & Michael Stabler	ISBN: 1-56884-188-4	$19.95 USA/$26.95 Canada
dBASE For Windows® For Dummies®	by Scott Palmer	ISBN: 1-56884-179-5	$19.95 USA/$26.95 Canada
dBASE 5 For Windows® Programming For Dummies®	by Ted Coombs & Jason Coombs	ISBN: 1-56884-215-5	$19.99 USA/$26.99 Canada
FoxPro 2.6 For Windows® For Dummies®	by John Kaufeld	ISBN: 1-56884-187-6	$19.95 USA/$26.95 Canada
Paradox 5 For Windows® For Dummies®	by John Kaufeld	ISBN: 1-56884-185-X	$19.95 USA/$26.95 Canada
DESKTOP PUBLISHING/ILLUSTRATION/GRAPHICS			
CorelDRAW! 5 For Dummies®	by Deke McClelland	ISBN: 1-56884-157-4	$19.95 USA/$26.95 Canada
CorelDRAW! For Dummies®	by Deke McClelland	ISBN: 1-56884-042-X	$19.95 USA/$26.95 Canada
Desktop Publishing & Design For Dummies®	by Roger C. Parker	ISBN: 1-56884-234-1	$19.99 USA/$26.99 Canada
Harvard Graphics 2 For Windows® For Dummies®	by Roger C. Parker	ISBN: 1-56884-092-6	$19.95 USA/$26.95 Canada
PageMaker 5 For Macs® For Dummies®	by Galen Gruman & Deke McClelland	ISBN: 1-56884-178-7	$19.95 USA/$26.95 Canada
PageMaker 5 For Windows® For Dummies®	by Deke McClelland & Galen Gruman	ISBN: 1-56884-160-4	$19.95 USA/$26.95 Canada
Photoshop 3 For Macs® For Dummies®	by Deke McClelland	ISBN: 1-56884-208-2	$19.99 USA/$26.99 Canada
QuarkXPress 3.3 For Dummies®	by Galen Gruman & Barbara Assadi	ISBN: 1-56884-217-1	$19.99 USA/$26.99 Canada
FINANCE/PERSONAL FINANCE/TEST TAKING REFERENCE			
Everyday Math For Dummies™	by Charles Seiter	ISBN: 1-56884-248-1	$14.99 USA/$22.99 Canada
Personal Finance For Dummies™ For Canadians	by Eric Tyson & Tony Martin	ISBN: 1-56884-378-X	$18.99 USA/$24.99 Canada
QuickBooks 3 For Dummies®	by Stephen L. Nelson	ISBN: 1-56884-227-9	$19.99 USA/$26.99 Canada
Quicken 8 For DOS For Dummies,® 2nd Edition	by Stephen L. Nelson	ISBN: 1-56884-210-4	$19.95 USA/$26.95 Canada
Quicken 5 For Macs® For Dummies®	by Stephen L. Nelson	ISBN: 1-56884-211-2	$19.95 USA/$26.95 Canada
Quicken 4 For Windows® For Dummies,® 2nd Edition	by Stephen L. Nelson	ISBN: 1-56884-209-0	$19.95 USA/$26.95 Canada
Taxes For Dummies,™ 1995 Edition	by Eric Tyson & David J. Silverman	ISBN: 1-56884-220-1	$14.99 USA/$20.99 Canada
The GMAT® For Dummies™	by Suzee Vlk, Series Editor	ISBN: 1-56884-376-3	$14.99 USA/$20.99 Canada
The GRE® For Dummies™	by Suzee Vlk, Series Editor	ISBN: 1-56884-375-5	$14.99 USA/$20.99 Canada
Time Management For Dummies™	by Jeffrey J. Mayer	ISBN: 1-56884-360-7	$16.99 USA/$22.99 Canada
TurboTax For Windows® For Dummies®	by Gail A. Helsel, CPA	ISBN: 1-56884-228-7	$19.99 USA/$26.99 Canada
GROUPWARE/INTEGRATED			
ClarisWorks For Macs® For Dummies®	by Frank Higgins	ISBN: 1-56884-363-1	$19.99 USA/$26.99 Canada
Lotus Notes For Dummies®	by Pat Freeland & Stephen Londergan	ISBN: 1-56884-212-0	$19.95 USA/$26.95 Canada
Microsoft® Office 4 For Windows® For Dummies®	by Roger C. Parker	ISBN: 1-56884-183-3	$19.95 USA/$26.95 Canada
Microsoft® Works 3 For Windows® For Dummies®	by David C. Kay	ISBN: 1-56884-214-7	$19.99 USA/$26.99 Canada
SmartSuite 3 For Dummies®	by Jan Weingarten & John Weingarten	ISBN: 1-56884-367-4	$19.99 USA/$26.99 Canada
INTERNET/COMMUNICATIONS/NETWORKING			
America Online® For Dummies,® 2nd Edition	by John Kaufeld	ISBN: 1-56884-933-8	$19.99 USA/$26.99 Canada
CompuServe For Dummies,® 2nd Edition	by Wallace Wang	ISBN: 1-56884-937-0	$19.99 USA/$26.99 Canada
Modems For Dummies,® 2nd Edition	by Tina Rathbone	ISBN: 1-56884-223-6	$19.99 USA/$26.99 Canada
MORE Internet For Dummies®	by John R. Levine & Margaret Levine Young	ISBN: 1-56884-164-7	$19.95 USA/$26.95 Canada
MORE Modems & On-line Services For Dummies®	by Tina Rathbone	ISBN: 1-56884-365-8	$19.99 USA/$26.99 Canada
Mosaic For Dummies,® Windows Edition	by David Angell & Brent Heslop	ISBN: 1-56884-242-2	$19.99 USA/$26.99 Canada
NetWare For Dummies,® 2nd Edition	by Ed Tittel, Deni Connor & Earl Follis	ISBN: 1-56884-369-0	$19.99 USA/$26.99 Canada
Networking For Dummies®	by Doug Lowe	ISBN: 1-56884-079-9	$19.95 USA/$26.95 Canada
PROCOMM PLUS 2 For Windows® For Dummies®	by Wallace Wang	ISBN: 1-56884-219-8	$19.99 USA/$26.99 Canada
TCP/IP For Dummies®	by Marshall Wilensky & Candace Leiden	ISBN: 1-56884-241-4	$19.99 USA/$26.99 Canada

Scholastic requests & educational orders please Educational Sales at 1. 800. 434. 2086

FOR MORE INFO OR TO ORDER, PLEASE CALL ▶ 800. 762. 2974

For volume discounts & special orders please call Tony Real, Special Sales, at 415. 655. 3048

The Internet For Macs® For Dummies,® 2nd Edition	by Charles Seiter	ISBN: 1-56884-371-2	$19.99 USA/$26.99 Canada
The Internet For Macs® For Dummies® Starter Kit	by Charles Seiter	ISBN: 1-56884-244-9	$29.99 USA/$39.99 Canada
The Internet For Macs® For Dummies® Starter Kit Bestseller Edition	by Charles Seiter	ISBN: 1-56884-245-7	$39.99 USA/$54.99 Canada
The Internet For Windows® For Dummies® Starter Kit	by John R. Levine & Margaret Levine Young	ISBN: 1-56884-237-6	$34.99 USA/$44.99 Canada
The Internet For Windows® For Dummies® Starter Kit, Bestseller Edition	by John R. Levine & Margaret Levine Young	ISBN: 1-56884-246-5	$39.99 USA/$54.99 Canada

MACINTOSH

Mac® Programming For Dummies®	by Dan Parks Sydow	ISBN: 1-56884-173-6	$19.95 USA/$26.95 Canada
Macintosh® System 7.5 For Dummies®	by Bob LeVitus	ISBN: 1-56884-197-3	$19.95 USA/$26.95 Canada
MORE Macs® For Dummies®	by David Pogue	ISBN: 1-56884-087-X	$19.95 USA/$26.95 Canada
PageMaker 5 For Macs® For Dummies®	by Galen Gruman & Deke McClelland	ISBN: 1-56884-178-7	$19.95 USA/$26.95 Canada
QuarkXPress 3.3 For Dummies®	by Galen Gruman & Barbara Assadi	ISBN: 1-56884-217-1	$19.99 USA/$26.99 Canada
Upgrading and Fixing Macs® For Dummies®	by Kearney Rietmann & Frank Higgins	ISBN: 1-56884-189-2	$19.95 USA/$26.95 Canada

MULTIMEDIA

Multimedia & CD-ROMs For Dummies,® 2nd Edition	by Andy Rathbone	ISBN: 1-56884-907-9	$19.99 USA/$26.99 Canada
Multimedia & CD-ROMs For Dummies,® Interactive Multimedia Value Pack, 2nd Edition	by Andy Rathbone	ISBN: 1-56884-909-5	$29.99 USA/$39.99 Canada

OPERATING SYSTEMS:

DOS

MORE DOS For Dummies®	by Dan Gookin	ISBN: 1-56884-046-2	$19.95 USA/$26.95 Canada
OS/2® Warp For Dummies,® 2nd Edition	by Andy Rathbone	ISBN: 1-56884-205-8	$19.99 USA/$26.99 Canada

UNIX

MORE UNIX® For Dummies®	by John R. Levine & Margaret Levine Young	ISBN: 1-56884-361-5	$19.99 USA/$26.99 Canada
UNIX® For Dummies®	by John R. Levine & Margaret Levine Young	ISBN: 1-878058-58-4	$19.95 USA/$26.95 Canada

WINDOWS

MORE Windows® For Dummies,® 2nd Edition	by Andy Rathbone	ISBN: 1-56884-048-9	$19.95 USA/$26.95 Canada
Windows® 95 For Dummies®	by Andy Rathbone	ISBN: 1-56884-240-6	$19.99 USA/$26.99 Canada

PCS/HARDWARE

Illustrated Computer Dictionary For Dummies,® 2nd Edition	by Dan Gookin & Wallace Wang	ISBN: 1-56884-218-X	$12.95 USA/$16.95 Canada
Upgrading and Fixing PCs For Dummies,® 2nd Edition	by Andy Rathbone	ISBN: 1-56884-903-6	$19.99 USA/$26.99 Canada

PRESENTATION/AUTOCAD

AutoCAD For Dummies®	by Bud Smith	ISBN: 1-56884-191-4	$19.95 USA/$26.95 Canada
PowerPoint 4 For Windows® For Dummies®	by Doug Lowe	ISBN: 1-56884-161-2	$16.99 USA/$22.99 Canada

PROGRAMMING

Borland C++ For Dummies®	by Michael Hyman	ISBN: 1-56884-162-0	$19.95 USA/$26.95 Canada
C For Dummies,® Volume 1	by Dan Gookin	ISBN: 1-878058-78-9	$19.95 USA/$26.95 Canada
C++ For Dummies®	by Stephen R. Davis	ISBN: 1-56884-163-9	$19.95 USA/$26.95 Canada
Delphi Programming For Dummies®	by Neil Rubenking	ISBN: 1-56884-200-7	$19.99 USA/$26.99 Canada
Mac® Programming For Dummies®	by Dan Parks Sydow	ISBN: 1-56884-173-6	$19.95 USA/$26.95 Canada
PowerBuilder 4 Programming For Dummies®	by Ted Coombs & Jason Coombs	ISBN: 1-56884-325-9	$19.99 USA/$26.99 Canada
QBasic Programming For Dummies®	by Douglas Hergert	ISBN: 1-56884-093-4	$19.95 USA/$26.95 Canada
Visual Basic 3 For Dummies®	by Wallace Wang	ISBN: 1-56884-076-4	$19.95 USA/$26.95 Canada
Visual Basic "X" For Dummies®	by Wallace Wang	ISBN: 1-56884-230-9	$19.99 USA/$26.99 Canada
Visual C++ 2 For Dummies®	by Michael Hyman & Bob Arnson	ISBN: 1-56884-328-3	$19.99 USA/$26.99 Canada
Windows® 95 Programming For Dummies®	by S. Randy Davis	ISBN: 1-56884-327-5	$19.99 USA/$26.99 Canada

SPREADSHEET

1-2-3 For Dummies®	by Greg Harvey	ISBN: 1-878058-60-6	$16.95 USA/$22.95 Canada
1-2-3 For Windows® 5 For Dummies,® 2nd Edition	by John Walkenbach	ISBN: 1-56884-216-3	$16.95 USA/$22.95 Canada
Excel 5 For Macs® For Dummies®	by Greg Harvey	ISBN: 1-56884-186-8	$19.95 USA/$26.95 Canada
Excel For Dummies,® 2nd Edition	by Greg Harvey	ISBN: 1-56884-050-0	$16.95 USA/$22.95 Canada
MORE 1-2-3 For DOS For Dummies®	by John Weingarten	ISBN: 1-56884-224-4	$19.99 USA/$26.99 Canada
MORE Excel 5 For Windows® For Dummies®	by Greg Harvey	ISBN: 1-56884-207-4	$19.95 USA/$26.95 Canada
Quattro Pro 6 For Windows® For Dummies®	by John Walkenbach	ISBN: 1-56884-174-4	$19.95 USA/$26.95 Canada
Quattro Pro For DOS For Dummies®	by John Walkenbach	ISBN: 1-56884-023-3	$16.95 USA/$22.95 Canada

UTILITIES

Norton Utilities 8 For Dummies®	by Beth Slick	ISBN: 1-56884-166-3	$19.95 USA/$26.95 Canada

VCRS/CAMCORDERS

VCRs & Camcorders For Dummies™	by Gordon McComb & Andy Rathbone	ISBN: 1-56884-229-5	$14.99 USA/$20.99 Canada

WORD PROCESSING

Ami Pro For Dummies®	by Jim Meade	ISBN: 1-56884-049-7	$19.95 USA/$26.95 Canada
MORE Word For Windows® 6 For Dummies®	by Doug Lowe	ISBN: 1-56884-165-5	$19.95 USA/$26.95 Canada
MORE WordPerfect® 6 For Windows® For Dummies®	by Margaret Levine Young & David C. Kay	ISBN: 1-56884-206-6	$19.95 USA/$26.95 Canada
MORE WordPerfect® 6 For DOS For Dummies®	by Wallace Wang, edited by Dan Gookin	ISBN: 1-56884-047-0	$19.95 USA/$26.95 Canada
Word 6 For Macs® For Dummies®	by Dan Gookin	ISBN: 1-56884-190-6	$19.95 USA/$26.95 Canada
Word For Windows® 6 For Dummies®	by Dan Gookin	ISBN: 1-56884-075-6	$16.95 USA/$22.95 Canada
Word For Windows® For Dummies®	by Dan Gookin & Ray Werner	ISBN: 1-878058-86-X	$16.95 USA/$22.95 Canada
WordPerfect® 6 For DOS For Dummies®	by Dan Gookin	ISBN: 1-878058-77-0	$16.95 USA/$22.95 Canada
WordPerfect® 6.1 For Windows® For Dummies,® 2nd Edition	by Margaret Levine Young & David Kay	ISBN: 1-56884-243-0	$16.95 USA/$22.95 Canada
WordPerfect® For Dummies®	by Dan Gookin	ISBN: 1-878058-52-5	$16.95 USA/$22.95 Canada

For scholastic requests & educational orders please call Educational Sales at 1. 800. 434. 2086

FOR MORE INFO OR TO ORDER, PLEASE CALL ▶ 800. 762. 2974

For volume discounts & special orders please Tony Real, Special Sales, at 415. 655. 3048

Fun, Fast, & Cheap!™

NEW!

The Internet For Macs® For Dummies® Quick Reference
by Charles Seiter

ISBN:1-56884-967-2
$9.99 USA/$12.99 Canada

NEW!

Windows® 95 For Dummies® Quick Reference
by Greg Harvey

ISBN: 1-56884-964-8
$9.99 USA/$12.99 Canada

SUPER STAR

Photoshop 3 For Macs® For Dummies® Quick Reference
by Deke McClelland

ISBN: 1-56884-968-0
$9.99 USA/$12.99 Canada

SUPER STAR

WordPerfect® For DOS For Dummies® Quick Reference
by Greg Harvey

ISBN: 1-56884-009-8
$8.95 USA/$12.95 Canada

Title	Author	ISBN	Price
DATABASE			
Access 2 For Dummies® Quick Reference	by Stuart J. Stuple	ISBN: 1-56884-167-1	$8.95 USA/$11.95 Canada
dBASE 5 For DOS For Dummies® Quick Reference	by Barrie Sosinsky	ISBN: 1-56884-954-0	$9.99 USA/$12.99 Canada
dBASE 5 For Windows® For Dummies® Quick Reference	by Stuart J. Stuple	ISBN: 1-56884-953-2	$9.99 USA/$12.99 Canada
Paradox 5 For Windows® For Dummies® Quick Reference	by Scott Palmer	ISBN: 1-56884-960-5	$9.99 USA/$12.99 Canada
DESKTOP PUBLISHING/ILLUSTRATION/GRAPHICS			
CorelDRAW! 5 For Dummies® Quick Reference	by Raymond E. Werner	ISBN: 1-56884-952-4	$9.99 USA/$12.99 Canada
Harvard Graphics For Windows® For Dummies® Quick Reference	by Raymond E. Werner	ISBN: 1-56884-962-1	$9.99 USA/$12.99 Canada
Photoshop 3 For Macs® For Dummies® Quick Reference	by Deke McClelland	ISBN: 1-56884-968-0	$9.99 USA/$12.99 Canada
FINANCE/PERSONAL FINANCE			
Quicken 4 For Windows® For Dummies® Quick Reference	by Stephen L. Nelson	ISBN: 1-56884-950-8	$9.95 USA/$12.95 Canada
GROUPWARE/INTEGRATED			
Microsoft® Office 4 For Windows® For Dummies® Quick Reference	by Doug Lowe	ISBN: 1-56884-958-3	$9.99 USA/$12.99 Canada
Microsoft® Works 3 For Windows® For Dummies® Quick Reference	by Michael Partington	ISBN: 1-56884-959-1	$9.99 USA/$12.99 Canada
INTERNET/COMMUNICATIONS/NETWORKING			
The Internet For Dummies® Quick Reference	by John R. Levine & Margaret Levine Young	ISBN: 1-56884-168-X	$8.95 USA/$11.95 Canada
MACINTOSH			
Macintosh® System 7.5 For Dummies® Quick Reference	by Stuart J. Stuple	ISBN: 1-56884-956-7	$9.99 USA/$12.99 Canada
OPERATING SYSTEMS:			
DOS			
DOS For Dummies® Quick Reference	by Greg Harvey	ISBN: 1-56884-007-1	$8.95 USA/$11.95 Canada
UNIX			
UNIX® For Dummies® Quick Reference	by John R. Levine & Margaret Levine Young	ISBN: 1-56884-094-2	$8.95 USA/$11.95 Canada
WINDOWS			
Windows® 3.1 For Dummies® Quick Reference, 2nd Edition	by Greg Harvey	ISBN: 1-56884-951-6	$8.95 USA/$11.95 Canada
PCs/HARDWARE			
Memory Management For Dummies® Quick Reference	by Doug Lowe	ISBN: 1-56884-362-3	$9.99 USA/$12.99 Canada
PRESENTATION/AUTOCAD			
AutoCAD For Dummies® Quick Reference	by Ellen Finkelstein	ISBN: 1-56884-198-1	$9.95 USA/$12.95 Canada
SPREADSHEET			
1-2-3 For Dummies® Quick Reference	by John Walkenbach	ISBN: 1-56884-027-6	$8.95 USA/$11.95 Canada
1-2-3 For Windows® 5 For Dummies® Quick Reference	by John Walkenbach	ISBN: 1-56884-957-5	$9.95 USA/$12.95 Canada
Excel For Windows® For Dummies® Quick Reference, 2nd Edition	by John Walkenbach	ISBN: 1-56884-096-9	$8.95 USA/$11.95 Canada
Quattro Pro 6 For Windows® For Dummies® Quick Reference	by Stuart J. Stuple	ISBN: 1-56884-172-8	$9.95 USA/$12.95 Canada
WORD PROCESSING			
Word For Windows® 6 For Dummies® Quick Reference	by George Lynch	ISBN: 1-56884-095-0	$8.95 USA/$11.95 Canada
Word For Windows® For Dummies® Quick Reference	by George Lynch	ISBN: 1-56884-029-2	$8.95 USA/$11.95 Canada
WordPerfect® 6.1 For Windows® For Dummies® Quick Reference, 2nd Edition	by Greg Harvey	ISBN: 1-56884-966-4	$9.99 USA/$12.99/Canada

Macworld® Mac® & Power Mac SECRETS,™ 2nd Edition

by David Pogue & Joseph Schorr

HOT!

This is the definitive Mac reference for those who want to become power users! Includes three disks with 9MB of software!

ISBN: 1-56884-175-2
$39.95 USA/$54.95 Canada

Includes 3 disks chock full of software.

WINNERS 1994-95
TECHNICAL PUBLICATIONS AND ART COMPETITIONS OF THE SOCIETY FOR TECHNICAL COMMUNICATION

NEWBRIDGE BOOK CLUB SELECTION

Macworld® Mac® FAQs™

by David Pogue

HOT!

Written by the hottest Macintosh author around, David Pogue, *Macworld Mac FAQs* gives users the ultimate Mac reference. Hundreds of Mac questions and answers side-by-side, right at your fingertips, and organized into six easy-to-reference sections with lots of sidebars and diagrams.

ISBN: 1-56884-480-8
$19.99 USA/$26.99 Canada

Macworld® System 7.5 Bible, 3rd Edition

by Lon Poole

ISBN: 1-56884-098-5
$29.95 USA/$39.95 Canada

NATIONAL BESTSELLER!

Macworld® ClarisWorks 3.0 Companion, 3rd Edition

by Steven A. Schwartz

ISBN: 1-56884-481-6
$24.99 USA/$34.99 Canada

NATIONAL BESTSELLER!

Macworld® Complete Mac® Handbook Plus Interactive CD, 3rd Edition

by Jim Heid

BMUG SPRING 1995 CHOICE PRODUCT

ISBN: 1-56884-192-2
$39.95 USA/$54.95 Canada

Includes an interactive CD-ROM.

NEWBRIDGE BOOK CLUB SELECTION

Macworld® Ultimate Mac® CD-ROM

by Jim Heid

ISBN: 1-56884-477-8
$19.99 USA/$26.99 Canada

CD-ROM includes version 2.0 of QuickTime, and over 65 MB of the best shareware, freeware, fonts, sounds, and more!

Macworld® Networking Bible, 2nd Edition

by Dave Kosiur & Joel M. Snyder

ISBN: 1-56884-194-9
$29.95 USA/$39.95 Canada

XI WINNER

Macworld® Photoshop 3 Bible, 2nd Edition

by Deke McClelland

ISBN: 1-56884-158-2
$39.95 USA/$54.95 Canada

Includes stunning CD-ROM with add-ons, digitized photos and more.

WINNERS 1994-95
TECHNICAL PUBLICATIONS AND ART COMPETITIONS OF THE SOCIETY FOR TECHNICAL COMMUNICATION

NEW!

Macworld® Photoshop 2.5 Bible

by Deke McClelland

ISBN: 1-56884-022-5
$29.95 USA/$39.95 Canada

NATIONAL BESTSELLER!

Macworld® FreeHand 4 Bible

by Deke McClelland

ISBN: 1-56884-170-1
$29.95 USA/$39.95 Canada

Macworld® Illustrator 5.0/5.5 Bible

by Ted Alspach

ISBN: 1-56884-097-7
$39.95 USA/$54.95 Canada

Includes CD-ROM with QuickTime tutorials.

Unauthorized Windows® 95: A Developer's Guide to Exploring the Foundations of Windows "Chicago"
by Andrew Schulman

ISBN: 1-56884-169-8
$29.99 USA/$39.99 Canada

Unauthorized Windows® 95 Developer's Resource Kit
by Andrew Schulman

ISBN: 1-56884-305-4
$39.99 USA/$54.99 Canada

Best of the Net
by Seth Godin

ISBN: 1-56884-313-5
$22.99 USA/$32.99 Canada

Detour: The Truth About the Information Superhighway
by Michael Sullivan-Trainor

ISBN: 1-56884-307-0
$22.99 USA/$32.99 Canada

PowerPC Programming For Intel Programmers
by Kip McClanahan

ISBN: 1-56884-306-2
$49.99 USA/$64.99 Canada

Foundations™ of Visual C++ Programming For Windows® 95
by Paul Yao & Joseph Yao

ISBN: 1-56884-321-6
$39.99 USA/$54.99 Canada

Heavy Metal™ Visual C++ Programming
by Steve Holzner

ISBN: 1-56884-196-5
$39.95 USA/$54.95 Canada

Heavy Metal™ OLE 2.0 Programming
by Steve Holzner

ISBN: 1-56884-301-1
$39.95 USA/$54.95 Canada

Lotus Notes Application Development Handbook
by Erica Kerwien

ISBN: 1-56884-308-9
$39.99 USA/$54.99 Canada

The Internet Direct Connect Kit
by Peter John Harrison

ISBN: 1-56884-135-3
$29.95 USA/$39.95 Canada

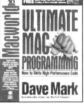

Macworld® Ultimate Mac® Programming
by Dave Mark

ISBN: 1-56884-195-7
$39.95 USA/$54.95 Canada

The UNIX®-Haters Handbook
by Simson Garfinkel, Daniel Weise, & Steven Strassmann

ISBN: 1-56884-203-1
$16.95 USA/$22.95 Canada

Learn C++ Today!
by Martin Rinehart

ISBN: 1-56884-310-0
34.99 USA/$44.99 Canada

Type & Learn™ C
by Tom Swan

ISBN: 1-56884-073-X
34.95 USA/$44.95 Canada

Type & Learn™ Windows® Programming
by Tom Swan

ISBN: 1-56884-071-3
34.95 USA/$44.95 Canada

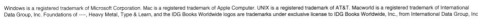

For scholastic requests & educational orders please call Educational Sales, at 1. 800. 434. 2086

FOR MORE INFO OR TO ORDER, PLEASE CALL ▶ 800. 762. 2974

For volume discounts & special orders pleas Tony Real, Special Sales, at 415. 655. 3048

**COMPUTER
BOOK SERIES
FROM IDG**

For Dummies
who want
to program...

**Delphi Programming
For Dummies®**
by Neil Rubenking

ISBN: 1-56884-200-7
$19.99 USA/$26.99 Canada

**Access Programming
For Dummies®**
by Rob Krumm

ISBN: 1-56884-091-8
$19.95 USA/$26.95 Canada

TCP/IP For Dummies®
*by Marshall Wilensky &
Candace Leiden*

ISBN: 1-56884-241-4
$19.99 USA/$26.99 Canada

HTML For Dummies®
by Ed Tittel & Carl de Cordova

ISBN: 1-56884-330-5
$29.99 USA/$39.99 Canada

**Windows® 95 Programming
For Dummies®**
by S. Randy Davis

ISBN: 1-56884-327-5
$19.99 USA/$26.99 Canada

**Mac® Programming
For Dummies®**
by Dan Parks Sydow

ISBN: 1-56884-173-6
$19.95 USA/$26.95 Canada

**PowerBuilder 4 Programming
For Dummies®**
by Ted Coombs & Jason Coombs

ISBN: 1-56884-325-9
$19.99 USA/$26.99 Canada

Visual Basic 3 For Dummies®
by Wallace Wang

ISBN: 1-56884-076-4
$19.95 USA/$26.95 Canada

Covers version 3.

ISDN For Dummies®
by David Angell

ISBN: 1-56884-331-3
$19.99 USA/$26.99 Canada

Visual C++ "2" For Dummies®
*by Michael Hyman &
Bob Arnson*

ISBN: 1-56884-328-3
$19.99 USA/$26.99 Canada

Borland C++ For Dummies®
by Michael Hyman

ISBN: 1-56884-162-0
$19.95 USA/$26.95 Canada

C For Dummies,® Volume I
by Dan Gookin

ISBN: 1-878058-78-9
$19.95 USA/$26.95 Canada

C++ For Dummies®
by Stephen R. Davis

ISBN: 1-56884-163-9
$19.95 USA/$26.95 Canada

**QBasic Programming
For Dummies®**
by Douglas Hergert

ISBN: 1-56884-093-4
$19.95 USA/$26.95 Canada

**dBase 5 For Windows®
Programming For Dummies®**
by Ted Coombs & Jason Coombs

ISBN: 1-56884-215-5
$19.99 USA/$26.99 Canada

holastic requests & educational orders please
ucational Sales, at 1. 800. 434. 2086

FOR MORE INFO OR TO ORDER, PLEASE CALL ▶ 800. 762. 2974

For volume discounts & special orders please call
Tony Real, Special Sales, at 415. 655. 3048

Official Hayes Modem Communications Companion
by Caroline M. Halliday

ISBN: 1-56884-072-1
$29.95 USA/$39.95 Canada

Includes software.

1,001 Komputer Answers from Kim Komando
by Kim Komando

ISBN: 1-56884-460-3
$29.99 USA/$39.99 Canada

Includes software.

PC World Excel 5 For Windows® Handbook, 2nd Edition
by John Walkenbach & Dave Maguiness

ISBN: 1-56884-056-X
$34.95 USA/$44.95 Canada

Includes software

PC World WordPerfect® 6 Handbook
by Greg Harvey

ISBN: 1-878058-80-0
$34.95 USA/$44.95 Canada

Includes software.

PC World DOS 6 Command Reference and Problem Solver
by John Socha & Devra Hall

NATIONAL BESTSELLER

ISBN: 1-56884-055-1
$24.95 USA/$32.95 Canada

Client/Server Strategies™: A Survival Guide for Corporate Reengineers
by David Vaskevitch

SUPER STAR

ISBN: 1-56884-064-0
$29.95 USA/$39.95 Canada

Internet SECRETS™
by John Levine & Carol Baroudi

ISBN: 1-56884-452-2
$39.99 USA/$54.99 Canada

Includes software.

Network Security SECRETS™
by David Stang & Sylvia Moon

ISBN: 1-56884-021-7
Int'l. ISBN: 1-56884-151-5
$49.95 USA/$64.95 Canada

Includes software.

PC SECRETS™
by Caroline M. Halliday

ISBN: 1-878058-49-5
$39.95 USA/$52.95 Canada

Includes software.

...SECRETS®

IDG BOOKS
WORLDWIDE

Here's a complete listing of PC Press Titles

Title	Author	ISBN	Price
BBS SECRETS™	by Ray Werner	ISBN: 1-56884-491-3	$39.99 USA/$54.99 Canada
Creating Cool Web Pages with HTML	by Dave Taylor	ISBN: 1-56884-454-9	$19.99 USA/$26.99 Canada
DOS 6 SECRETS™	by Robert D. Ainsbury	ISBN: 1-878058-70-3	$39.95 USA/$52.95 Canada
Excel 5 For Windows® Power Programming Techniques	by John Walkenbach	ISBN: 1-56884-303-8	$39.95 USA/$52.95 Canada
Hard Disk SECRETS™	by John M. Goodman, Ph.D.	ISBN: 1-878058-64-9	$39.95 USA/$52.95 Canada
Internet GIZMOS™ For Windows®	by Joel Diamond, Howard Sobel, & Valda Hilley	ISBN: 1-56884-451-4	$39.99 USA/$54.99 Canada
Making Multimedia Work	by Michael Goodwin	ISBN: 1-56884-468-9	$19.99 USA/$26.99 Canada
MORE Windows® 3.1 SECRETS™	by Brian Livingston	ISBN: 1-56884-019-5	$39.95 USA/$52.95 Canada
Official XTree Companion 3rd Edition	by Beth Slick	ISBN: 1-878058-57-6	$19.95 USA/$26.95 Canada
Paradox 4 Power Programming SECRETS™, 2nd Edition	by Gregory B. Salcedo & Martin W. Rudy	ISBN: 1-878058-54-1	$44.95 USA/$59.95 Canada
Paradox 5 For Windows® Power Programming SECRETS™	by Gregory B. Salcedo & Martin W. Rudy	ISBN: 1-56884-085-3	$44.95 USA/$59.95 Canada
PC World DOS 6 Handbook, 2nd Edition	by John Socha, Clint Hicks & Devra Hall	ISBN: 1-878058-79-7	$34.95 USA/$44.95 Canada
PC World Microsoft® Access 2 Bible, 2nd Edition	by Cary N. Prague & Michael R. Irwin	ISBN: 1-56884-086-1	$39.95 USA/$52.95 Canada
PC World Word For Windows® 6 Handbook	by Brent Heslop & David Angell	ISBN: 1-56884-054-3	$34.95 USA/$44.95 Canada
QuarkXPress For Windows® Designer Handbook	by Barbara Assadi & Galen Gruman	ISBN: 1-878058-45-2	$29.95 USA/$39.95 Canada
Windows® 3.1 Configuration SECRETS™	by Valda Hilley & James Blakely	ISBN: 1-56884-026-8	$49.95 USA/$64.95 Canada
Windows® 3.1 Connectivity SECRETS™	by Runnoe Connally, David Rorabaugh & Sheldon Hall	ISBN: 1-56884-030-6	$49.95 USA/$64.95 Canada
Windows® 3.1 SECRETS™	by Brian Livingston	ISBN: 1-878058-43-6	$39.95 USA/$52.95 Canada
Windows® 95 A.S.A.P.	by Dan Gookin	ISBN: 1-56884-483-2	$24.99 USA/$34.99 Canada
Windows® 95 Bible	by Alan Simpson	ISBN: 1-56884-074-8	$29.99 USA/$39.99 Canada
Windows® 95 SECRETS™	by Brian Livingston	ISBN: 1-56884-453-0	$39.99 USA/$54.99 Canada
Windows® GIZMOS™	by Brian Livingston & Margie Livingston	ISBN: 1-878058-66-5	$39.95 USA/$52.95 Canada
WordPerfect® 6 For Windows® Tips & Techniques Revealed	by David A. Holzgang & Roger C. Parker	ISBN: 1-56884-202-3	$39.95 USA/$52.95 Canada
WordPerfect® 6 SECRETS™	by Roger C. Parker & David A. Holzgang	ISBN: 1-56884-040-3	$39.95 USA/$52.95 Canada

For scholastic requests & educational orders please call Educational Sales, at 1. 800. 434. 2086

FOR MORE INFO OR TO ORDER, PLEASE CALL ▶ **800. 762. 2974**

For volume discounts & special orders please Tony Real, Special Sales, at 415. 655. 3048

IDG BOOKS WORLDWIDE™

Order Center: **(800) 762-2974** *(8 a.m.–6 p.m., EST, weekdays)*

Quantity	ISBN	Title	Price	Total

Shipping & Handling Charges

	Description	First book	Each additional book	Total
Domestic	Normal	$4.50	$1.50	$
	Two Day Air	$8.50	$2.50	$
	Overnight	$18.00	$3.00	$
International	Surface	$8.00	$8.00	$
	Airmail	$16.00	$16.00	$
	DHL Air	$17.00	$17.00	$

*For large quantities call for shipping & handling charges.
**Prices are subject to change without notice.

Ship to:

Name _____

Company _____

Address _____

City/State/Zip_____

Daytime Phone _____

Payment: ☐ Check to IDG Books Worldwide (US Funds Only)

☐ VISA ☐ MasterCard ☐ American Express

Card # _____ Expires _____

Signature _____

Subtotal _____

CA residents add applicable sales tax _____

IN, MA, and MD residents add 5% sales tax _____

IL residents add 6.25% sales tax_____

RI residents add 7% sales tax_____

TX residents add 8.25% sales tax_____

Shipping_____

Total _____

Please send this order form to:
IDG Books Worldwide, Inc.
7260 Shadeland Station, Suite 100
Indianapolis, IN 46256

Allow up to 3 weeks for delivery.
Thank you!

IDG BOOKS WORLDWIDE REGISTRATION CARD

RETURN THIS REGISTRATION CARD FOR FREE CATALOG

Title of this book: Access For Windows 95 For Dummies

My overall rating of this book: ❑ Very good [1]   ❑ Good [2]   ❑ Satisfactory [3]   ❑ Fair [4]   ❑ Poor [5]

How I first heard about this book:

❑ Found in bookstore; name: [6]   ❑ Book review: [7]

❑ Advertisement: [8]   ❑ Catalog: [9]

❑ Word of mouth; heard about book from friend, co-worker, etc.: [10]   ❑ Other: [11]

What I liked most about this book:

What I would change, add, delete, etc., in future editions of this book:

Other comments:

Number of computer books I purchase in a year: ❑ 1 [12]   ❑ 2-5 [13]   ❑ 6-10 [14]   ❑ More than 10 [15]

I would characterize my computer skills as: ❑ Beginner [16] ❑ Intermediate [17] ❑ Advanced [18] ❑ Professional [19]

I use ❑ DOS [20]   ❑ Windows [21]   ❑ OS/2 [22]   ❑ Unix [23]   ❑ Macintosh [24]   ❑ Other: [25]_____
(please specify)

I would be interested in new books on the following subjects:
(please check all that apply, and use the spaces provided to identify specific software)

❑ Word processing: [26]   ❑ Spreadsheets: [27]

❑ Data bases: [28]   ❑ Desktop publishing: [29]

❑ File Utilities: [30]   ❑ Money management: [31]

❑ Networking: [32]   ❑ Programming languages: [33]

❑ Other: [34]

I use a PC at (please check all that apply): ❑ home [35]   ❑ work [36]   ❑ school [37]   ❑ other: [38] _____

The disks I prefer to use are ❑ 5.25 [39]   ❑ 3.5 [40]   ❑ other: [41]_____

I have a CD ROM: ❑ yes [42]   ❑ no [43]

I plan to buy or upgrade computer hardware this year: ❑ yes [44]   ❑ no [45]

I plan to buy or upgrade computer software this year: ❑ yes [46]   ❑ no [47]

Name: _____   Business title: [48] _____   Type of Business: [49] _____

Address (❑ home [50] ❑ work [51]/Company name: _____)

Street/Suite# _____

City [52]/State [53]/Zipcode [54]: _____   Country [55] _____

❑ **I liked this book!** You may quote me by name in future
   IDG Books Worldwide promotional materials.

My daytime phone number is _____

IDG BOOKS

THE WORLD OF
COMPUTER
KNOWLEDGE

❏ YES!

Please keep me informed about IDG's World of Computer Knowledge.
Send me the latest IDG Books catalog.